HANDBOOK OF

INTEGRATED RISK MANAGEMENT for E-BUSINESS

Measuring, Modeling, and Managing Risk

Edited by
Abderrahim Labbi

J.ROSS
PUBLISHING

Copyright ©2005 by J. Ross Publishing, Inc.

ISBN 1-932159-07-X

Printed and bound in the U.S.A. Printed on acid-free paper
10 9 8 7 6 5 4 3 2 1

Library of Congress Cataloging-in-Publication Data

Handbook of integrated risk management for e-business / edited by Abdel
Labbi.—1st ed.
   p. cm.
  Includes and index.
  ISBN 1-932159-07-X (hardback : alk. paper)
  1. Electronic commerce. 2. Risk management. I. Labbi, Abdel.
  HF5548.32.H355 2004
  658.15'5—dc22   2004013334

    Direct all inquiries to J. Ross Publishing, Inc., 6501 Park of Commerce Blvd., Suite 200, Boca Raton, Florida 33487.

Phone: (561) 869-3900
Fax: (561) 892-0700
Web: www.jrosspub.com

TABLE OF CONTENTS

FOREWORD

Today's increasingly competitive environment is causing companies to transform their businesses into more efficient and dynamic entities. Such businesses will, among other things, need the ability to quickly respond to outside forces, increase their variable-to-fixed-cost ratio, and be resilient to unexpected and potentially catastrophic events. Much of this will require a thorough understanding of risk, how to model and manage it, and finally, how to turn such knowledge into competitive advantage. It is easy to see that oversubscription of resources to accommodate peak demand is inefficient and results in much higher fixed costs. But it is another matter entirely to understand and weigh the consequences of not meeting service level agreements for some period of time and to set a lower level of fixed resources accordingly. Likewise, it is straightforward to specify a system or process to be resilient to both internal and external factors. But what price is one willing to pay for this? Once again, a thorough understanding of the likelihood of an event, be it malicious or otherwise, and the risk (consequences) associated with it is critical to optimally answering this question and implementing a solution.

The importance of risk management is further magnified by the fact that decisions are taken increasingly frequently and with greater consequence than ever before. This is partly because of the availability of often real-time data from sensors, systems, and related processes, as well as the dynamic nature of the business processes themselves. It is worthwhile to note that there are two fundamental types of variability that need to be considered: internal variability within the system and external variability imposed upon the system. For example, in the power generation industry, internal variability may correspond to the variable output of individual power plants in a grid, while external variability may be due to the weather or the spot market price for power. Such problems have led to an increased awareness of the need to model the variability in most processes with a greater degree of reliability. Recent advances in analytical decision support systems have resulted in more reliable modeling and are routinely used to model this variability and the ensuing risk.

This handbook on risk management provides a comprehensive overview of the various kinds of risk — operational, security, service level, etc. — in real-world settings. While much has been written on the actual topic of integrated risk management, this is one of the first instances where the tools and technologies that allow for the implementation of solutions to solve specific problems are outlined. One could say that this book provides a recipe for the practical application of technology. When considering real problems, it becomes clear that one cannot treat individual sources of risk in isolation. The interconnected nature of processes and their often global nature lead to an interaction of risks that necessitates an integrated risk management solution. In fact, this is one of the key messages of this book.

The business need for the study of this topic makes this work very topical. Not only are businesses transforming themselves in order to drive increased revenue and profit, but they are also doing so to enhance the visibility into their own systems. Integrated risk management or enterprise risk management is a key step toward this transformation.

Dr. Krishna Nathan
Vice President and Director
IBM Research – Zurich Research Laboratory

ABOUT THE EDITOR

Dr. Abdel Labbi received a Ph.D. in Applied Mathematics in 1993 from the University of Grenoble, France. He is currently a Research Program Leader at the IBM Zurich Research Laboratory in Rüschlikon, Switzerland. Over the last four years, he has been leading several projects in the areas of operational risk management and customer relationship and supply chain risk management using advanced mathematical and statistical models. Prior to joining IBM Research, Dr. Labbi was Assistant Professor at the University of Geneva, Switzerland, where he led several research and development projects on mathematical modeling and data mining with scientific and industrial organizations. He has published more than 30 articles on subjects related to this book in international conferences and journals and holds four patents on related technologies.

CONTRIBUTORS

Naoki Abe
IBM T.J. Watson Research Center
Yorktown Heights, New York

Chid Apte
IBM T.J. Watson Research Center
Yorktown Heights, New York

Vicki Bier
Department of Industrial Engineering
University of Wisconsin-Madison
Madison, Wisconsin

Richard Boedi
IBM Zurich Research Laboratory
Rüschlikon, Switzerland

Pascale Carayon
Department of Industrial Engineering
University of Wisconsin-Madison
Madison, Wisconsin

Giorgos Cheliotis
McKinsey & Company
Zurich, Switzerland

Louis Anthony Cox, Jr.
Cox Associates
Denver, Colorado

Marcelo G. Cruz
RiskMath, Inc.
Jersey City, New Jersey

Michel Cuendet
Lab for Inorganic Chemistry
ETH Hönggerberg
Zurich, Switzerland

Wei Fan
IBM T.J. Watson Research Center
Yorktown Heights, New York

William Grey
IBM Retirement Funds
White Plains, New York

Christopher M. Kenyon
IBM Zurich Research Laboratory
Rüschlikon, Switzerland

Alan J. King
IBM T.J. Watson Research Center
Yorktown Heights, New York

Sara Kraemer
Department of Industrial Engineering
University of Wisconsin-Madison
Madison, Wisconsin

Abderrahim Labbi
IBM Zurich Research Laboratory
Rüschlikon, Switzerland

Edwin Pednault
IBM T.J. Watson Research Center
Yorktown Heights, New York

Ulrich Schimpel
IBM Zurich Research Laboratory
Rüschlikon, Switzerland

Samir Shah
Tillinghast-Towers Perrin
Rosslyn, Virginia

Dailun Shi
IBM T.J. Watson Research Center
Hawthorne, New York

Mark S. Squillante
IBM T.J. Watson Research Center
Yorktown Heights, New York

Haixun Wang
IBM T.J. Watson Research Center
Yorktown Heights, New York

Andreas Wespi
IBM Zurich Research Laboratory
Rüschlikon, Switzerland

Bianca Zadrozny
IBM T.J. Watson Research Center
Yorktown Heights, New York

ENTERPRISE RISK MANAGEMENT: A VALUE CHAIN PERSPECTIVE

William Grey and Dailun Shi

1.1. INTRODUCTION

In March of 2000, lightning struck a semiconductor manufacturing facility owned by Philips Electronics (see, e.g., Latour, 2001). It caused a fire that lasted about 10 minutes and shut down the plant for only a few weeks. But the plant was the sole source of critical semiconductor devices used by Nokia and Ericsson to produce mobile phone handsets. The resulting supply disruption threatened to halt cell phone production for both firms.

At Nokia, the event received immediate executive-level attention. Nokia launched a textbook crisis management program. Within two weeks, Nokia officials were in Asia, Europe, and the United States securing alternative sources of supply. Despite the fire, Nokia experienced only minimal production disruptions.

Ericsson was far slower to react. It had no contingency plans in place to manage the disruption. Information about the event percolated slowly up to executive management. By the time the company began to mount a serious response, it was already too late. Nokia had locked in all alternative sources of supply.

The business impact on Ericsson was devastating. The firm reported over $400 million in lost revenue as a result of the supply shortages, and its stock price declined by over 14%. Nokia gained three points of market share, largely at Ericsson's expense. Some time later, Ericsson stopped manufacturing cell phone handsets and outsourced production to a contract manufacturer.

The Ericsson case is not an isolated incident. Firms face a wide variety of business risks, many related to their extended value chains. Poor demand planning and risky purchasing contracts at Cisco Systems recently precipitated $2.5 billion in inventory write-offs and led to massive layoffs (Berinato, 2001). Difficulties implementing supply chain management software at Nike led to severe inventory shortages, impacting third-quarter revenue by $100 million and shaving almost 20% off the firm's market capitalization (see, e.g., Piller, 2001; Wilson, 2001). In a case subject to widespread public scrutiny, quality problems with Ford Explorers using Firestone tires resulted in more than 100 highway fatalities and forced massive tire recalls (see, e.g., Aeppel et al., 2001; Bradsher, 2001; Kashiwagi, 2001). This not only created a potential multibillion-dollar legal exposure for the two firms, but also led to significant loss of brand valuation.

The pace of business has been accelerating, leading to increased risk. There have been dramatic shifts in the way companies interact, driven both by new technologies and new business methods. Increased use of information technology has raised productivity, while simultaneously introducing new sources of uncertainty and complexity. Value chains are leaner and far more dependent on the carefully orchestrated coordination of a complex network of supply chain partners. Product life cycles are shorter, and in many industries rapid product obsolescence is the norm. Business processes have become more automated, and without proper monitoring and management, small problems can easily escalate. Increased outsourcing has not only made firms more dependent on third parties, but also made it more difficult to detect and respond to risk events.

The consequences of failing to manage risk effectively have also increased. The interconnectedness of current value chains means that a small mistake by a single entity can have a ripple effect that impacts multiple trading partners. The equity markets are equally unforgiving. Failure to meet financial targets can result in dramatic declines in market value, even for well-managed firms. According to one study, firms reporting supply chain difficulties typically lost about 10% of their market capitalization in the two days following announcement of the event (Hendricks and Singhal, 2000).

In this chapter, risks that an enterprise faces in its business processes and ways to manage them are discussed. An overview of current practices in enterprise risk management is provided, followed by a discussion of how this integrated approach to risk management can be used to manage risks in an enterprise's extended value chain. Finally, a general risk management framework is introduced and how it can be applied to identify, characterize, and manage value chain risks is discussed.

As the Nokia and Ericsson case demonstrates, effective risk management can provide protection against significant financial losses. However, risk management does not only add value during times of crisis. Strategic, operational, and organizational changes can help firms to not only improve their financial performance and increase customer satisfaction, but also position themselves to exploit new business opportunities as they arise.

1.2. ENTERPRISE RISK MANAGEMENT

Enterprises have traditionally failed to manage risk in an integrated fashion. Many risks are managed only at the corporate level, and attempts to effectively assess and manage risk across organizational boundaries are hindered by the absence of a consistent set of risk metrics. Interactions and potential correlations between risk factors are often ignored. This makes it difficult for firms to understand their total risk exposure, much less measure, manage, or control it.

Enterprise risk management is a technique for managing risk holistically and for closely linking risk management to the financial and business objectives of a firm. It begins by defining, at a strategic level, the firm's appetite for risk. Risk factors affecting the enterprise are addressed using a consistent methodology for measurement, management, and control. Risk is managed in an integrated fashion, across business units, business functions, and sources of risk.

Executive interest in enterprise risk management programs is growing. In a survey of more than 200 CEOs and senior executives at firms from a diverse set of industries (E.I.U., 2001), more than 40% of the respondents reported that they were managing risk on a formal enterprise risk management basis. Almost 20% more planned to do so within a year, and more than 70% planned to do so within five years. At present, only 15% of the firms managed risk on a corporate-wide basis. However, more than 40% expected to do so within three years.

Enterprises face many risks, including market risk, credit risk, operational risk, and business risk. *Market risk* is uncertainty caused by fluctuations in the market prices of financial or nonfinancial assets. For example, when a firm has operations in multiple countries, changes in foreign exchange rates can have a significant impact on both the income statement and the balance sheet. Changes in interest rates can affect a firm's interest expense, the value of its loan portfolio, and the market value of its debt. Price changes for commodities such as heating oil and electricity can have an impact on the cost of keeping factories and office buildings running, and price changes for commodities like steel and copper can affect the cost of goods sold.

Credit risk is the risk that parties to which an enterprise has extended credit will fail to fulfill their obligations. Customer defaults, or delays in making anticipated payments, can have varying impacts on an enterprise. These range from transient effects on liquidity to ratings downgrades or even bankruptcy. It might seem that credit risk should primarily be a concern for financial services firms, but this is not the case. As recent experience in the telecommunications and computer industries has shown, a heavy credit concentration in a risky customer segment can sometimes lead to severe financial repercussions even for industrial firms.

Operational risk refers to risks caused by the way a firm operates its business. It includes risks associated with technical failures, losses caused by processing errors, and quality and cost problems caused by production errors. It also includes losses due to human error, such as fraud, mismanagement, and failure to control and monitor operations effectively.

Business risk is caused by uncertainty associated with key business drivers. Business risks tend to be more strategic than other risks and can be the most difficult to manage. Business risk factors include the overall state of the economy, fluctuations in customer demand, supply disruptions, competitive actions by rivals, technological change, legal liabilities, and regulatory changes.

There are a number of reasons why it is important to analyze and manage risk in a global, integrated fashion. Examining risk factors in isolation makes it difficult to understand interaction effects. This can increase risk management costs, since firms may unnecessarily hedge certain risks that are in reality offset by others. A fragmented approach to risk management also increases the likelihood of ignoring important risks. Even for known risks, it is important to consider the impact for the organization as a whole. Otherwise, mitigation attempts may only introduce new risks or shift the risk to less visible parts of the organization.

Failure to consider risk interactions can also cause firms to grossly underestimate their risk exposures. For example, the precipitous decline in capital investments by telecommunications firms several years ago increased risk for telecommunications equipment manufacturers along multiple dimensions. The manufacturers faced additional business risk, as uncertainty regarding demand for their products increased dramatically. They faced increased credit risk. Loans extended to high-flying customers deteriorated rapidly in credit quality as many customers neared default. They also faced increased market risk as equity values for recent strategic acquisitions declined precipitously, forcing multibillion-dollar write-downs.

1.3. VALUE CHAIN RISK MANAGEMENT

Traditionally, risk management has been the domain of the corporate treasury function, which had the primary responsibility for managing exposures to foreign exchange fluctuations, changes in interest rates, credit downgrades, and the risks of hazards such as fires, earthquakes, and liability lawsuits. Today, corporate treasurers have at their disposal an evolving but well-defined set of risk management tools and techniques (e.g., Crouhy et al., 2001).

Business risks, on the other hand, are more difficult to manage. They can be difficult to quantify, and managers often have to be satisfied with qualitative assessments of risk based on little more than intuition. Business risks can be difficult to identify, and their complex interactions with business processes make them difficult to characterize. Unlike financial risk, there are fewer well-defined risk management tools and techniques. Firms typically manage business risk in an ad hoc fashion.

Business risks can arise virtually anywhere in an enterprise's extended value chain. They affect — and are affected by — all of a firm's business processes. Successful risk management can play a critical role in improving business performance from the moment a new product is conceived until its effective end of life.

Two major trends have the potential to transform the way firms manage risk in their extended value chains. The first is increased financial innovation. In the traditional domains of insurance and financial derivatives, new products are emerging that enable firms to manage risks such as sensitivity to changes in the weather, bandwidth prices, and energy costs (Pilipovic, 1998). The financial markets have developed innovative ways to transfer and repackage risks so they can be resold to a broad set of investors. Furthermore, increased use of auctions and spot markets is increasing opportunities for supplier diversification. It is also providing greater price transparency for a wide range of products and services. This will make it easier for firms to quantify a broad set of risk factors. It will also drive the creation of new risk management products.

The second major trend is improved access to enterprise information. Widespread deployment of enterprise-level software packages to support business processes such as enterprise resource planning and supply chain management has provided firms with unprecedented access to fairly standardized information. These systems are becoming more tightly integrated, both within the enterprise and between value chain partners. Firms will soon reach the point where they have end-to-end visibility into their supply chains, from the early stages of product design to after-market support. This will enable them to detect risk events earlier and to respond more effectively.

This trend will also make it possible to more accurately analyze and characterize enterprise risks and to develop new systems and business practices to manage and mitigate risk. In particular, the integration of financial and operational systems will enable firms to use sophisticated analytics to create a tighter coupling between the high-level financial objectives of a firm and its underlying business processes.

1.4. RISK MANAGEMENT FRAMEWORK

In this section, a framework for managing enterprise risks from the perspective of an extended supply chain is introduced. As shown in Figure 1.1, the framework has three stages: risk identification, risk characterization, and risk management. Risk identification is the process of identifying the key risks that affect an organization. Once risks have been identified, they are characterized and classified. This step assesses the nature and importance of different risks and their collective impact on the organization. After risks have been identified and characterized, an effective risk management program can be established.

A risk management program is basically an action plan that specifies which risks can be addressed and how to address them. Firms have a number of "levers" they can use to manage their risk exposure. For risks that can be

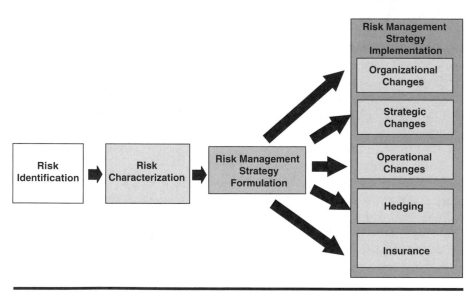

Figure 1.1.   Risk management framework.

controlled, implementing changes in strategy or operations is an effective means of risk mitigation. Other categories of risk may require the introduction of new business practices and organizational controls. Certain risks cannot be controlled. For these, a firm must determine what level of risk can be tolerated and adjust its business plans or financial risk management programs accordingly. This process may entail limiting risk exposure by transferring some or all of its risk to another party, by using either financial derivatives or insurance (Doherty, 2000). In cases where derivatives and insurance are either unavailable or too costly, it could also mean foregoing certain business opportunities, exiting particular product or customer segments, or divesting certain business units.

1.5. RISK IDENTIFICATION

This section presents a number of risk identification techniques which have been broadly applied in the financial services industry (see, e.g., Crouhy et al., 2001). These approaches include scenario analysis, historical analysis, and process mapping. A risk taxonomy that is useful for categorizing value chain risks is also introduced.

1.5.1. Risk Identification Techniques

When performing a top-down strategic risk assessment, it often makes sense to start with *scenario analysis*. Scenario analysis typically begins with a series of brainstorming sessions that uncover key economic, technological, cultural, and economic trends that could affect the business performance of an enterprise. These are then used to identify potential future states of the world. Once these states of the world have been identified, each one is analyzed to understand the implications for the firm. This exercise can then be used to enumerate a broad set of existing and potential risk factors.

At a strategic level, scenario analysis is particularly effective at identifying game-changing risks that result from new technologies, changes in industry structure and dynamics, or economic shifts. Scenario analysis can also be applied at a more tactical level to explore the likely impact of existing risk factors and their interactions with risk factors looming just over the horizon.

Another way to identify potential risk factors is through *historical analysis*. This technique examines historical events to gain insight into potential future risks. In general, events with negative outcomes are identified and then categorized by determining the underlying risk factor or factors that triggered the event. If possible, the analysis considers events that had the potential for a negative outcome, even if no actual losses were incurred. Including such events can be quite useful, since they often point to latent risks that need to be addressed. In a value chain context, events could include parts shortages, sudden shifts in customer demand, production problems, and quality difficulties.

One drawback of historical analysis is that significant risk events are often infrequent. This difficulty can be at least partially overcome by including in the analysis events affecting other companies with similar business characteristics. Another problem with historical analysis is that by definition it can only identify risk factors that have caused difficulty in the past. This leaves open the possibility that important risk factors will be overlooked, especially those related to changes in technology, business practices, or industry dynamics.

Risks can also be identified using *process mapping*. This technique begins by creating a business process map, a visual display that resembles a flowchart showing business work flows for different business functions. Process maps are comprehensive: they provide an end-to-end view of the organization or value chain processes being analyzed. Each step on the map describes an individual business process, providing details about its objective, how it is performed, who performs it, and what, if anything, can go wrong.

Once the process map is complete, it is analyzed for control gaps, potential failure points, and vulnerabilities. Special attention is paid to risks that could arise during hand-offs between (and within) departments or organizations. The analysis seeks to identify missing control procedures, such as a missing approval process, that do not show up on the process map. It also looks for steps where ill-defined tasks or duties could lead to processing errors or a breakdown in control.

Process mapping is particularly useful for identifying risks associated with poor execution. Unlike historical analysis, process mapping can identify risks with a large potential impact before an actual loss occurs. It also can help to clarify the likely impact of a potential risk exposure on the organization as a whole.

Certain risk identification methods are best suited for identifying specific classes of risk. Both process mapping and historical analysis are useful for identifying operational risks, as well as potential risks associated with value chain interactions. Market risk, on the other hand, is almost always analyzed using historical analysis. Historical analysis is also typically the technique of choice for estimating the frequency and magnitude of risk events, although it can be difficult to apply for risks to intangibles such as reputation. Historical analysis is also the best way to identify a number of value chain risks, including quality, quantity, and price risk. Finally, scenario analysis serves as a versatile tool for identifying major risks at the enterprise level.

1.5.2. Value Chain Risk Taxonomy

Successful risk management requires a consistent framework for communicating and thinking about risk. Figure 1.2 introduces a risk taxonomy that serves as the basis for a value chain perspective on enterprise risk management. As shown in the figure, enterprise risks are divided into core and noncore risks. Core risks are tightly woven into the business fabric of the firm and usually cannot be managed using financial derivatives or insurance. In contrast, noncore risks are less central to a firm's business, but can still have a significant impact.

A number of value chain risks are worth discussing in detail. Firms face risk when buying goods and services from their suppliers, developing and manufacturing new offerings, and selling goods and services to their customers. *Price risk,* for example, is the result of uncertainty about the cost of goods and services required for production and uncertainty about the prices that a firm will ultimately realize for its products in the marketplace. A related risk is *quantity risk* — the risk that the desired quantity of a good or service may not be available for purchase or sale. Sometimes quantity risk can be severe, as is the case during a supply disruption. In other cases, it is merely the result of normal supply variability. Firms also face quantity risk associated with inventories of raw materials and components, goods in the production pipeline, and inventories held to meet anticipated customer demand. Sometimes referred to as *inventory risk,* this represents the risk associated with having too much or too little inventory. Excess inventory exposes a firm to price fluctuations or product obsolescence that can impair the value of its inventory. Inventory shortages, on the other hand, can prevent a firm from meeting customer demand (Ervolina et al., 2001).

Risk factors such as quality risk and complexity risk affect a broad set of business processes. *Quality risk* is the risk associated with variability in quality, reliability, or execution. Quality risk can relate to procured goods and services, as well as to the goods and services produced or sold by a firm. It can also apply to a wide variety of value chain processes, including design, logistics, and customer support. Similarly, *complexity risk* results from product complexity, supply chain complexity, or even business process complexity.

1.6. RISK CHARACTERIZATION

Once the risk identification process is complete, the next step is to assess the nature, impact, and importance of risk factors. First the risk characterization process and a set of risk metrics are described, followed by a discussion of how risk factors interact with business processes and how they propagate through an enterprise's value chain.

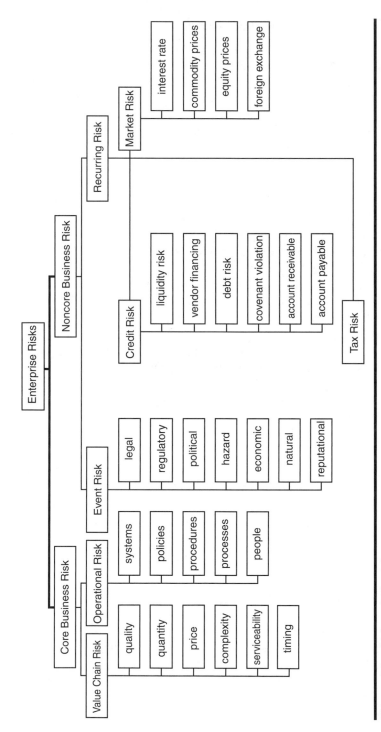

Figure 1.2.   Value chain risk taxonomy.

1.6.1. Risk Characterization Process

When assessing the magnitude of a risk event, the two most important factors to consider are the probability of occurrence and the severity of the expected loss (Grimmett and Stirzaker, 1982; Lewin, 2000). If historical data are available, they are used to estimate both the size and frequency of risk events. Sometimes complete probability distributions can be constructed for each risk factor, providing a rich sense of the likelihood of an unfavorable event. When only a limited number of observations are available, specialized techniques such as extreme value analysis (Hertz, 1979) can be applied.

If quantification is impossible, either because historical data are not available or are perceived not to be suitable, a qualitative approach must be used (Bazerman, 1997). In its simplest form, qualitative analysis involves eliciting information from subject matter experts about the probability of a risk event and its likely consequences. Qualitative analysis is sometimes used in conjunction with a quantitative analysis. Typically this entails developing mathematical models similar to those described above, then using domain experts to generate model inputs based on their experience and intuition.

Even when mathematical models can be applied, risk characterization often requires considerable judgment on the part of the analyst, not only to define the model's structure and assumptions but also to assess the relevance of historical data for estimating future risks (Bazerman, 1997; Kahneman and Tversky, 1979).

The next step in the risk characterization process is to group and prioritize risks. Typically this is done by assigning risks to one of four categories based on their severity of impact and probability of occurrence (see Figure 1.3). This approach not only helps determine which risks require immediate action, but also provides insight into how individual risks can be managed. Risks in region

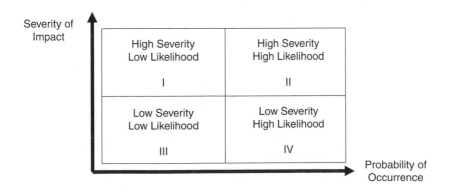

Figure 1.3.   Risk characterization.

I occur infrequently but have a high impact. If possible, steps should be taken to mitigate these risks, and contingency plans should be established. As will be discussed later, insurance is frequently used for these risks.

Risks in region II are the most pressing: they have a high likelihood of occurrence and a high impact. Typically these risks are too expensive to insure, so steps should be taken to reduce either their frequency or severity. If the risks are tied to a particular product or product line, attempts should be made to verify that they are profitable enough to justify continued production.

Risks in region III have low likelihood and low severity and consequently do not require immediate attention. Nevertheless, they should be subject to periodic monitoring and review to make sure that there has been no change in their status. The high-likelihood, low-severity risks in region IV are typically managed by introducing operational changes and controls to reduce their frequency.

1.6.2. Value at Risk

Different business units typically have different risk measures, making it difficult to understand the risk exposure of a firm as a whole. A common set of risk metrics can help firms make better investments, since capital can be allocated in a fashion that accurately reflects the trade-off between risk and reward. Standardized measurements also make it possible to evaluate business lines and executives on a risk-adjusted basis. It is therefore important to establish a common framework for communicating information about risk throughout the organization.

A metric called *value at risk* is particularly useful for characterizing enterprise risks (Duffie and Pan, 1997; Jorion, 1997). Although value at risk was originally intended for assessing the risk of a portfolio of financial assets (Crouhy et al., 2001), it can also be applied to analyze multiple risks faced by a global firm. One of its key strengths is its ability to provide a common metric for comparing and managing risks across an enterprise.

Value at risk is a statistical measure of the risk associated with an investment or set of investments. It provides an estimate, usually in dollars or another unit of currency, of the most a firm can expect to lose on an investment over a specified time period at a given confidence level. For example, suppose a bank owns a highly risky portfolio of stocks. The bank analyzes the risk of the portfolio and estimates that 95% of the time it will at most lose $100 million on the portfolio in a given year. The value at risk for this risky portfolio at the 95% confidence level is then $100 million. A similar calculation on a less risky portfolio might conclude that 95% of the time, annual losses would not exceed $50 million. The value at risk for the less risky portfolio would be only $50 million.

In an enterprise setting, value at risk can be used to model the interactions of different risk factors and risk exposures. For a firm with multiple business units, the risks in different business units tend to partially offset each other in much the same way that diversification reduces the riskiness of a stock portfolio. Value at risk basically treats a firm as a portfolio of investments with different risk factors and analyzes them in the same way as a portfolio of financial assets.

One of the drawbacks of value at risk is that it can sometimes lead to a false sense of security. Although value at risk provides an estimate of how much a firm is likely to lose at a given confidence level, it does not let management know how much it could lose in the case of a very unlikely event. Although value at risk provides insight into expected losses under "normal" business conditions, it may not help much for analyzing the potential impact of truly catastrophic events.

A technique called *stress testing* can compensate for this weakness in value at risk (Committee on the Global Financial System, 2000). Stress testing develops a set of worst-case scenarios and then estimates their effect on the financial performance of a firm or a financial portfolio. When sufficient data are available, inputs to worst-case scenarios are derived using analysis of actual catastrophic events, such as earthquakes or stock market crashes. Models are then run to assess the impact of shocks similar to those during the catastrophe. Stress testing can be extremely effective as long as the model faithfully captures interactions between risk factors and considers all key risk factors.

1.6.3. Risk Interactions with Value Chain Processes

In characterizing value chain risks, it is important to understand *which* business processes they affect. Value chain risk factors often have a broad impact. For example, quantity risk affects almost the entire value chain. Parts shortfalls impact procurement, as management attention is directed toward identifying alternate sources of supply and qualifying and negotiating additional capacity with new suppliers. Parts shortages also disrupt production, causing temporary drops in utilization. They can reduce production efficiency, especially if normal operations are interrupted to expedite commitments for impacted products. Input shortages can also prevent companies from meeting customer demand, thus reducing revenue and damaging a firm's reputation. Logistics costs and complexity may increase because shipments must be expedited. Even after-market support and service can be affected because supply shortages may limit the availability of spare parts.

In characterizing risks, it is also important to understand *how* they affect different business processes. Table 1.1 shows the impact of a number of risks

Table 1.1. Risk Impact on Value Chain Processes

	Sourcing	Manufacturing	Marketing and Sales	Distribution and Logistics	Support
Quantity	■ Component shortfalls impact production, hurting sales and potentially damaging reputation for service and reliability.	■ Poor capacity planning constrains production output. ■ Poor production planning results in production constraints or excess inventory.	■ Poor demand forecasts result in either missed revenue opportunities or excess inventory throughout the supply chain.	■ Poor supply chain design and execution lead to excess inventory. ■ Poor inventory positioning prevents products from reaching customers, hurting revenue.	■ Poor warranty forecasting leads to understocking of spare parts. This causes poor customer satisfaction and loss of market share.
Price	■ Unexpected price volatility in procured components increases revenue and profit variability.	■ Excess capacity increases production costs.	■ Poor pricing decisions hurt market share, resulting in foregone profit margins or excess inventory.	■ Poor supply chain design and execution increase the need for expediting, thus increasing logistics costs.	■ Poor support network design and execution increase expediting, causing higher logistics costs.
Quality	■ Low-quality purchased parts impact manufacturing yields, hurting sales. Also affects customer satisfaction and reputation and increases warranty and support costs.	■ Low yields can constrain production output, reducing revenue. ■ Poor quality affects customer satisfaction and reputation and increases warranty and support costs. ■ Poor quality affects obsolescence and creates obstacles for marketing and sales.		■ Poor supply chain design or execution results in poor serviceability, reducing customer satisfaction and limiting ability to fulfill service models such as vendor-managed inventory and just in time.	■ Poor quality of support execution affects customer satisfaction, damaging firm's reputation.

Serviceability	■ Selecting suppliers with poor or erratic service affects production, reducing revenue and damaging reputation.	■ High production cycle time variability affects ability to deliver products to meet commitments.	■ Certain sales processes work well for certain customer segments, but are too costly to address other segments. Revenue and profit decline.	■ See entry under "Quality."	■ See entry under "Quality."
Obsolescence	■ Overordering parts characterized by rapid obsolescence results in costly inventory write-downs.	■ Obsolete production technology makes a firm uncompetitive in terms of cost structure and product portfolio.		■ Poorly positioned inventory is exposed to obsolescence, leading to inventory write-downs.	■ Obsolete products in the field can be uneconomical to support under existing maintenance agreements. ■ Inventories for obsolete spare parts result in inventory write-downs.
Complexity	■ Too many suppliers make it difficult to manage supplier relations and coordinate logistics.	■ Complex manu-facturing processes increase throughput variability. This impacts quality and increases cycle time variability.	■ Complex sales processes make it difficult to do business, resulting in missed market-ing opportunities and lost revenue.	■ Long logistics cycle times impact service-ability and increase inventory. This reduces customer satisfaction and increases inventory obsolescence risk.	■ Complex products make support more expensive, increasing warranty costs. ■ Complex support organizations are difficult to manage, making them unresponsive to customer needs. ■ Complex or unique processes make it difficult to hire staff and increase training requirements.

at different stages of the value chain. In general, the earlier in the chain an event occurs, the greater its impact.

1.6.4. Risk Propagation

Some risks propagate through the value chain in a comparatively well-behaved manner, making their effect on value chain partners fairly constant. Other risks are less well behaved. As they move along the value chain, their impact is amplified, sometimes with catastrophic consequences.

One comparatively well-behaved value chain risk is price risk. Assume there is a price increase of one dollar for a production input such as a computer chip. As the chip moves through the value chain, costs increase by about one dollar for anyone buying the chip either in its original state or in an intermediate product containing the chip. There may be additional cost increases to reflect profit margins, but the overall effect will be small.

Now consider how risk becomes amplified when a problem with a faulty semiconductor device is detected at different stages of the value chain. If the problem is discovered when the device is purchased, the loss will be comparatively small — approximately the cost of the device. However, if the problem is detected only after the device has been installed on a printed circuit board, the impact will be greater because the circuit board will have to be either reworked or scrapped. The impact will be greater still if the defect goes undetected and the circuit board is installed in a high-end computer. Servicing a machine in the field is costly, and field failures can cause significant financial hardship for the owner of the machine. If the defect is not an isolated incident, the costs to the computer manufacturer can increase significantly, sometimes leading to damage to its brand and reputation.

Another case where risk propagates in a nonlinear fashion is supply risk. For a product assembled from multiple components, a shortage for even a single component can halt the production of the entire product. This can lead to situations where a small, inexpensive component effectively stops production. Revenue losses associated with such shortages can be orders of magnitude larger than the cost of the constrained part.

1.7. RISK MANAGEMENT

Once a firm has characterized its risk exposure, it can begin to develop a comprehensive plan for managing, mitigating, and transferring risk. Enterprise risk can be managed in a number of ways. Changes to organizational structure and controls can reduce execution errors and improve a firm's ability to respond to a crisis. Strategic approaches to risk management include changes to an enterprise's financial and operating leverage as well as modifications to its portfolio of customers, products, and suppliers. Operationally, a firm can manage or mitigate risk by applying risk-based analytics to a broad set of value chain processes, ranging from product design to demand planning. Financially, risk can be managed using financial derivatives such as futures, swaps, and options (Hull, 1997). Firms can also use a number of different insurance products to limit losses, particularly those associated with severe, low-frequency events.

1.7.1. Organizational Structure and Controls

One of the first steps in establishing an effective risk management program is to make sure that a firm's organizational structure is appropriate to the risks faced by the firm. This involves a number of steps, including defining the firm's risk objectives, clarifying the role of senior management, establishing effective monitoring systems, and creating a set of appropriate internal controls. Senior managers play a central role in implementing an effective risk management program. They are responsible for specifying the risks the firm is willing to bear and the firm's tolerance for risk. They are also responsible for making sure that the organization has the necessary skills and resources to support the firm's risk management strategy.

By creating an appropriate organizational structure, senior management also defines appropriate roles and responsibilities for personnel either directly or indirectly involved in risk management (Knight and Pretty, 2000). In the financial services industry, there has been a trend toward consolidation of the risk function in the office of a chief risk officer, who has the overall responsibility for developing and nurturing a firm's risk management strategy. Many nonfinancial firms are also adopting this approach.

One of the key systems that must be implemented is an integrated risk measurement and management framework. As part of this process, it is critical to establish systems for measuring and reporting different types of risk, so that a firm can effectively monitor and manage its overall risk exposure. Firms also need to establish risk assessment and audit processes coupled with a benchmarking process to provide a vehicle for keeping informed about industry best practices.

Core resources and capabilities required for effective risk management can be grouped into three broad categories: policies, methodologies, and infrastructure (see Figure 1.4). They help support a range of risk management activities, including measuring, monitoring, reporting, controlling, and mitigating risk.

Policies	Methodologies	Infrastructure
■ Risk tolerance	■ Risk profiling	■ People
■ Risk limits	■ Risk modeling	■ Data
■ Approvals processes	■ Pricing and valuation	■ Decision support systems
■ Business continuity	■ Investment analysis	■ Communications systems
■ Disclosure policies	■ Performance measurement	
■ Internal controls		

Figure 1.4. Core risk management resources and capabilities.

Risk management policies define and implement an organization's risk management strategy along multiple dimensions. At a high level, they define a firm's tolerance for risk and provide principles for evaluating the trade-off between risk and return within the context of the firm's overall business objectives. They also provide specific guidelines and procedures to disseminate a firm's risk management strategy throughout the organization.

Disclosure policies provide guidelines to help senior managers understand and report the risks inherent in their businesses. Disclosure policies clearly state the duties and responsibilities for each business unit and specify the relevant internal controls, including self-management, that must be established.

Certain policies are designed to help a firm manage unusual situations and to keep the business operating smoothly when catastrophe strikes. A continuity of business policy specifies a set of operating procedures for addressing risky events. It provides guidelines on how to respond during times of crisis and describes contingency plans, risk monitoring techniques, and procedures to recover from a business interruption.

Risk management methodologies comprise a common set of frameworks, models, tools, and analytics that support a broad range of risk management activities, including risk characterization, risk modeling, and valuation. Methodologies go beyond the mere mechanics of risk analysis; they provide guidelines and procedures for estimating different types of risk and for constructing and validating models. Valuation methodologies are used to evaluate strategic acquisitions and to perform capital budgeting. They also provide important insights when negotiating and structuring joint ventures, strategic alliances, and outsourcing deals. A comprehensive set of risk management methodologies helps a firm consistently account for risk in decision making, particularly when computing risk-adjusted returns for individual divisions and projects and when adjusting performance measurements to account for risk.

An adequate infrastructure is necessary to support risk management business processes. People are probably the most critical infrastructure component, since they supply a broad range of capabilities to effectively detect, analyze, and mitigate risk. Risk management is data intensive and requires accurate and timely information to support effective decision making. The technological infrastructure of a firm can play a significant role in effectively processing and disseminating information about risk incidents and events.

Enterprise risk management often requires information that crosses both functional and system boundaries. In the past, this posed significant challenges for firms forced to reconcile and link data from multiple disparate legacy systems. The widespread adoption (and increased integration) of software solutions such as enterprise resource planning, supply chain management, and customer relationship management makes it easier to develop data repositories to support risk management.

Development of a cross-enterprise risk management backbone for integrating and disseminating risk management data can help companies improve their effectiveness at managing risk. This backbone would provide information to support more advanced risk management methodologies, including risk analytics and rule-based systems for detecting and responding to risk.

1.7.2. Strategic Risk Management

In this section, a number of ways to incorporate risk management into strategic decision making are discussed. First, a number of strategic approaches for altering a firm's level of risk are considered. Then several modeling and analysis techniques that support decision making under uncertainty are described.

A number of techniques have been broadly applied in the financial world to manage risk. These include leverage, diversification, and hedging. Financial forms of these techniques — as well as their strategic analogues — can be applied to modify a firm's risk profile.

Financial leverage alters risk by changing a firm's capital structure — its mix of debt and equity. Carrying more debt increases leverage — and risk. Besides issuing debt, firms can increase their financial leverage in a number of ways, including the use of capital leases and by issuing preferred stock. Firms have considerable latitude and flexibility in determining their degree of financial leverage, and techniques for determining an optimal capital structure have been widely studied and applied.

Operating leverage is determined by a firm's cost structure, rather than its capital structure. The higher a firm's fixed costs, the greater its operating leverage. One of the primary determinants of a firm's cost structure is its choice of production technology. Capital-intensive firms tend to have higher fixed costs, since they need to cover depreciation expense on their assets. This makes their earnings more sensitive to changes in customer demand, since a larger portion of revenue must be allocated to cover fixed expenses. Capital-intensive production processes also tend to have lower unit costs. This means that at low production volumes, they are less profitable. At high production volumes, however, they have much higher profitability. Decisions about capital invest-ments thus involve a trade-off between the risk of increasing operating leverage and the potential for higher profits.

A number of value chain decisions can have a major effect on a firm's operating leverage. Investments in highly automated production and distribution facilities increase fixed costs and hence risk. Outsourcing arrangements affect operating leverage, with the magnitude of the change determined by how the deal is structured. A long-term contract to outsource warehousing to a third-party logistics provider would have little effect on a firm's operating leverage if predetermined payments to the provider merely substitute for the fixed costs of company-owned warehouses. An agreement to outsource production to a contract manufacturer, on the other hand, could reduce operating leverage sig-nificantly, as long as contractual volume commitments are relatively low. Joint ventures and strategic alliances often entail shared investments and funding commitments and hence can affect operating leverage. The way a firm struc-tures its supplier and customer contracts can also have a significant impact on its risk profile. Contracts with volume commitments, such as take-or-pay supply contracts,* increase operating leverage by increasing fixed charges.

An enterprise can also manage risk strategically through *diversification.* *Financial diversification* is used to reduce the risk of portfolios of financial assets. It is based on the premise that changes in the prices of securities like stocks and bonds do not move precisely in tandem, since different securities are subject to different risk factors. By constructing portfolios consisting of stocks and bonds that tend to move in different directions, price movements tend to cancel out, reducing portfolio volatility.

Operational diversification can be broadly applied to a variety of business processes at both the strategic and tactical level. Enterprises can diversify by acquiring new businesses in unrelated industries, targeting diverse market seg-ments, broadening their product portfolios, and marketing in multiple geo-graphic regions and to multiple customer segments.

Finance theory has developed a rich set of techniques for effectively man-aging portfolios of financial assets. These can be applied to strategic decision making as well. Doing so is particularly important in complex business situ-

---

* A take-or-pay contract obliges the customer to pay for a specified minimum number of parts or components, even if the customer actually purchases less than that minimum.

ations where it is difficult to effectively diversify using only simple analyses and intuition. Firms are now gathering and capturing more detailed information about their customers, products, and suppliers. This information can be mined to discover patterns that can be exploited to develop more efficient portfolios.

The third cornerstone of strategic risk management is *hedging*. In a process related to diversification, *financial hedging* reduces the effect of one or more risk factors on an asset such as a financial portfolio or physical commodity. A hedge is created by first identifying a security whose price movements directly track the risk factor being hedged. This security is then used to offset the impact of the risk factor. Corporations use financial hedging to reduce the uncertainty associated with a broad range of risks, including foreign exchange rates, interest rates, and commodities prices.

Operational hedging uses a similar approach, but instead of transforming risk with a financial instrument, it does so by changing a firm's strategy or operations. A simple example shows how this works. Consider a hypothetical U.S. automobile manufacturer selling cars in Japan. It has a sales and distribution network located in Japan, but no local production facilities. As a result, the company has substantial revenue denominated in yen, but most of its costs are in dollars. Its net foreign exchange exposure is the gap between the amount of yen it receives and the amount of yen it pays out. Since this gap is large, the company has considerable foreign exchange risk.

If the company establishes local production facilities in Japan, payments for running the facilities will be made in yen, as will labor costs and purchases from local suppliers. As a result of this change, a much larger percentage of the firm's costs are denominated in yen. This reduces its net yen exposure. It now has less foreign exchange risk.

A natural hedge can also be more robust than a financial hedge. Hedging revenues financially can be difficult in practice, since at the time the hedge is being executed, a firm may not know exactly how large its revenues will be. For a natural hedge, this is less of an issue, since costs tend to track revenue closely.

The decision to build a new production facility abroad clearly has many strategic implications that might outweigh the benefits of reducing foreign exchange risk. However, there are many ways to apply operational hedging that are simpler to implement and require far less investment.* For example, instead

---

* This is not to say that firms should ignore opportunities to establish operational hedges when making decisions about where to locate production facilities. The potential benefits of reducing foreign exchange rate risk should be carefully weighed, along with other evaluation criteria.

of moving production abroad to change its foreign exchange exposure, a firm can sometimes achieve a similar result simply by changing suppliers or by altering the terms of its supply contracts.

Other forms of operational hedges can also be constructed. The process of managing supply and demand can be improved by optimally matching supply and demand to ensure that financial performance is less sensitive to a variety of value chain risks. The approach can also be applied to contract management and to the balancing of investments in production capacity with investments in sales and marketing activity.

Another way that firms can reduce risk is through value chain restructuring. Restructuring improves the efficiency of a firm's extended value chain by removing or consolidating redundant or inefficient stages. It does so by eliminating intermediaries, simplifying business processes, or introducing new types of interactions between value chain partners. New approaches for value chain restructuring enabled by information technologies have emerged in the past few years, including middleware to support business process integration as well as the use of on-line marketplaces and collaboration networks to conduct transactions and exchange information.

Value chain restructuring can reduce risk in a number of ways. A shorter value chain means that goods spend less time being processed and thus have less exposure to risk. This is especially important for technology products and fashion goods, where every extra minute in the supply pipeline increases the risk of price declines and obsolescence. Uncertainty tends to increase over time, so the longer a product takes to reach the final customer, the greater the risk.

Value chain restructuring also decreases risk by reducing value chain complexity. This helps eliminate execution errors and reduces supply risk by making it easier to coordinate activities with suppliers. With fewer intermediaries between an enterprise and its final customers, the firm also receives more timely information about demand and supply fluctuations. Inventory and production assets can thus be utilized more efficiently.

Changing the nature of value chain interactions can also reduce risk. Often this works by altering information flows and incentives. For example, collaborative business models such as vendor-managed inventory provide suppliers with greater inventory visibility without physically shortening the value chain. Nevertheless, the supplier still receives more accurate and timely information about customer demand.

The approaches discussed here for strategically managing risk can be applied to a broad range of business processes. A number of applications of these techniques are illustrated in Table 1.2. Many of these decisions entail trade-offs, since reducing one form of risk can introduce others. For example, supplier diversification reduces the risk of supply disruptions, but it can also increase supply chain complexity, leading to higher costs and more execution errors. Similarly, geographical diversification to reduce labor price risk may require investments in countries with high political uncertainty, increasing political, legal, and regulatory risk.

1.7.3. Operational Risk Management

Developing integrated risk management systems that link strategy, planning, and execution requires the deployment of systems, measurements, and processes for managing and mitigating operational risk. Drawing on best practices in the financial services industry, several key features of an operational risk management program will be described. Then a high-level systems architecture is presented for an integrated risk management system that integrates risk management at an operational level with an enterprise's strategy and plans.

The objective of operational risk management is to minimize business disruptions, improve the response to crises, and constrain the adverse consequence of risky events. This is accomplished by integrating several forms of risk management functionality into business operations. Many of the risk management approaches discussed here can be directly applied to reduce execution errors and improve crisis management. They can serve as a model for implementing information systems to monitor and respond to risky supply chain events. They also describe a hierarchical approach to establishing risk limits that can be applied in a production setting and provide a useful set of measurements for monitoring and tracking operational risks.

Operational risk management begins by determining how much risk a firm is willing to absorb. This is defined in terms of the amount of money the firm is willing to lose due to risky activities. Since a firm's profit potential depends on its appetite for risk, acceptable losses are determined within the context of a firm's overall financial objectives, including its profit and revenue targets.

Once acceptable risk levels have been established for the firm as a whole, risk limits are defined at the business unit level, where business managers have the ability to influence and control risk. Risk limits are often expressed in terms of value at risk, with acceptable loss levels specified for different time horizons. Establishing these limits typically involves analyzing the unit's business activities and their fit with the firm's overall tolerance for risk. Setting appropriate limits is something of a balancing act. The aim is to control the risks taken by business units without placing constraints that unnecessarily limit flexibility. If risk limits are too conservative, they can hinder the business unit's ability to meet its overall revenue and profit targets. In evaluating the performance of

Table 1.2. Approaches for Strategically Managing Risk

	Leverage	Diversification	Hedging	Restructuring
Value chain design	■ Modify using changes in production technology ■ Modify by outsourcing production	■ Geographical diversification to reduce hazard risk ■ Political unit diversification to reduce political risk and tax risk ■ Geographical diversification to reduce labor price risk	■ Natural hedging of foreign exchange risk ■ Matching inbound and outbound supply chain capacity and flexibility ■ Matching supply chain capacity to marketing capability ■ Matching supply chain flexibility to customer demand volatility	■ Value chain restructuring ■ Alternative value chain interactions ■ Supply chain redesigned to reduce cycle time and inventory ■ Value chain simplification to reduce complexity risk ■ Create growth and flexibility options
Strategic sourcing strategy	■ Increase by selecting vendors requiring capacity commitments ■ Reduce by consolidating spending to improve flexibility terms	■ Vendor diversification to reduce supply and price risk ■ Vendor diversification to reduce hazard risk	■ Hedge demand volatility with supply-demand matching ■ Natural hedging of foreign exchange risk	■ Single-source selected components to reduce complexity ■ Increase information sharing with core suppliers ■ Improve planning coordination and synchronization ■ Increase flexibility with spot market buys ■ Create growth and flexibility options
Supply and sales contract portfolio design	■ Modify by changing contract terms	■ Manage portfolio of flexibility options ■ Manage portfolio of embedded options	■ Hedge demand volatility with supply flexibility terms ■ Hedge price and foreign exchange risk with embedded options	■ Improve information sharing with contract incentives

	Modify	Diversify	Hedge	Create options
Product portfolio design	■ Modify by making changes in portfolio composition ■ Modify by considering relationship with strategic sourcing	■ Diversify to improve portfolio risk-return trade-off	■ Hedge demand volatility with product choices ■ Parts commonality to hedge supply risk	■ Create learning, growth, and flexibility options
Strategic acquisitions	■ Modify by acquiring new production facilities ■ Modify by acquiring new production technology	■ Customer and market segment diversification to reduce demand risk ■ Geographical diversification to reduce demand risk ■ Technological diversification to reduce product risk	■ Hedge demand volatility with complementary product lines ■ Hedge supply risk with complementary suppliers	■ Create learning, growth, and flexibility options
Outsourcing, strategic partnerships, and alliances	■ Modify by investing in new joint production facilities ■ Modify by obtaining access to new production technology	■ Customer and market segment diversification to reduce demand risk ■ Geographical diversification to reduce demand risk ■ Technological diversification to reduce product risk	■ Hedge technology risk by placing multiple bets ■ Hedge demand volatility with new products ■ Hedge demand volatility by targeting new geographies and market segments	■ Create learning, growth, and flexibility options

business units and individuals, risk must be quantified and priced to verify that superior performance is not the result of taking on excessive risk. When assessing operational performance, it is thus common to use metrics such as risk-adjusted revenue or risk-adjusted profit.

Effective risk management requires extensive information. Capturing inputs directly from business operations, systems track information required to analyze risk and to support appropriate management controls. By taking a modular approach to risk management, the risk management process can be structured so risks can be managed collectively. This allows multitasking, enabling different parts of an organizations to effectively coordinate their risk management actions. Ideally, an operational risk management system should also include means for capturing and structuring organizational learning about risk.

Effective operational risk management requires continuous monitoring, not only of risks but also of the effectiveness of the program itself. Metrics for benchmarking program effectiveness include losses avoided, opportunities capitalized, the speed of new product introduction, level of management comfort, efficiency of control, and overall enterprise risk-return profile. Operational risk management programs also establish a capability for managing business contingencies. These include not only backup systems, but also procedures for handling extreme conditions. Their key aim is to establish a balance between risk control and business flexibility, while ensuring the speedy resolution of a crisis.

1.7.4. Financial Risk Management

Historically, firms have used the financial markets to manage a broad range of market risks, including foreign exchange, interest rates, equity prices, and commodity prices. As financial engineering techniques have evolved, new derivatives products have emerged to protect against a broad range of new risks (Hull, 1997). Some of these products are standardized, while others can be highly customized to meet the specific needs of a particular party.

Financial risk management is concerned primarily with risk transfer — shifting risk from one party to another. In a corporate setting, a firm typically seeks to transfer some or all of its risk to a third party, such as a bank, an insurance company, a speculator, or an investor. Risk transfers do not always reduce risk. Sometimes a firm will actually assume additional risk as part of its financial management strategy. In other cases, a firm may keep its total risk exposure constant, instead of merely transforming one form of risk into another.

In analyzing whether it makes sense to hedge a particular risk using derivatives, a firm should consider a number of factors. The first is the likely impact of the risk factor on the business. If prices for a particular risk factor are not especially volatile, or if a firm's profitability or market value is not particularly sensitive to changes in the risk factor, then it probably does not make sense to hedge. Event though a firm's costs may be very sensitive to changes in the price of a particular part or commodity, it does not always make sense to hedge. For example, if a firm is able to pass along price increases for procured components to its customers, it may not make sense to hedge.* However, if a firm needs to hold substantial inventories of a part or commodity, this creates a risk exposure, and hedging might be appropriate.

Another factor to consider is the likelihood of being able to establish an effective hedge. Sometimes the instruments used to manage risk do not precisely offset the risk faced by a company. This could happen, for example, for an electronics firm purchasing a special type of gold for electrical interconnects. The price it pays its gold fabricator may not precisely track the price of gold traded on a commodities exchange. This introduces basis risk, the difference between price changes of the asset being hedged and price changes in the hedging instrument.

Ineffective hedges have two primary disadvantages. First, if basis risk is large, hedging not only becomes ineffective but also can actually increase risk. Furthermore, ineffective hedges may not qualify for hedge accounting treatment for financial accounting purposes. When this is the case, offsetting price changes in the hedging instrument and the asset being hedged may be reported at different times. This can have the effect of increasing the volatility in reported earnings, even though cash flows are actually less volatile in purely economic terms.

Firms also have to consider the costs associated with hedging. Transaction costs can be high, especially for options. Furthermore, it can often be difficult to completely understand all of the costs (and risks) associated with managing risk financially. This raises the possibility of incurring significant unexpected losses if certain unanticipated events transpire.

In some cases, it may be difficult to get a fair price for derivatives. This is usually not the case for exchange-traded derivatives or for widely traded over-the-counter instruments such as foreign exchange options and forward contracts. However, prices for custom derivatives products are notoriously difficult to model. This can make it difficult to determine whether an offered price is fair, especially since comparison shopping for highly custom products can be difficult. A similar problem arises for thinly traded over-the-counter derivatives in emerging markets for underlying assets such as bandwidth, electronic compo-

---

* In fact, when a firm can naturally offset its risk in this fashion, hedging is counterproductive. It actually increases the firm's risk, since it creates an exposure to price changes in the hedging instrument.

nents, and weather. Derivatives brokers and dealers often have significant information advantages that they can exploit with their customers, since their traders are exposed to a far broader range of marketplace transactions.

Firms also have to consider the strategic implications of their risk management activities. In low-margin industries, the cost of hedging with options may leave little room for profit. A firm locking in the prices of procured components using futures or forwards contracts may remove uncertainty about its costs, but it may increase the uncertainty of its earnings. For example, a personal computer manufacturer buying DRAM swaps to fix the price of its computer memory purchases may find its cost structure uncompetitive if DRAM prices drop dramatically. Competitors will have the advantage of buying at low market prices, while the firm has to continue paying the higher fixed price established by the swaps contract.

Supply contract terms and conditions frequently have characteristics that make them behave much like financial derivatives. Examples include price adders linked to commodities prices and pricing pegged to a particular foreign currency. Embedded derivatives effectively transfer risk between value chain partners, such as suppliers and their customers. Embedded derivatives can be exploited in several ways. Often they provide a particularly effective hedge, since the amount of risk transferred changes depending on the actual quantity of goods or services purchased through the contract. They are also sometimes mispriced. This presents an opportunity for one value chain partner to transfer away risk more cheaply than would be possible using traditional financial derivatives.

One interesting trend is the emergence of new risk management products that can be used to hedge risks closely linked to a firm's operating profits. An example is weather derivatives, financial instruments whose payoff is pegged to temperature changes at particular geographical locations. Derivatives are also emerging for electricity, telecommunications bandwidth, and electronic components such as computer memory chips. The increasing availability of such derivatives products will enable firms to manage a broader set of risks, many of which are central to their business performance.

1.7.5. Insurance

A wide variety of insurance products are available, many of which can be customized to meet particular customer needs. In addition, new products are evolving that share characteristics of both insurance and financial products. These hybrids seek to combine the efficiency of the financial markets with the specialization of insurance.

Conventional insurance focuses primarily on indemnifying a firm against losses. Insurance policies are available to protect against numerous hazards, including property damage, injuries, theft, and a variety of potential liabilities.

Insurance companies offer a grab bag of products that are loosely referred to as nontraditional insurance or alternative risk transfer (ART) products. In general, these offerings seek to address significant risks whose management requires specialized expertise not available from noninsurance firms. Examples include structured deals that offer special accounting or tax treatments, insurance against operational risk, and protection against exposures such as credit risk and the weather. These products often seek to address a firm's requirement for capital after significant business losses and are specifically designed to limit downside risk on a firm's income statement or balance sheet.

Many ART products are a special form of debt where payments are contingent on a certain event. For example, forgivable debt, such as "catastrophe bonds," is structured so that principal or interest payments are waived following a predefined event such as a natural disaster. For structured debt, principal or interest payment is linked to the market price of oil or another commodity. Other ART offerings are hybrids of debt and equity. For example, reverse convertible debt can be converted to equity at the option of the issuer to reduce its financial leverage when cash is short.

Structured deals or finite risk insurance (FRI) are products that limit the amount of risk transferred. They often also involve packaging multiple risks. FRI also usually includes a profit-sharing mechanism that allows for an ex-post adjustment in the insurance premium based on the claim experience of the purchasing firm. FRI has a longer term than conventional insurance products, with coverage typically lasting for three to five years.

It is often difficult to distinguish between insurance and financial risk management products. Furthermore, the boundary between the two is constantly shifting. Risk needs to be fairly standardized to develop liquidity in the financial markets. It also needs to be fairly easy to price, so different market participants can readily trade it. For risks that the financial markets cannot absorb, insurance can be an effective alternative. For example, weather insurance used to be the domain of insurers, but has now largely shifted to the financial markets. Since weather risk can be fairly easily standardized, and can be modeled using existing options pricing models, liquid markets for weather derivatives have quickly developed.

Firms have a number of choices regarding the types of risks to insure and how to insure them. This is illustrated in Figure 1.5, which shows appropriate risk management vehicles for risks with different frequency and severity (Dickinson, 2000; Williams et al., 1997). Insurance tends to be more expensive

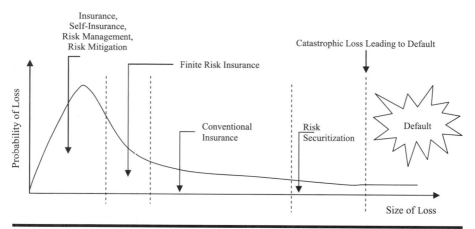

Figure 1.5. Risk coverage spectrum.

than financial forms of risk management. Insurance is therefore typically used to manage residual risk — risk that cannot effectively be addressed either operationally or through financial risk management.

For frequent, low-severity losses, firms typically use self-insurance and other risk management techniques. Since such losses are usually fairly predictable, and their consequences limited, they do not contribute significant uncertainty.

When losses are infrequent, risk tends to be harder to model. Insurance companies have developed specialized expertise that enables them to price these risks effectively. For example, estimating the expected losses associated with extremely rare events can be extraordinarily difficult and is one of the core competencies of commercial insurers and reinsurers. In particular, for rare events with extremely high potential losses, insurance may be the only option, since firms typically do not have enough capital to self-insure.

FRI and structured deals can be used as a layer between self-insurance and conventional insurance for securing postloss funding. Firms sometimes also retain some of this risk, but typically cap their potential losses through reinsurance.

Risk securitization can be used for extremely rare events that are especially severe.* Finally, there are certain business risks that cannot be insured or managed financially. These are the risks that equity holders are paid to bear. If too large a loss occurs, insurance will not be able to cover it, and the firm has no choice but bankruptcy.

Insurance innovation may some day enable insurers to offer nontraditional products targeted specifically at value chain risks, such as parts shortages or

---

* Risk securitization is the packaging of risk for sale in financial markets. Such products are therefore financial-insurance hybrids.

unexpected drops in customer demand.* New models will be required to estimate the potential losses from such disruptions and their frequency of occurrence. However, some of the analytics discussed earlier in the section on operational risk management could be extended to price these risks. In addition, the presence of appropriate risk-monitoring systems could be used to justify lower premiums and could provide data necessary for an insurer to assess its risk exposure prior to extending coverage.

REFERENCES

Aeppel, T., White, J. B., and Power, S. (2001). Firestone quits as tire supplier to Ford — Auto company is accused of refusing to concede to SUV safety concerns, *The Wall Street Journal*, May 22.

Bazerman, M. H. (1997). *Judgment in Managerial Decision-Making*, 4th ed., Wiley, New York.

Berinato, S. (2001). What went wrong at Cisco, *CIO Magazine*, August 1.

Bradsher, K. (2001). Ford and Firestone wrangle over rollovers and tires, *The New York Times*, May 24.

Clemen, R. (1996). *Making Hard Decisions*, Duxbury Press, Belmont, CA.

Committee on the Global Financial System (2000). Stress Testing by Large Financial Institutions: Current Practice and Aggregation Issues, Committee on the Global Financial System, Basel, March (available at http://www.bis.org/publ/cgfs14.htm).

Crouhy, M., Galai, D., and Mark, R. (2001). *Risk Management*, McGraw-Hill, New York.

Dickinson, G. (2000). Insurance finds a blend of innovation and tradition, *Financial Times*, Mastering Risk Series, Part VII, June 6.

Doherty, N. (2000). Insurance and finance: New vehicles for driving value, *Financial Times*, Mastering Risk Series, Part IV, May 16.

Duffie, D. and Pan, J. (1997). An overview of value at risk, *Journal of Derivatives*, 4(3), 7–49, Spring.

E.I.U. (2001). Enterprise Risk Management: Implementing New Solutions, Technical Paper, The Economist Intelligence Unit Limited, London and MMC Enterprise Risk, New York.

Ervolina, T., Ettl, M., Grey, W., Kalagnanam, J., Katircioglu, K., Ramachandran, B., and Shi, D. (2001). Supply Chain Risk Management Decision Support Tools and Applications, IBM Technical Paper.

Grimmett, G. R. and Stirzaker, D. R. (1982). *Probability and Random Processes,* Oxford University Press, Oxford, U.K.

Hendricks, K. and Singhal, V. R. (2000). Report on Supply Chain Glitches and Shareholder Value Destruction, Working Paper, DuPree College of Management, Georgia Institute of Technology, Atlanta, December.

---

* Such policies would be similar to existing offerings, such as business interruption insurance and surety insurance.

Hertz, D. (1979). Risk analysis in capital investment, *Harvard Business Review*, September–October.

Hull, J. (1997). *Options, Futures and Other Derivatives*, Prentice Hall, Upper Saddle River, NJ.

Johnson, M. E. and Pyke, D. F. (1999). Supply Chain Management, Working Paper, The Tuck School of Business, Dartmouth College, Hanover, NH.

Jorion, P. (1997). *Value at Risk*, McGraw-Hill, New York.

Kahneman, D. and Tversky, A. (1979). Prospect theory: An analysis of decision under risk, *Econometrica*, 47, 262–290.

Kashiwagi, A. (2001). Recalls cost Bridgestone dearly — Firestone parent's profit drops 80%, *The Washington Post*, February 23.

Knight, R. and Pretty, D. (2000). Philosophies of risk, shareholder value and the CEO, *Financial Times*, Mastering Risk Series, Part X, June 27.

Kogut, B. and Kulatilaka, N. (1994). Options thinking and platform investments: Investing in opportunity, *California Management Review*, 36, 52–71.

Latour, A. (2001). A fire in Albuquerque sparks crisis for European cell-phone giants — Nokia handles shock with aplomb as Ericsson of Sweden gets burned, *The Wall Street Journal Interactive Edition*, January 29.

Law, A. M. and Kelton, W. D. (1991). *Simulation Modeling & Analysis*, McGraw-Hill, New York.

Lewin, C. (2000). Refining the art of the probable, *Financial Times*, Mastering Risk Series, Part II, May 2.

Markowitz, H. M. (1952). Portfolio selection, *Journal of Finance*, 7(1), 77–91.

Pilipovic, D. (1998). *Energy Risk*, McGraw-Hill, New York.

Piller, C. (2001). E-business: Meeting the technology challenge; with big software projects, firms find haste makes waste, *Los Angeles Times*, April 2.

Stulz, R. (2000). Diminishing the threats to shareholder wealth, *Financial Times*, Mastering Risk Series, Part I, April 25.

Trigeorgis, L. (1997). *Real Options*, MIT Press, Cambridge, MA.

Williams, C. A., Smith, M. L., and Young, P. C. (1997). *Risk Management and Insurance*, 8th ed., McGraw-Hill, New York.

Wilson, T. (2001). Supply chain debacle — Nike faces yearlong inventory problem after I2 implementation fails, *Internetweek*, March 5.

INTEGRATED RISK MANAGEMENT

Samir Shah

2.1. INTRODUCTION

Over the past decade, risk management has witnessed explosive growth and increased specialization. The maturity of the financial engineering discipline has fueled a frenzy in the banking sector to create ever-more exotic forms of risk packaging and risk transfer products. Banks continue to compete aggressively on the basis of their ability to transfer clients' financial risks to the capital markets. There has also been some innovation in the insurance market as insurers have developed custom products to securitize the risk of natural disasters and protect against emerging risks such as weather, cyber crime, rogue trading, and terrorism. Companies have also become more expert at self-insuring their own risks through a variety of onshore and offshore captive insurance companies. This proliferation of risk management activities occurred simultaneously with an increased specialization of risk management products and markets.

Companies at the forefront of the advances in risk management have organized their risk management function to mirror the specialization of products and markets. There are typically separate risk managers for each major category of risk (e.g., interest rate risk, foreign exchange risk, commodity price risk, credit risk, operational risk, and insurable property and casualty risks). The risk management decisions are typically not coordinated, although the overall investment in risk management activity is consolidated in the finance function. In the process, companies have lost sight of the interaction among risks. The consequence of this "silo" approach to risk management is a strategy that does not meet its objectives and costs too much.

This chapter presents the motivation and methodology for integrating risk management decisions. It does this first by describing the internal and external forces that drive an increasing number of companies to adopt a holistic view of risk management. A mathematical example comparing the performance of the silo approach to the integrated approach for risk management clarifies the tangible benefits of integrated risk management. The example also provides a window into the mathematics underlying such an analysis. Then the process of modeling and managing risks in an integrated fashion is described. Each step of the process discusses the details that are not transparent in the example. The notes and references at the end of the chapter provide clarification and options for anyone wishing to pursue the topic at a higher level.

2.2. MOTIVATION FOR ENTERPRISE RISK MANAGEMENT

Some organizations are adopting enterprise risk management in response to direct and indirect pressure from corporate governance bodies and institutional investors. Failures in corporate risk management, some well publicized, have led to efforts by regulators, rating agencies, stock exchanges, institutional investors, and corporate governance oversight bodies to insist that senior management and directors take greater responsibility for managing risks on an enterprise-wide scale. These efforts span virtually all the developed countries and they encompass virtually all industries.

- In the United Kingdom, the London Stock Exchange has adopted a set of principles, the Combined Code, which makes directors responsible for reviewing risk management controls and their effectiveness.
- In Germany, a mandatory bill, the KonTraG, which became law in 1998, requires the management board to establish supervisory systems for risk management and to report on these systems to the supervisory board. Auditors appointed by the supervisory board must examine the implementation of risk management.
- In Canada, the Dey report, commissioned by the Toronto Exchange, and the clarifying "Guidance on Control" (CoCo report), produced by the Canadian Institute of Chartered Accountants, specifies that internal control should include the process of enterprise risk assessment and risk management.
- In the United States, the Securities and Exchange Commission requires companies to describe risks that may have a material impact on future financial performance within 10-K and 10-Q statements.

- The American Institute of Certified Public Accountants produced an analysis entitled "Improving Business Reporting — A Customer Focus" (also known as the Jenkins Report), in which it recommends that reporting of risks be improved to include a discussion of all risks/opportunities that (1) are current, (2) are of serious concern, (3) have an impact on earnings or cash flow, (4) are specific or unique, and (5) have been identified and considered by management.
- In the Netherlands, the Peters Report made 40 recommendations on corporate governance, including one that the management board submit an annual report to the supervisory board on a corporation's objectives, strategy, related risks, and control systems.
- In the United States, a committee of five major professional accounting associations (COSO) published an integrated framework for enterprise risk management.

There are additional external pressures unique to the financial sector. Since financial institutions are in the business of buying, holding, and selling risks faced by the rest of industry, it is vital to all commerce that their risk management is based on a solid foundation. It should come as no surprise that financial institutions were among the first to embrace the concept of enterprise risk management.

- In the United Kingdom, the Financial Services Authority (the recently created regulator of all U.K. financial services business) is introducing a system of risk-based supervision that will create a single set of prudential requirements organized by risk rather than by type of business. Regulated businesses will have to demonstrate that they have identified all material risks and have adequate systems and financial resources to manage and finance such risks, including market risk, credit risk, operational risk, and insurance risk.
- The Basel Committee on Banking Supervision has proposed a New Basel Capital Accord (a.k.a. Basel II) intended to become the new capital framework for large banks worldwide. The new capital framework includes an explicit capital charge for operational risks. The charge reflects the committee's "realization that risks other than market and credit" can be substantial. Operational risk is broadly defined as "the risk of direct and indirect loss resulting from inadequate or failed internal processes, people and systems or from external events."
- The European Commission is working on Solvency II, a new risk-based approach for solvency requirements for insurance companies. Solvency II is an interpretation for the insurance sector of Basel II in the banking sector.

- The International Actuarial Association, in its publication *Insurance Liabilities — Valuation & Capital Requirements*, classifies risk into eight types: credit, transfer, market, business, operational, mortality, morbidity, and property and casualty. It states that "...the calculation of economic capital should be based on the expected ruin probabilities or default rates, taking into account all the risks to which the company is subject."

- In Canada, the Office of Superintendent of Financial Institutions, in its *Supervisory Framework: 1999 and Beyond*, defines "inherent risk" to include credit risk, market risk, insurance risk, operational risk, liquidity risk, legal and regulatory risk, and strategic risk.

Whereas some organizations are motivated primarily by external forces, other organizations simply regard enterprise risk management as good business. These organizations view systematic anticipation of material threats to their strategic plans as integral to executing those plans and operating their businesses. They seek to eliminate the inefficiencies built into managing risk within individual "silos," and they appreciate that their cost of capital can be reduced through managing earnings volatility. Publicly traded companies, in particular, know the keen and increasing desire of their investors for stable earnings.

There are many real-world examples from which to draw observations on the need to integrate risk management:

- An insurance company providing directors and officers (D&O) liability insurance coverage to a conglomerate was also investing in the securities of the same company. D&O coverage provides reimbursement to directors and officers of a company for losses due to claims made against them by shareholders. To make matters worse, the insurance company had also entered into a reinsurance treaty with a subsidiary of the conglomerate. It is quite likely that if a major event resulted in insurance losses due to successful lawsuits against the directors and officers of the conglomerate, it would also result in investment losses due to a drop in the stock price and potentially credit losses on commitments made by the reinsurance subsidiary.

  The underwriter (responsible for writing D&O policies), the investment manager (responsible for investing insurance company assets), and the director of reinsurance (responsible for purchasing reinsurance) do not coordinate their decisions, as these activities are conducted in distinct organizational units. The result is an overconcentration of exposure to insurance risk, market risk, and credit risk to a single event, namely, the demise of the parent company. If this scenario seems farfetched, see Enron, WorldCom, Barings, Andersen Consulting, et al.

■ The current pension crisis faced by many companies in the United States is similarly the result of the interaction of multiple risks. Pension liabilities are exposed to interest rate risks: as interest rates decrease, liabilities increase due to the decrease in the discount rate used to determine the present value of future pension payments. Pension assets are exposed to equity market risks, as pension asset portfolios are typically weighted toward equities. Company profitability is exposed to business cycle risks. The environment in 2003 of low interest rates, depressed equity markets, and a recession created a "perfect storm," resulting in significant pension underfunding and requiring companies to substantially increase their pension contributions at a time when they can least afford to do so.

Making matters worse, many employees, close to retirement and fearing company failure, are retiring early and selecting the option of receiving their entire pension as a lump sum immediately. This "run on the bank" has created liquidity risks for many pension plans, further exacerbating the situation.

■ A major energy company managed its exposure to commodity prices, foreign exchange fluctuations, and property and casualty risks through separate departments. The commodity price risks were managed through active trading in the capital markets by two separate trading groups, one focused on natural gas price risk and the other on oil price risk; foreign exchange risks were managed by the treasurer; and the property and casualty risks were managed by a risk manager through purchase of insurance. Although the combined impact on earnings was a result of the interaction among these risks, surprisingly, none of the groups coordinated their decisions. An exploratory study on the possible benefits of integrating the risk management decisions revealed that by not reflecting the correlation among these risks, the company had significantly overspent on hedging its risks and not met its risk reduction objectives.

■ Senior management of a life insurance company did not anticipate that the interaction of product design risk, ratings risk, and liquidity risk could interact in such a way as to result in the failure of the company. Moody's Investors Service, a rating agency, downgraded the company from A2 to A3, citing the liquidity of the company's investment portfolio. The lower rating is below the rating that most institutional investors will accept (ratings risk). The downgrade resulted in 37 institutional investors seeking withdrawal of contracts valued at billions of dollars within the seven days stipulated in their contracts (product design risk). When the insurer failed to meet its obligations (liquidity risk), Moody's downgraded the company's rating to B1, as did other rating agencies. Since the ability of a financial institution to generate revenue through new sales is directly linked to its credit rating, the downgrade precluded the company from solving its liquidity crunch through new business. In a matter of days, the company was put under administrative supervision of the state regulator and was ultimately acquired by another insurer in an eleventh-hour rescue. All this in a matter of days!

■ A telephone company operating in California suffered huge losses due to an earthquake in the region. Fortunately, the losses were insured. However, the company did not anticipate an upward spike in the number of telephone calls resulting from the earthquake. These were presumably placed by people calling to check on the well-being of their friends and relatives living in the area of the earthquake. The calls resulted in an unexpected, significant increase in revenues, which offset the losses suffered in the earthquake! The natural hedge resulting from the interaction of earthquake risk and revenue risk could possibly have allowed the company to self-insure some of the earthquake risk and reduce its hefty risk premium.

Several observations are worth noting:

■ Investors, rating agencies, and regulatory bodies hold senior management accountable for managing risks on an enterprise-wide basis.
■ Often, it is not one risk that results in catastrophic losses but the interaction of multiple risks. In each of the examples above, companies were in a position to respond well to each risk in isolation; however, they had not anticipated the compounding of losses due to the interaction of multiple risks.
■ Integrating risk management decisions can create opportunities to reduce costs by recognizing natural hedges, as in the case of the telephone company, and/or diversification benefits, as in the case of the oil company.

2.3. MATHEMATICAL EXAMPLE OF INTEGRATED RISK MANAGEMENT

The easiest way to demonstrate the advantages of integrating risk management decisions is through a hypothetical example. The example also illustrates the analytics for integrating risk management decisions.

Let us start simply by first looking at how a company might manage a single risk. We will then add a second source of risk and compare the management of both risks on a silo basis with an integrated approach. The example strives to illustrate a real-world risk management task. However, many details that must be considered in the real world but are ancillary to the analysis have been omitted in order to present a clear and concise illustration of the main theme. These omissions do not materially affect the analysis or the results.

Risk 1. Oil Price Risk Management

Let us assume that an enterprise's earnings are subject to oil price risk such that increases in oil price will decrease earnings. This risk can be managed effectively through the capital markets by purchase of derivatives such as forwards, futures, or call options.

Many companies can estimate the amount of oil they will need over the near term. For example, an airline will be able to estimate how much jet fuel it will need to purchase over the next quarter. In this case, it is relatively easy to determine the company's exposure to oil price risk.

However, for many companies, it will not be so simple. For a large company in particular, it may be difficult to estimate the amount of its direct purchase of oil. Also, it may be exposed to secondary or indirect effects of oil price movements through the broader impact on the economy. Oil prices may indirectly affect the cost of goods if suppliers are adversely affected and sales volume and price competition if consumers are affected. These effects can be significant for individual companies as well as national economies (so much so that some countries are willing to go to war in order to control their oil supply). In these situations, in order for a company to manage the risk of increasing oil prices, it must first develop a financial model of earnings (or other pertinent financial measure) as a function of oil prices.

The traditional silo approach to managing commodity price risk (or other risks that can be hedged through the capital markets) is to determine the optimal hedge ratio (see Kolb, 1997). The *hedge ratio* is the ratio of the notional value of the hedge contracts and the value of the underlying portfolio that is being hedged. The *optimal* hedge ratio is one that will minimize the volatility of the portfolio. In our example, the hedge ratio (HR) is therefore:

$$ HR \equiv \frac{\text{total notional value of forward contracts}}{\text{expected earnings}} = \frac{\text{\# of forward contracts} \times \text{notional value}}{\text{expected earnings}} $$

The optimal hedge ratio (HR_o) is calculated as follows:

$$\text{HR}_o \; = \; -\rho_{ep} \frac{\sigma_e}{\sigma_p}$$

$$= \; -\rho_{ep} \frac{(\sigma_{\Delta e/e} \times \text{ expected earnings})}{(\sigma_{\Delta p/p} \times \text{ \# of forward contracts } \times \text{ notional value})}$$

where ρ_{ep} = correlation coefficient between rate of change in oil prices and rate of change in earnings, $\sigma_{\Delta e/e}$ = standard deviation of rate of change in earnings, and $\sigma_{\Delta p/p}$ = standard deviation of rate of change in oil prices.

A more intuitive approach to determine the optimal hedge ratio is to develop a regression model of the rate of change in earnings ($\Delta e/e$) as a function of the rate of change in oil price ($\Delta p/p$):

$$\frac{\Delta e}{e} \; = \; \beta_p \frac{\Delta_p}{p} + \varepsilon$$

where β_p = the beta based on a least-squares estimate.

The optimal hedge ratio is equal to the negative of the beta value, $-\beta_p$. To understand why, recall that β_p is determined such that it minimizes the squared deviations of earnings, a measure of earnings variance. Naturally, if the company purchased $-\beta_p$ forward contracts, it would cancel out the effect of oil prices on earnings. This would not eliminate all the volatility in earnings because the regression model indicates that there is residual risk represented by the error term, ε.

The advantage of determining the hedge ratio in terms of a regression model is that it clarifies how much each risk factor contributes to the earnings risk (as measured by variance of earnings). It also provides a measure for the effectiveness of the hedge. The portion of the earnings variability that cannot be explained by oil price volatility is measured by the variance of the error term. The hedge eliminates the variance that can be explained by the regression terms.

$$\text{Effectiveness of hedge} \; = \; \sigma_p^2/\sigma_e^2 \; = \; R^2$$

The following calculations illustrate this approach for managing the earnings exposure to oil price risk.

Let us assume that a regression of the rate of change in earnings on the rate of change in oil price produces the following results:

$$\beta_p = -0.623$$

$$R^2 = 0.706$$

$$\mu_{\Delta e/e} = 0.0, \ \sigma_{\Delta e/e} = 0.199$$

$$\mu_{\Delta p/p} = 0.0, \ \sigma_{\Delta p/p} = 0.268$$

$$\rho_{ep} = -0.840$$

Let us assume that expected earnings = \$100,000, and the oil price risk will be hedged using the following forward contracts on oil price:

Current price of forward contract = \$25
Number of barrels of oil in each forward contract = 1000
Notional value of 1 forward contract = \$25,000
Optimal hedge ratio, HR_o = 0.623

The optimal number of forward contracts to purchase is

$$N = \left[-\rho_{ep} \frac{\sigma_e}{\sigma_p} \right] \times \left[\frac{\text{expected earnings}}{\text{notional value of forward contract}} \right]$$

$$= \left[-(-0.840) \frac{0.199}{0.268} \right] \times \left[\frac{\$100,000}{\$25} \right] = 2491$$

The optimal number is positive because the purchase of forwards will produce earnings as the oil price increases to offset the losses in earnings.

Let us also examine the effectiveness of the hedge, as follows. Earnings variance before hedge:

$$\sigma_e^2 = (\sigma_{\Delta e/e} \times \text{expected earnings})^2 = (0.199 \times \$100,000)^2 = 394,412,490$$

$$\sigma_e = (394,412,490)^{0.5} = \$19,860$$

Earnings variance after hedge equals the variance of the residual term. The forward contracts cancel out the effect of the oil price movements, leaving only the residual variance:

$$\sigma_{e,\text{hedged}}^2 = \sigma_\varepsilon^2 = \sigma_e^2 - \sigma_p^2$$

$$= \sigma_e^2 - (\sigma_{\Delta p/p} \times N \times \text{notional value of 1 contract})^2$$

$$\sigma_{e,\text{hedged}}^2 = 394,412,490 - (0.268 \times 2491 \times \$25)^2 = 116,027,937$$

$$\sigma_{e,\text{hedged}} = (116,027,937)^{0.5} = \$10,772$$

The effectiveness of the hedge =

$$1 - \frac{\sigma_e^2}{\sigma_{e,\text{hedged}}^2} = 1 - \frac{116,027,937}{394,412,490} = 0.706 = 71\%$$

Note that this also equals $R^2 = 0.706 = 71\%$. This means that approximately 71% of the variance in earnings has been hedged. The fact that the hedge was constructed using an optimal variance minimizing hedge ratio means that this is the most the earnings variance can be reduced using oil forward contracts.

Often a company's objective is not just to reduce earnings variance, which reduces upside potential as well as downside shortfall, but to only reduce the risk that earnings will be much lower than expected (i.e., minimizing only downside risk). One measure of downside risk is earnings value at risk (VaR). VaR is defined in terms of the earnings distribution. A 95% VaR is defined as the expected earnings minus the earnings value at the fifth percentile. This is interpreted as the maximum loss with 95% confidence. VaR can also be defined using other levels of confidence (e.g., 90%, 99%) to suit a risk manager's preferences for or aversion to risk.

Let us look at the impact of the above variance minimizing hedge on earnings VaR. For the sake of illustration, we will assume that both earnings and oil price changes are normally distributed. The results for the earnings VaR at various percentiles are as follows:

Confidence Level	Earnings VaR Before Hedging	Earnings VaR After Hedging
90%	$25,451	$13,804
95%	$32,666	$17,718
99%	$46,201	$25,058

The earnings VaR before hedging is based on a normal distribution of earnings with a mean of $100,000 and a standard deviation of $19,860, that is, $N(\$100,000, \$19,860)$. The earnings VaR after hedging is based on $N(\$100,000, \$10,772)$.

Risk 2. Weather Risk Management

Let us now consider that the company's earnings are also exposed to another major risk factor: weather risk. Weather risk can be managed using forward contracts and options (see Dischel, 2002). If the weather risk is related to temperature fluctuations (as opposed to rain, snow, etc.), a forward contract based on heating degree days (HDD) or cooling degree days (CDD) can be purchased. HDD and CDD are defined as follows:

$$HDD \equiv max[0,65 - T_{avg}]$$

and

$$CDD \equiv max[,0,T_{avg} - 65]$$

where T_{avg} is the average of daily high and low temperatures.

Presumably, when the temperature is below 65 degrees Fahrenheit, there is a need to provide heating, and when it is above 65, there is a need for cooling. The HDD and CDD are associated with specific weather stations that record local temperature. A forward contract can be created based on the sum of the daily HDD during a winter at a specific weather station in Chicago, for example. The contract is assigned a value of $100 per HDD.

For our example, let us assume that the company is adversely affected by abnormally cold winters. When the temperature is very low, the company may suffer higher costs of operation as well as reduced demand for its products as customers are reluctant to venture out of their homes. To protect against weather risk, the company will purchase a HDD forward contract.

Let us assume that weather risk is managed separately from oil price risk and by a different group of employees, a scenario not uncommon in many companies. Using the same approach as used for oil price risk, the key results are as follows.

The regression equation is

$$\frac{\Delta e}{e} = \beta_w \frac{\Delta w}{w} + \varepsilon$$

where β_w = the beta based on a least-squares estimate.

The regression results are

$$\beta_w = -0.519$$

$$R^2 = 0.320$$

$$\mu_{\Delta e/e} = 0.0, \ \sigma_{\Delta e/e} = 0.199$$

$$\mu_{\Delta w/w} = 0.0, \ \sigma_{\Delta w/w} = 0.216$$

$$\rho_{ew} = -0.566$$

Expected earnings = $100,000, and the weather temperature risk will be hedged using the following forward contracts on HDD:

Current HDD forward index = 3500
Index value = $0.100 per HDD
Notional value of 1 forward contract = $350
Optimal hedge ratio, HR_o = 0.519

Optimal number of forward contracts to purchase is

$$N = \left[-\rho_{ep}\frac{\sigma_e}{\sigma_p}\right] \times \left[\frac{\text{expected earnings}}{\text{notional value of forward contract}}\right]$$

$$= \left[-(-0.566)\frac{0.199}{0.216}\right] \times \left[\frac{\$100,000}{\$350}\right] = 148$$

The optimal number is positive because the purchase of forwards will produce earnings as HDD increases to offset the losses in earnings.

The effectiveness of the hedge = R^2 = 0.320 = 32%. This means that the earnings variance was reduced by only 32%.

Confidence Level	Earnings VaR Before Hedging	Earnings VaR After Hedging
90%	$25,451	$20,986
95%	$32,666	$26,935
99%	$46,201	$38,094

Risk 1 + Risk 2. Integrated Risk Management of Oil Price and Weather Risks

The group managing oil price risk and the group managing weather risk at this state may be satisfied that they have done what they could to minimize earnings volatility. However, the following illustrates that the groups working in isolation have *not* in fact minimized earnings.

Let us start by developing a regression model of rate of change in earnings as a function of rate of change in oil price and rate of change in HDD:

$$\frac{\Delta e}{e} = \beta_p\frac{\Delta p}{p} + \beta_w\frac{\Delta w}{w} + \varepsilon$$

The regression results are:

$$\beta_p = -0.545$$

$$\beta_w = -0.311$$

$$R^2 = 0.810$$

$$\mu_{\Delta e/e} = 0.0, \ \sigma_{\Delta e/e} = 0.199$$

$$\mu_{\Delta p/p} = 0.0, \ \sigma_{\Delta p/p} = 0.268$$

$$\mu_{\Delta w/w} = 0.0, \ \sigma_{\Delta w/w} = 0.216$$

$$\rho_{ep} = -0.840$$

$$\rho_{ew} = -0.566$$

$$\rho_{pw} = -0.308$$

Note that the beta-oil and beta-HDD are naturally not the same as in the single-factor regression models. The optimal variance-minimizing hedge based on these betas (calculated in the same manner as before) is 2182 forward contracts on oil price at a forward price of $25, 89 forward contracts on HDD at a forward index level of 3,500.

The effectiveness of the hedge measured by the R^2 of the regression model is 81%.

The following is a summary of the results comparing the silo approach to the integrated risk management approach:

	Without Hedging	Silo Approach	Integrated Approach
No. of oil contracts	0	2491	2182
No. of HDD contracts	0	148	89
Standard deviation of earnings, σ_e	$19,860	$10,260	$8657
Effectiveness of hedge in reducing variance	N/A	73%	81%

Next is a similar comparison in terms of earnings VaR:

Percentile	Without Hedging	Silo Approach	Integrated Approach
90%	$25,451	$13,148	$11,095
95%	$32,666	$16,876	$14,240
99%	$46,201	$23,868	$20,140

The integrated approach to managing both risks does a better job of minimizing the earnings volatility and the earnings VaR, and it does so while purchasing fewer contracts! It achieves this by explicitly recognizing the correlation between oil price risk and weather risk in determining the net effect on earnings.

Let us expand our example by considering the cost of risk management. There are many methods for managing risk, each with its own cost. Risk can be transferred to the capital markets by purchasing derivatives or securitization. Some derivatives such as options have an explicit premium, whereas others such as forwards and futures have an implicit cost based on the difference in strike price and expected future spot price. Both forms also have transaction costs due to the bid-ask spread. Risk can be transferred to insurance companies by paying the appropriate premiums. Risk can also be retained by a company and managed through self-insurance by setting aside the necessary capital. The cost of risk retention in this case is the cost of setting aside capital. Finally, risk can be managed internally through changes in business processes and technology with its commensurate cost. In all cases, there is a cost for managing risk that must be considered in setting goals for risk reduction.

For our example, let us develop the costs for risk management in a fairly simple way. Assume that underlying the expected earnings of $100,000 is an expected oil price of $23 per barrel. The forward price, however, is $25. Forward prices are affected by supply and demand of forward contracts, as opposed to the supply and demand of oil, so it is conceivable that they will differ from expected spot prices. If a company purchases forward contracts, it has the effect of fixing the oil price at $25. Therefore, the expected earnings will decrease by $2 (the difference between the forward price and the expected oil price) for each forward contract. This difference is the cost of reducing exposure to oil price risk.

By the same logic, let us assume that the expected level of HDD is 3300. Since the forward HDD index is 3500, the cost of reducing exposure to weather risk is $20 per contract (200 × index value of $0.1).

Applying these cost factors to the optimal integrated hedge produces the following results:

Expected earnings before hedging	$ 100,000
Number of oil price forward contracts purchased	2,182
Cost per contract	$2
Number of HDD forward contracts purchased	89
Cost per HDD contract	$20
Total cost of hedging	$6,144

Expected earnings after hedging	$93,856
Earnings standard deviation before hedge	$19,860
Earnings standard deviation after hedge	$8,657
Reduction in earnings standard deviation	$11,203

Now that we know how much it costs to manage oil price risk and weather risk, it is natural to consider whether the benefit of risk reduction is worth the cost of lower expected earnings. It may be helpful to analyze how the cost of risk management changes as the risk reduction objectives change. For example, how much less would it cost if, instead of minimizing the earnings variance, we settled for reducing the standard deviation by one-third, that is, to approximately $13,000?

There are many hedging strategies that will achieve the same earnings standard deviation. The optimal strategy is one that minimizes the cost of risk management or, equivalently, maximizes expected earnings. The optimal strategy can be determined analytically or by using optimization (linear programming). If the process is repeated for many different values for the earnings standard deviation, a risk-return efficient frontier can be created as shown in Figure 2.1. Each point on the efficient frontier corresponds to an optimal com-

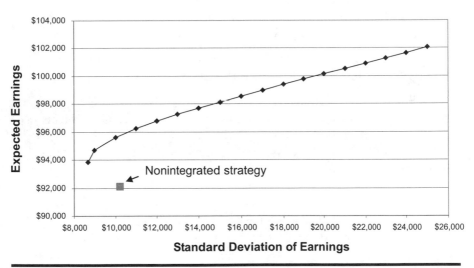

Figure 2.1. Efficient frontier of oil and weather forward contract purchases. Each point on the curve corresponds to a combination of oil and weather forward contracts which maximizes expected earnings for a given level of risk, as defined by standard deviation of earnings.

bination of oil and weather forward contract purchases to achieve a given earnings risk reduction objective.

This example illustrates the need to coordinate risk management activities among risk managers. A silo approach to risk management is not effective in achieving risk reduction objectives. It also does not allow managers to minimize the cost of risk management. To develop an optimal risk management strategy, it is necessary to reflect the interaction among risk factors and the relative cost of managing each risk. This can be achieved by integrating the risk management activities across a company.

2.4. INTEGRATED RISK MANAGEMENT MODELING PROCESS

The discussions thus far and the example provide the motivation for integrating risk management activities; now let us consider the process. The process of developing a strategy to manage risks on an integrated basis consists of the following logical steps:

1. State corporate financial objectives.
2. Identify and assess risk factors that threaten objectives.
3. Develop financial model linking risk factors to financial objectives.
4. Evaluate alternative strategies for managing risk factors.

Step 1. State Corporate Financial Objectives

It is common wisdom that in order to choose the best path, one must first know where one wants to arrive. Thus, stating clear and measurable objectives is critical to the selection of the optimal risk management strategy.

Companies typically have multiple, and sometimes conflicting, objectives for increasing value. Value is created by

- Increasing returns (e.g., EBITDA, ROE, ROA, earnings per share)
- Increasing the rate of growth (e.g., revenue, market share)
- Improving consistency of results (e.g., risk measures for returns and growth)

It is obvious that growth and improved returns increase value; however, it may be less apparent how consistency creates value. Risk-averse investors by definition will prefer companies that have greater consistency in results, *ceteris parabus*. Empirical research indicates that, holding constant the other drivers of value (growth and return), companies with relatively low historical volatility in results had significantly higher increases in market value compared with companies with high volatility (Miccolis and Shah, 2000, 2001). Markets have consistently penalized companies that have not met their quarterly earnings projections. There are many instances of companies whose stock price decreased when they announced quarterly earnings per share that were even one cent below expectations. Improving consistency through risk management is a critical component of increasing shareholder value.

Return and growth objectives are the focus of business strategy; consistency objectives are the focus of risk management strategy. The risk management task at hand is to find a way to allow the company to meet its objectives for consistency of results given the course it has set for business strategy.

There are many risk measures from which to choose to specify consistency objectives, as shown in Table 2.1. These risk measures can be applied to measures of return and growth.

Some examples of consistency objectives are:

- Minimize the earnings VaR at the 95% probability level
- Minimize the probability of achieving earnings below $X (shortfall risk)
- Minimize the downside standard deviation of revenue growth over the next five years
- Minimize standard deviation of earnings over the next five years

Often, the growth and return objectives are in conflict. For example, strategies that achieve long-term growth objectives may require investments that will be in conflict with short-term return objectives. In these cases, the objectives can be achieved by coordinating the business strategy with the risk management strategy. For example, the business strategy is set to achieve the primary objective of maximizing five-year growth in revenue. However, given investor expectations for short-term results, the risk management strategy is set to minimize the probability of achieving annual earnings below $X in each of the next two years.

For the sake of illustration, let us assume for the subsequent steps that the consistency objective is to minimize earnings VaR at the 95% probability level.

Step 2. Identify and Assess Risk Factors That Threaten Objectives

The process of identifying risk factors can be cumbersome given that most businesses are exposed to hundreds of risks. It is essential that the process focus on identifying only those risks that have a material impact on a company's

Table 2.1. Definitions of Risk Measures

Risk Measure	Definition
Standard deviation	$\sqrt{\dfrac{\sum_{i=1}^{n}(x_i - \bar{x})^2}{n}}$, where n is the number of simulation iterations and $\bar{x}$ is the average value. It is interpreted as the extent to which results deviate either above or below expectations. Note that equal weight is given to deviations of the same magnitude regardless of whether the deviation is favorable or unfavorable.
Shortfall risk	$\dfrac{\sum_{i=1}^{n}[\text{if } (x_i \le T) \text{ then 1, else 0}]}{n}$ * 100%, where n is the number of simulation iterations and T is the target value for the financial variable. It is interpreted as the probability that the financial variable will fall below a specified target level. This is an improvement over standard deviation because it reflects the fact that most people are risk averse (i.e., they are more concerned with unfavorable deviations than favorable deviations). This is also referred to as the probability of ruin when applied to insurance assets net of liabilities.
Value at risk	In VaR-type measures, the equation is reversed: the shortfall probability is specified first, and then the corresponding value of T is calculated (see Jorion, 1997).
Downside standard deviation	$\sqrt{\dfrac{\sum_{i=1}^{n}(\max[0, T - x_i])^2}{n}}$, where n is the number of simulation iterations and T is the target value for the financial variable. It is interpreted as the extent to which the financial variable could deviate below a specified target level. This is a further improvement over the prior measures because it focuses not only on the probability of an unfavorable deviation (as does shortfall risk) but also the extent of the deviation.

ability to meet the stated objectives in Step 1, in our case earnings VaR. All enterprise-wide risks that meet this criterion should be considered, whether they are

- **Market risks**, such as changes in interest rates, foreign exchange rates, and commodity prices
- **Credit risks** associated with customers and other counterparties to financial transactions, such as derivatives, swaps, and holdings of corporate debt

Table 2.1. Definitions of Risk Measures (continued)

Risk Measure	Definition
Below-target risk	Below-target risk is similar, but the argument is not squared and no square root taken.
Expected deficit	Expected deficit is similar to below-target risk, except that the denominator is equal to the number of simulation iterations in which x_i exceeds T. It is interpreted as the average downside deviation below the target level. This measure is often used in insurance to measure the expected policyholder deficit if an insurer fails.
Tail-conditional expectation	$$\frac{\sum_{i=1}^{\alpha} x_i}{\alpha}$$, where the simulation iterations are sorted in ascending order and α corresponds to a specified threshold percentile of least favorable outcomes (e.g., bottom 5% or 1%). It measures the expected value given that the value will fall below a specified probability threshold. This is similar to the expected deficit, except that the threshold is specified in terms of a probability rather than a value for the financial variable. Tail-conditional expectation has the advantage over the above risk measures in that it meets the axioms defining a "coherent" risk measure (see Artzner et al., 1999).

- **Weather risk**, such as excessive heat, cold, rain, and snow, which can disrupt sales and operations
- **Operational risks**, such as disruption of supply chain or technology infrastructure and transactional errors
- **People risks**, such as employee fraud and theft, loss of key employees, high turnover, inability to recruit critical talent, and prolonged employee strike
- **Regulatory risks**, such as changes in tax laws, accounting rules, tariffs, and international trade agreements
- **Competitor risks**, such as entry of new competitors or new competing products and services, and changes in competitor pricing
- **Legal risks**, such as class action lawsuits by customers, employees, or regulators
- **Political risks** associated with leadership and government of unstable countries or regions
- **Natural hazard**, such as earthquakes, hurricanes, and floods
- **Property risks**, such as fire, theft, and equipment breakdown
- **Intellectual capital risks**, such as loss of patent rights

This is not meant to be an exhaustive list, but rather to point out that risks can arise from many different sources that have not been considered by traditional risk management. The enterprise risk management movement is providing impetus for management to consider all risks as part of good corporate governance.

Those risks that are considered material should be reflected in the development of a risk management strategy. Material risks are those that can have a significant impact on the stated objectives and require significant investment to mitigate. If a risk does not require significant investment to mitigate, then it should be addressed immediately through normal channels. For example, let us assume that there is a risk that key employees will leave the company, either because they are dissatisfied or they are close to retirement age. This risk can be mitigated through the existing employee recruiting and benefit and compensation design activities within the human resources function by focusing on key positions or job types. This may be done without significant investment. However, if a prolonged employee strike could threaten earnings and averting it would require a significant investment in upgrading benefits and compensation programs for all employees, it should be considered a material risk. The risk mitigation options for all material risks should be evaluated in an integrated fashion to optimize the cost allocation of risk management. Steps 3 to 5 will describe how to integrate these risk management decisions.

First, however, the material risk factors that have been identified must be quantified. Risk typically is quantified as probability distributions of random variables. There are many methods available to model specific risks (see Figure 2.2). They can be broadly classified along the continuum of the extent to which they rely on historical data versus expert input.

Data Analysis	Modeling	Expert Input
■ Empirically from historical data	■ Stochastic differential equations	■ System dynamics simulation	■ Influence diagrams	■ Direct assessment of relative likelihood or fractiles
■ Fit parameters for theoretical pdf	■ Neural networks	■ Bayesian belief networks	■ Preference among bets or lotteries
■ Extreme value theory	■ Regression over variables that affect risk	■ Fuzzy logic	■ Delphi method

Figure 2.2.   There is a broad range of risk modeling methods that can be used depending on the relative availability of historical data versus expert input.

- Traditional methods used in the financial services sector for modeling risks are primarily statistical approaches based on historical data. These include, for example, stochastic differential equations (SDEs) to model the path of interest rates, commodity prices, and foreign exchange rates; actuarial methods based on fitting probability distributions on frequency and severity of losses; and extreme value theory to model tails of distributions.
- At the opposite end of the continuum are methods that rely almost exclusively on expert input. These include, for example, the Delphi method to assess risk based on a group of experts, preference among bets, and direct assessment of relative likelihood and fractiles used for decades in decisions and risk analysis.
- Between the two extremes are those methods that are effective in combining both historical data and expert input. These methods rely on expert input to fill the gaps in historical data. They include, for example, fuzzy logic and system dynamics used extensively in the engineering sciences and Bayesian belief networks, which make use of prior beliefs based on expert input.

Most market risk and weather risk factors can be modeled by applying one of the statistical methods to historical time series data. As noted in the earlier example, the risk of commodity price movement was represented as a normal distribution fitted to historical data on rate of change in oil prices. A more refined approach for modeling commodity price risk is to use the Schwartz-Smith two-factor model (see Schwartz and Smith, 2000), which uses SDEs to model the evolution of prices over time. There are several interest rate and foreign exchange models that are also expressed as SDEs (see Caouette et al., 2001; Panjer, 1998).

Credit risks can be modeled in several ways, one of which is to model the probability of default and the loss given default (actuarial method), the product of which provides a probability distribution of aggregate credit losses (see Caouette et al., 2001; Jorion, 2001). Probability of default can be derived from statistics maintained by rating bureaus such as Standard & Poor's and Moody's. They maintain tables based on historical data of the probability of default over a specified time period for a company with a given credit rating. A Markov process can also be used to reflect the probability that a company's credit rating may change over time and therefore affect its probability of default. The loss given default is the amount a company could lose if there were a default. This can be expressed as either a constant or a probability distribution. The mathematical convolution (product) of the probability distributions for default and loss given default provides a distribution of aggregate credit losses.

Insurable risks such as natural hazard, property risks, many legal risks, some operational risks, and people risks are also modeled using an actuarial approach. Historical data are used to model the frequency of losses and severity of loss given the occurrence of event. Insurance companies are able to model these risks because they can aggregate loss data across large populations to develop statistically credible models.

The remaining risks, such as political risk, competitor risk, intellectual capital risk, and some operational and people risks, are modeled by relying more on expert input. In these cases, there are typically some data, but they are not complete or representative. Nevertheless, they can be used as a starting point for experts to contribute their input. For example, for political risk, there are consulting firms that specialize in modeling the key factors that affect such risk. One firm generates a political risk index. This can be a starting point for experts to customize the risk factor to the unique circumstances facing a company.

It may not be possible or reasonable to express all risk factors as probability distributions when relying primarily on expert input. For example, it may be difficult to credibly assess the likelihood of a competitor entering the market, the passage of a key regulation, or the change in leadership of a developing country. In such a case, instead of forcing an artificial distribution, it is better to consider it as a separate scenario without attesting the likelihood of it occurring. For example, two scenarios could be considered for regulatory risk: one assuming the passage of key legislation and the other assuming it does not pass. In subsequent steps, scenario testing can be used to determine the impact of each scenario on achieving risk management objectives.

The output of Step 2 is a list of key risk factors quantified in terms of probability distributions or represented as alternative scenarios.

Step 3. Develop Financial Model Linking Risk Factors to Financial Objectives

At this point, we know the risk management objectives and the risk factors that threaten those objectives. The risk management objectives are stated in terms of risk measures (i.e., earnings VaR). Risk factors are expressed as probability distributions. In this step, the risk factors must be linked to earnings using a stochastic financial model. By linking the two, the model will take as input the distribution on each risk factor and output a distribution of earnings. The earnings VaR can then be measured at 95%, for example, to develop a baseline for the risk management objective.

The example earlier in this chapter showed how oil price risk and weather risk were linked to earnings using a regression model. This is a top-down approach based on a statistical relationship between the risk factors and the financial variable. However, it also was mentioned that if the company knew how much oil it was going to need, it would be possible to determine directly the impact of oil price movements on earnings. This is a bottom-up approach based on a real link between the risk factor and the financial variable.

The bottom-up approach is the preferred approach because it provides a more reliable way to measure the impact of a risk factor. It involves mapping a sequence of cause-effect relationships to link the risk factor to the financial variable.

As discussed previously, it is not feasible in many circumstances to develop a detailed map of cause-effect relationships linking the risk factor to financial outcomes. In these cases, a top-down approach must be used. A statistical model based on historical data must be constructed to quantify the links.

In our example, a simple regression model was used to link oil price risk and weather risk to earnings. Other models can be used. For example, an SDE can be used to model the evolution of earnings over a period of time. In any case, the parameters for the model are developed using statistical analysis, such as a maximum likelihood estimation. Care should be taken to eliminate the effects of the bottom-up risk factors from the financial variable before fitting the statistical model. For example, if information systems failure is modeled using a bottom-up approach, then major losses due to information systems failure must be removed from the historical earnings data before using the earnings history in a top-down approach.

In order to integrate risk factors in a common stochastic financial model, the correlation among risk factors must be recognized. It is easy to develop correlation coefficients among risk factors that were modeled in Step 1 based on historical data. However, for other risk factors correlation assumptions will have to be developed based on professional judgment and expert input. Sensitivity analysis can be performed on the correlation assumptions (as with any model assumption) to determine the impact they can have on decisions. In this manner, a correlation matrix (or covariance matrix) is developed to represent the interaction among all the risk factors.

Once a stochastic financial model is created, simulation is used to develop a distribution of outcomes for earnings (or any other financial measure selected in Step 1). Although in our example an analytical approach was used, it can be difficult and even impossible to use an analytical approach in a realistic setting. The risk factors are not always normally distributed; often the distributions are skewed. It may be difficult in this case to find closed form analytical solutions. Simulation provides greater flexibility since it is not dependent on specific forms of distributions.

The simulation must sample from the probability distribution for each risk factor in a way that reflects the correlation among the factors. For normally distributed variables, this can be done using Cholesky decomposition. For variables with skewed distributions, Spearman's rank order correlation and normal copula can be used (see Jorion, 2001; Alexander and Sheedy, 2004).

The output of the simulation model is a distribution on earnings. Since the consistency objective is to "minimize earnings VaR at 95%," earnings VaR at the 95% confidence level must be calculated. This is equal to the difference between the fifth percentile value and the mean from the cumulative distribution of earnings. At this stage, the output of the model provides earnings VaR before the use of any risk mitigation strategies. Alternative risk mitigation strategies will be evaluated in the next step.

Modeling the risk factor (Step 2) and developing the stochastic financial model (Step 3) represent the bulk of the analytical effort and pose the greatest analytical challenge in applying an integrated risk management approach. For this reason, it is sensible to start incrementally by narrowing the scope of risk factors that are considered. The Pareto principle, or the 80-20 rule, should be the guiding precept in completing Steps 2 and 3.

Step 4. Evaluate Alternative Strategies for Managing Risk Factors

The objective of this step is to consider various strategies for mitigating each of the material risk factors identified in Step 2 and modeled in Step 3. In general, there are several ways to mitigate risk. They were mentioned briefly in the example in the discussion of the cost of risk management.

Hedging in the capital markets. This involves entering into a derivatives transaction, for example, in futures or forwards, options, and swaps. This can be an effective way to transfer risk if there is a contract that closely tracks the risk factor to minimize basis risk and there is enough liquidity in the market to minimize transaction costs. However, if the transaction is executed in the over-the-counter market, as opposed to a securities exchange, the risk transfer also involves accepting credit risk.

Securitization. As with a derivatives transaction, securitization also involves transferring risk to the capital markets. An intermediary between the company wishing to transfer the risk and the capital markets, called a special-purpose vehicle, is created to issue a bond to the capital markets. The performance of the bond is linked to a risk factor, typically a natural hazard such as an earthquake or a windstorm. The bond continues to pay periodic coupon payments to bondholders if no risk events (i.e., earthquakes or windstorms) occur. If there is a risk event, the capital raised by the bond offering is used to cover the losses experienced by the company. Whatever capital remains after paying for losses is repaid to bondholders. If no risk event occurs, then the bondholders receive their full principal at maturity. To provide an incentive for bondholders to accept the risk, the bonds are priced to provide competitive returns.

Insurance. Most property and liability risks are transferred to insurers for a premium. Insurers can cost effectively diversify the risk among a large base of policyholders. Insurers can also offer insurance on a combination of risk factors. For example, a product can be structured such that it will pay for losses regardless of whether they are a result of oil price increase or abnormally cold weather. Such a product is priced to reflect the correlation between the two risk factors, oil price risk and weather risk. Other products can be designed to pay for losses for one risk factor only if there is also a loss due to another risk factor. For example, a product can pay for losses due to weather risk only if oil prices first went above $30. These are called multitrigger products because the weather risk protection is only triggered if the oil price first exceeds a threshold. This is useful in situations when oil price risk by itself is manageable, but if there also were losses due to weather, then the company would need protection. There are several variations on these two themes that involve varying the number of risk factors and the number of triggers. These commercial insurance products are typically custom designed to meet a company's specific needs and are particularly well suited for integrated risk management.

Contingent financing. In some instances, it is more cost effective to retain the risk and to simply borrow money when there is a loss, to be repaid later when the company has had enough time to recover. The problem is, of course, that when there is a loss, it is the most difficult time to obtain a bank loan. Therefore, it is better to arrange in advance for financing in case of a future loss due to a specified risk event.

Self-insurance. For large companies, it may be more cost effective to self-insure. This can be done either by earmarking certain funds to cover losses or through a company's own captive insurance company. A captive works just like an ordinary insurance company, but it is wholly owned by the company and provides insurance primarily to its parent company.

Internal management. Risk factors can be mitigated through changes in internal business processes, technology, and people. For example, information systems failure risk can be mitigated by investing in redundant systems or by shifting to a more decentralized systems architecture.

For each of the risk factors, there are one or more risk mitigation alternatives. For each alternative, the cost and payoff function are added to the sto-

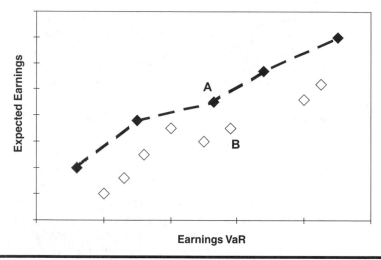

Figure 2.3. Plot of alternative strategies on risk/return grid. The strategy points in black dominate the strategy points in white because they offer either higher return for the same level of risk, lower risk for the same level of return, or both. Collectively, the dominant strategies form an efficient frontier of risk strategies.

chastic financial model developed in Step 3. Then all possible strategies consisting of combinations of alternatives are evaluated using simulation. For each strategy, the output of the simulation model is a distribution of earnings that reflects a combination (or portfolio) of risk mitigation alternatives. From these distributions, the earnings VaR can be calculated at the 95% confidence level.

Naturally, some strategies will produce a lower VaR than others. However, each strategy also has a cost of risk mitigation associated with it that decreases the expected earnings. The dual effect of each strategy is therefore a decrease in earnings VaR (positive effect) and a decrease in expected earnings (negative effect). Management must assess the relative worth of the positive and negative effects to determine the optimal risk management strategy.

Plotting the results for all strategies helps eliminate some strategies from consideration (see Figure 2.3). Note that strategy A in Figure 2.3 is better than strategy B because A has both higher expected earnings and lower earnings VaR. Strategy A is considered to be dominant over strategy B. This type of comparison can be made for all strategies to eliminate those that are dominated by at least one other strategy. The remaining strategies must have either lower earnings VaR or lower expected earnings, but not both, compared to all other strategies. Connecting these strategies reveals an efficient frontier of discrete strategies.

Management must decide among the remaining strategies, each of which constitutes a combination of risk mitigation alternatives. There are several technical approaches for deciding among strategies on the efficient frontier by either explicitly or implicitly reflecting the decision-makers' wealth utility functions. Stochastic dominance is one such technique that compares strategies along the entire range of the distribution of earnings, rather than just comparing results at specific points along the distribution (see Levy, 1998). However, these approaches are often perceived as "black boxes" and therefore regarded with suspicion by management.

A less technical but much more practical approach is simply to provide modeling results in a manner that facilitates discussion among decision-makers. Practical limitations on the investment in risk management activities often narrows the options down to a handful of strategies by eliminating strategies along the return dimension. This makes it relatively easy for decision-makers to reach a consensus and select a strategy from among the remaining few that provides the best trade-off between risk and return.

2.5. CONCLUSION

The enterprise risk management movement has prompted companies to consider their exposure to all categories of risks. Under the proposed Basel II rules, banks will have to consider operational risks in addition to market and credit risks in determining required capital. Insurance companies have also recognized that they are exposed to a broader range of operational, legal, regulatory, and business risks than previously recognized in determining capital. In the wake of the collapse of several mega-companies in the United States, companies in all sectors are under pressure from regulators to take seriously their corporate governance responsibility by diligently reviewing their exposure to all forms of risk. Companies that implement enterprise risk management must be careful to ensure that they coordinate their risk management activities across all categories of risks.

This chapter focused on the modeling aspects of integrated risk management. However, integrated risk management also requires changes to organization, business processes, and staffing. Integrated risk management centralizes risk management decision making to optimize the allocation of investment to various risk mitigation activities. Many companies have created the position of a chief risk officer, who reports to the chief executive officer, to oversee the management of risk across the enterprise. The shift in decision-making authority from line functions to the chief risk officer is likely to have political implications that should not be underestimated. New business processes must also be designed and implemented to manage the flow of information and decisions among the various risk management groups and the chief risk officer. It is also helpful to recruit or develop staff that has experience in a broad range of risk products and markets — risk management generalists — to overcome the trend toward specialization. Organizational, process, and staffing changes can prove to be a greater hurdle to overcome in implementing integrated risk management than the actual modeling.

Notwithstanding the analytical and organizational challenges in implementing integrated risk management, the benefits are worth it. The creation of a chief risk officer position in many companies indicates the critical role risk management plays in the current economic environment. Companies compete in their ability to manage risks as well as their ability to generate returns. Investors, analysts, rating bureaus, and regulators are now paying closer attention to companies' ability to control risks and are rewarding or penalizing them accordingly. An incremental approach to implementing integrated risk management that provides time to overcome its challenges, yet conveys to the markets the focus on risk management, provides the best balance between risk and opportunity.

REFERENCES AND RECOMMENDED READING

There is a rapidly growing list of papers, articles, and books on enterprise risk management. The following is by no means complete, and the references cited are not necessarily the definitive publications on the topics. However, these publications provide more detail on the concepts presented in this chapter and should prove useful for the reader who is interested in delving into these subjects more deeply.

Some of the material in this chapter was first published in the following two monographs on enterprise risk management:

Miccolis, J. and Shah, S. (2000). *Enterprise Risk Management — An Analytic Approach,* Tillinghast-Towers Perrin, Atlanta (www.tillinghast.com).
Miccolis, J. and Shah, S. (2001). *Risk Value Insights — Creating Value Through Enterprise Risk Management — A Practical Approach for the Insurance Industry,* Tillinghast-Towers Perrin, Atlanta (www.tillinghast.com).

The following references provide some background on corporate governance related to risk management:

American Institute of Certified Public Accountants (1994). Improving Business Reporting — A Customer Focus, AICPA, New York (www.aicpa.org/members/div/acctstd/ibr/index.htm).

Basel Committee on Banking Supervision (2003). Overview of the New Basel Capital Accord, Bank of International Settlements, April (www.bis.org/bcbs/cp3ov.pdf).

Committee on Corporate Governance (1997). Recommendations on Corporate Governance in the Netherlands, June.

The Institute of Chartered Accountants (1999). Internal Control — Guidance for Directors on the Combined Code, ICA, London, September (www.icaew.co.uk/viewer/index.cfm?AUB=TB21_6342).

International Actuarial Association, Insurance Liabilities — Valuation and Capital Requirements, IAA, Ottawa (www.actuaries.org/members/en/documents/submissions/IASC_Insurance_Issues/Fair_Value_Overview.pdf).

Superintendent of Financial Institutions, Canada (1999). Supervisory Framework: 1999 and Beyond, Office of the Superintendent of Financial Institutions, Canada.

The following publications describe various risk modeling methods:

Alexander, C. and Sheedy, E. (2004). *The Professional Risk Manager's Handbook: A Comprehensive Guide to Current Theory and Best Practices,* PRMIA (www.prmia.org).

Caouette, J. B., Altman, E. I., and Narayanan, P. (2001). *Managing Credit Risk: The Next Great Financial Challenge,* John Wiley and Sons, Hoboken, NJ.

Clemen, R. T. (1996). *Making Hard Decisions,* 2nd ed., Duxbury Press, Belmont, CA.

Coles, S. (2001). *An Introduction to Statistical Modeling of Extreme Values,* 1st ed., Springer-Verlag, Berlin, December.

Dischel, R. S. (2002). *Climate Risk and the Weather Market: Financial Risk Management with Weather Derivatives,* Risk Books, London.

Jorion, P. (2001). *Financial Risk Manager Handbook,* John Wiley and Sons, Hoboken, NJ.

Kolb, R. (1997). *Understanding the Futures Market,* 5th ed., Blackwell, Oxford, U.K.

Linstone, H. A. and Turoff, M. (1975). *The Delphi Method: Techniques and Applications,* Addison-Wesley, Boston.

Panjer, H. (1998). *Financial Economics: With Applications to Investments, Insurance and Pensions,* The Actuarial Foundation, Schaumburg, IL.

Schwartz, E. and Smith, J. E. (2000). Short-term variations and long-term dynamics in commodity prices, *Management Science,* 46, 893–911.

Shah, S. (2003). *Measuring Operational Risk Using Fuzzy Logic Modeling,* International Risk Management Institute, Dallas, September (www.irmi.com/expert/articles/shah005.asp).

Smith, R. L. (1990). Extreme value theory, in *Handbook of Applicable Mathematics, Supplement,* Wiley, Hoboken, NJ.

Smithson, C. W. (1998). *Managing Financial Risk: Guide to Derivative Products, Financial Engineering, and Value Maximization,* 3rd ed., McGraw-Hill, New York.

von Winterfeldt, D. and Edwards, W. (1986). *Decision Analysis and Behavioral Research,* Cambridge University Press, Cambridge, U.K.

The following publications provide guidance on selecting risk measures in order to evaluate alternative risk strategies:

Artzner, P., Delbaen, F., Eber, J. M., and Heath, D. (1999). Coherent risk measures, *Mathematical Finances,* 9(3), 203–228, July.
Jorion, P. (1997). *Value at Risk,* McGraw-Hill, New York.
Levy, H. (1998). *Stochastic Dominance: Investment Decision Making Under Uncertainty,* Kluwer Academic Publishers, Dordrecht, Netherlands.

The following publication provides an excellent summary of methods for transferring, financing, transforming, and retaining risks:

Lane, M. (2002). *Alternative Risk Strategies,* Risk Books, London.

HUMAN FACTORS ISSUES IN COMPUTER AND E-BUSINESS SECURITY

Pascale Carayon, Sara Kraemer, and Vicki Bier

3.1. INTRODUCTION

The 2002 "Computer Crime and Security Survey," conducted by the Computer Security Institute (CSI) and the Federal Bureau of Investigation (FBI), shows that 90% of the survey respondents (mainly large companies and government agencies) detected computer security breaches within the past year. A range of attacks and abuses was detected: system penetration from the outside (40%), denial of service attacks (40%), employee abuse of Internet access (78%), and computer viruses (85%). The CSI/FBI survey is a nonscientific, informal survey, and therefore, the survey results should not be considered representative of computer security problems. However, the survey provides an interesting snapshot of security problems experienced by companies, in particular because they emphasize the variety as well as the diverse sources of security problems.

As shown in the 2002 CSI/FBI survey, computer system vulnerabilities and security breaches are growing rapidly, maybe faster than our ability to respond (Computer Science and Telecommunications Board–National Research Council, 2002). Why is this? Schneier (2000) describes four characteristics of computer systems that make computer security challenging: (1) computer systems are complex; (2) they interact with each other, forming even larger systems; (3) the resulting systems have "emergent" properties (i.e., they do things that are not anticipated by the users or designers); and (4) they suffer from bugs and failures. These characteristics have a major impact on the security of computer systems.

To ensure the security of computer systems, three activities are necessary: prevention, detection, and reaction (Schneier, 2000). Prevention typically involves the installation and implementation of computer security methods. This chapter examines the human factors issues involved in the usability and implementation of such methods. Many security breaches bypass prevention mechanisms. Therefore, detection and reaction are critical. Understanding and characterizing attacker behavior can help prevent, detect, and react to such threats.

The area of human factors in computer security is still new, so there are currently few if any quantitative models. However, quantitative and predictive models are starting to be developed in other areas of computer security. For example, Soo Hoo (2000) discusses the limitations of current nonquantitative or semiquantitative approaches to computer security analysis, such as scenario analysis and the use of best practices. He proposes a risk- and decision-analytic approach that explicitly takes into account both the likelihood of particular types of attacks and the consequences if those attacks are successful as a way to identify and prioritize the most cost-effective security improvements. Based on the results of a hypothetical case study constructed using data from the CSI/FBI 1999 computer crime survey, he proposes that some relatively inexpensive computer security measures (such as screen locking, communications content screening, and intrusion detection) are highly cost effective, while other measures (such as central access control) may not be cost justified. Longstaff et al. (2000) also propose a simple model for "assessing the efficacy of risk management."

Similarly, Bilar (forthcoming) has developed a risk analysis method for evaluating the weaknesses of the software running on a given computer network and proposing measures to improve the security of the network. The risk management options considered in this methodology include either replacing particular software packages with more secure software performing the same functions or removing software from the network if it poses an excessive security risk, based on a database of known software characteristics and vulnerabilities. Optimal risk management actions are identified based on the solution of an integer-programming problem, subject to upper bounds on cost and risk and lower bounds on needed functionality. Future work may also consider changes in system structure and topology as possible risk management strategies.

More general risk assessment methods can also be applied or adapted for use in analyzing the risks of interconnected computer systems, even though they were not specifically developed with computer security in mind. See, for example, Bier (1997), Ezell et al. (2000), and Pate-Cornell and Guikema (2002).

3.2. ATTACKER BEHAVIOR/ADVERSARY PERSPECTIVE

It is important to realize that protecting something of value against an intelligent and adaptable adversary is fundamentally different from protecting it against acts of nature or accidents. For example, an earthquake will not become stronger or smarter just because buildings have been equipped with earthquake protection measures. By contrast, an intelligent and determined adversary is likely to adopt a different offensive strategy once a particular set of protective measures has been put in place. For example, if one point of entry into a system is protected and made essentially invulnerable, an adversary is likely to target an alternative point of entry instead. Therefore, good defensive strategies must take the goals and behavior of potential adversaries into account.

The requirement to take adversary behavior into account in selecting defensive strategies means that it is important to think about the goals, motivations, and capabilities of the likely adversaries against which we wish to protect our systems. In fact, that is one of the advantages of contributions from ex-hackers, such as the book by Mitnick and Simon (2002). Howard and Longstaff (1998) and Schneier (2000) identify several classes of attackers that may be of general concern, as well as their objectives. Although their taxonomies and terminology are not entirely consistent, a review of the classes of attackers they identify is nonetheless useful (see Table 3.1). For example, Howard and Longstaff (1998) distinguish between hackers (who attack computers for challenge, status, or the thrill of obtaining access) and vandals (who attack computers to cause damage). Schneier might categorize these groups as either hackers or malicious insiders, depending on their motivation (e.g., obtaining access versus causing damage) and whether they operate from outside or inside the organization being attacked. Similarly, professional criminals attack computers for personal financial gain (Howard and Longstaff, 1998). Schneier (2000) distinguishes further between individual criminals and organized crime (which typically has greater financial and organizational resources at its disposal).

Other attackers are motivated not so much by causing damage or reaping personal financial gain as by the desire to obtain information. Howard and Longstaff (1998) divide this group into spies (e.g., national intelligence organizations — motivated by political gain) and corporate raiders (engaged in industrial espionage). Schneier (2000) also notes that police and members of

Table 3.1. Taxonomy of Attacker Attributes and Characteristics

Attributes	Specific Examples	Characteristics
Attacker type (Howard and Longstaff, 1998; Schneier, 2000)	Hackers Vandals Professional criminals Spies Terrorists	Motivated by challenge, status, or thrill Motivated to cause damage Motivated by personal financial gain Motivated by political or industrial espionage Motivated to cause fear
Insider status (Anderson et al., 2000)	Insider Outsider	May have extensive knowledge and privileges May range from a novice to a government organization
Choice of targets	Opportunistic Determined	Looking for easy targets Not deterred by difficulty
Sophistication (Hutchinson and Skroch, 2001)	Novices Individual hackers Hacker coalitions Cyber-terrorists Intelligence organizations	
System access (Hutchinson and Skroch, 2001)	Physical access only User privileges System operator privileges	
Resource availability (Schudel and Wood, 2000)	Money Information Software Hardware Personnel	Can obtain other resources Examples: system design knowledge, passwords Cracking tools, etc. Number of compromised computers for use in denial of service attack, etc. Number of people, expertise, professionalism, creativity, cleverness
Risk aversion (Duggan, 2000; Wood, 2002b)	Hit-and-run attacks Leave system more slowly Attack until caught	Minimize probability of detection Allow opportunity to assess effects of attack Maximize damage

the press may sometimes attempt to gain access to information that companies would prefer to keep private. While such individuals may perceive their motives as positive or even noble, companies that find that newsworthy but proprietary information has suddenly been made public may not necessarily share this view.

Finally, Howard and Longstaff (1998) identify terrorists as individuals who attempt to cause fear for financial gain. Schneier (2000) notes further that we may also need to be concerned with information warriors. Thus, he distinguishes between individual acts of cyber-terrorism (such as politically moti-vated denial of service attacks) and organized information warfare (which at-tempts to undermine the target's ability to wage war by attacking the informa-tion or network infrastructure).

Legitimate e-businesses may not often need to be concerned with police or intelligence investigations and information warfare. However, even relatively sophisticated businesses are potentially vulnerable to many other types of at-tacks, ranging from vandalism by hackers or disgruntled insiders, to theft of company or client information by criminals, to corporate espionage by competi-tors (Power, 2002). For example, organizations including the *New York Times* (Poulsen, 2002) and Western Union (Lemos, 2000; Stokes, 2000) have had insecure databases containing information such as home phone numbers, Social Security numbers, and credit-card numbers. In the case of Western Union, these problems resulted in the theft of more than 15,000 customer credit-card num-bers. Theft of proprietary information or trade secrets, such as source code or databases, has resulted in losses of up to $200 million, as well as criminal convictions and even prison sentences (e.g., *USA Today*, 2001; U.S. Department of Justice, 2001a). Banks and major e-commerce sites such as PayPal have been victimized for a total of as much as $700,000 through credit-card fraud (U.S. Department of Justice, 2002), and an insider attack at Cisco Systems resulted in illegal issuance of almost $8 million in stock to the perpetrators (U.S. Department of Justice, 2001b). British intelligence and military organizations have experienced theft of laptops containing classified and/or secret information (Schneier, 2000); a laptop containing confidential information belonging to Qualcomm's chairman was also stolen (Khan, 2001; Vijayan, 2000).

Hutchinson and Skroch (2001) categorize attackers by their level of sophis-tication. Thus, outsiders can range from novices to experienced and knowledge-able individual hackers to coalitions of hackers and still further to organized criminals, cyber-terrorists, and foreign intelligence organizations. For malicious insiders, Hutchinson and Skroch categorize attackers based on the level of access they have to the computer system, ranging from physical access only (e.g., an employee who works on the premises but does not have any particular knowledge about or access to the computer system), to users and computer operators (who may have substantial knowledge about and privileges on the computer system), to system administrators with full system design knowledge.

Several researchers and practitioners in the computer security area have proposed that other attacker characteristics should be considered in system defense (Duggan, 2000; Schneier, 2000; Schudel and Wood, 2000; Wood, 2002a, 2002b). In addition to those discussed above (insider/outsider status, sophisti-cation, level of system privileges, and motivation or goals), these include re-source availability (e.g., money, information, personnel, software, and hardware), risk aversion (e.g., how hard the adversary avoids detection [Duggan, 2000; see also Wood, 2002b]), and attributes such as professionalism, creativity, and cleverness (Schudel and Wood, 2000).

Among the various possible attacker characteristics, insider threats are often considered to be a particular area of concern (see, for example, Anderson et al., 2000). In particular, insiders may already have access to (and knowledge about) many aspects of an organization's computer system. In addition, insiders can often easily gain access to (and information about) additional areas, since they may be known and trusted by others in the organization. Thus, for example, Knight (2000) discusses "social engineering" (e.g., gaining access to a computer system by manipulation of people's trust) as a significant source of vulnerability in computer systems. (Note, however, that social engineering need not be limited to use by insiders and can be used for a variety of purposes ranging from internal sabotage to corporate sabotage to extortion.) Finally, insiders may have different avenues of attack available to them than outsiders. For example, an insider may be able to influence the life cycle of a particular product by influencing developers or individuals with access to the product's development (Schudel and Wood, 2000, p. 52), interfering during the process of product distribution, and so on.

One characteristic that has not yet been discussed explicitly in the literature, to the authors' knowledge, but is crucial to understanding and modeling attacker behavior is the distinction between what can be called *opportunistic* and *determined* attackers. Essentially, opportunistic attackers may have a wide range of targets that would be of interest to them (e.g., defacing any of numerous popular Web sites, launching a denial of service attack against any of numerous Internet retailers) and will generally have little or no reason to prefer one to another. An opportunistic attacker is merely looking for an easy target and will be deflected to an easier target if one target becomes too difficult or costly to attack successfully. Thus, for example, Martz and Johnson (1987) note that increasing the survivability of an attack may actually decrease the vulnerability to an attack by deterring potential attackers. Against such an attacker, an effective system defense may require merely that one particular system be more substantially difficult to attack successfully than those of other similar organizations. Ordinary vandalism typically falls into this category; similarly, many computer hackers may not care exactly which Internet businesses they disrupt.

By contrast, realistic levels of difficulty or cost will not deter a determined attacker from the preferred target (or a small set of desirable targets). Examples of determined attackers might include military adversaries or terrorists attempting to attack a particular U.S. military computer system, unethical business competitors attempting to steal a particular trade secret, or simply disgruntled current or former employees determined to damage a particular company's assets or reputation. Such attackers might perceive even an extremely difficult attack as being potentially worthwhile. Thus, for example, Schudel and Wood (2000) claim that cyber-terrorists have "specific targets or goals in mind when they attack a given system. Unlike hackers or naïve adversaries, the cyber-terrorist will attempt to target the exact host or system that must be compromised to accomplish their mission."

However, it should be noted that an attacker's level of determination versus opportunism is not necessarily related to the attacker's sophistication (e.g., naïve hacker versus sophisticated cyber-terrorist). For example, some hackers are extremely determined, not because they have any particular military or terrorist goal in mind, but only because the most difficult targets make for the most prestigious or notorious successes. Consider the following story, possibly apocryphal. Several years ago, before the days of personal computers, crashing the student computer system was a favorite recreational activity for Massachusetts Institute of Technology hackers. The consequence of this was that system administrators spent a great deal of time and effort attempting to make the computer system harder to crash, only to find each time that, within a few weeks, some determined hacker had once again outwitted them. According to this story, the problem was ultimately solved not by better system programming but by social engineering: the system administrators simply implemented a command called "kill system." Once any novice could crash the system with a dozen keystrokes, it was no longer appealing for hackers to spend days and weeks looking for increasingly ingenious and sophisticated ways of accomplishing the same goal.

The purpose of this story is not to argue that good security measures are unnecessary but rather to suggest that determination (the property of being undeterred by difficulty) is not limited to cyber-terrorists, but rather is common to many types of adversaries. By contrast, military or terrorist adversaries may be opportunistic in their choice of targets in some circumstances. To illustrate this point, consider the following example. First, imagine that a group of environmental extremists, or so-called eco-terrorists, are interested in blowing up the headquarters (or disabling the computer system) of Corporation X, which they define as environmentally "evil." In this case, if their preferred target becomes invulnerable due to improved security, they are unlikely to shift their attack to blow up the local senior citizen center or disable the computer system of the municipal social services department. Of course, terrorists might also prefer Corporation X to these other targets, but may be quite willing to damage other buildings or computer systems if successful attacks against X become too difficult.

Defending against opportunistic adversaries is a much less formidable challenge than defending against determined attackers. It's like the old joke about the campers who see a bear: You don't have to run faster than the bear; you just have to run faster than the other potential victims! Thus, if most adversaries are of the opportunistic variety, it may be acceptable merely to adopt security practices that are better than the average of other similar companies or facilities. In this type of situation, defenses need not be impenetrable as long as they are strong enough to discourage possible attacks. Defending something of value from a truly determined attacker is a much more difficult challenge, however, since, as pointed out above, the asset must be defended against all plausible attacks, which is more difficult than merely shoring up a few weak links.

Because attacker characteristics are so important in determining the nature and severity of computer security threats, human factors have an important part to play in understanding attacker behavior, much the same as understanding the behavior of legitimate computer users. For example, at a workshop organized by Rand (Anderson et al., 2000), analysis of human factors was suggested as a way to develop tools for early detection of the insider "going bad." Specific aspects of human factors that would need to be understood and successfully modeled in order to fully define computer security threats include human performance, behavior, knowledge, and motivation (Anderson et al., 2000).

This is obviously a formidable research challenge. In fact, Brannigan and colleagues (Brannigan et al., 2001; Brannigan and Smidts, 1998) use the term *intentional uncertainty* to highlight the difficulty of predicting human actions. Thus, while some attacker goals, motivations, and tactics may be relatively straightforward to anticipate, others will be driven by unique circumstances (e.g., the fact that a particular server has the same name as a hacker's estranged ex-spouse) that will be virtually impossible to predict.

In the absence of good formal models for attacker behavior, the use of *red teams* (Schudel and Wood, 2000) and so-called *ethical hacking* (see, for example, Palmer, 2001) are *important mechanisms for detecting system vulnerabilities and hence enhancing security*, since they allow system defenders to see the system weaknesses from the adversary perspective. Red teaming is defined as "an independent and threat-based effort by an interdisciplinary, simulated opposing force which, after proper safeguards are established, uses both active and passive capabilities on a formal, time-bounded tasking to expose and exploit information assurance vulnerabilities of friendly forces as a means to improve the readiness of DOD components" (see "A Management Process for a Defense-wide Information Assurance Program," November 1997, cited by Sandia National Laboratories, 2000). Similarly, Palmer (2001, p. 770) states that "organizations came to realize that one of the best ways to evaluate the intruder threat to their interests would be to have independent computer security professionals attempt to break into their computer systems."

3.3. HUMAN ERROR IN E-SECURITY

In e-business security, the consequences of human error on business may be devastating. Some direct consequences of errors contributing to vulnerabilities and security breaches may include loss of assets, compromised confidential information, lost work time, and loss of resources (i.e., employee overtime costs, opportunity costs of rebuilding/restoring systems). These can also have major implications for the strategic goals of an organization, such as brand value, customer retention, and profit. In a case involving Avery Dennison, theft of one secret formula was estimated to result in more than $40 million in losses, counting only the cost of the actual investment. Adding lost profits and competitive advantage, trade secrets can be worth much more. Loss of reputation alone may be worth more than $50 million (Power, 2002). Understanding the human performance link between individuals or organizations and the strategic goals can thus have significant implications for business sustainability.

Furthermore, organizational weaknesses have been recognized to have a sizable impact on security. In addition to poorly implemented security measures and substandard audit trails, there are also problems with inadequate or non-existent security procedures (Power, 2002). Lack of appropriate organizational controls, methods, and practices can be a direct cause of security problems.

For example, in the fall of 2000, Western Union was victim to an attack that was attributed to human error rather than a design flaw. A hacker electronically entered one of Western Union's computer servers without permission and stole about 15,700 customer credit-card numbers. The incident occurred after the system had been taken down for routine maintenance, and a file containing the credit-card information had inadvertently been left unprotected when the system was returned to operation (Stokes, 2000). Similarly, in August 2002, an on-line market research company, OpinionWorld, accidentally revealed the e-mail addresses of 13,000 of its subscribers in a mass mailing. The addresses were inserted as plain text in the main body of the message, because a programmer had inserted the subscribers' e-mail message instead of an invitation to take part in a survey. This was done in a last-minute change to a draft mail message, after the programmer had previously sent a clean test message to himself. He mistakenly assumed that the second version would be error free and sent it to the entire subscriber list without further checks (Hayday, 2002).

These examples illustrate the role of human error in e-business security and the extensive possible ramifications of these errors. These incidents can lead to substantial damage to both customer data and company image. Investigation into the organizational factors leading up to and causing these errors can reveal how to eliminate or reduce errors, thereby improving security.

Table 3.2. Taxonomy of Error Types

Acts	Actions		Error Types
Insecure actions	Unintended actions	Slips	Skill-based errors ■ Incorrect security actions in tasks that are routine and require only occasional conscious checks; these errors are related to the attention of the individual performing the security action ■ Memory failures in security actions, such as omitting a planned action, losing one's place, or forgetting security-relevant intentions
		Lapses	Rule-based errors ■ Misapplication of good security rule ■ Failure to apply good security rule ■ Application of bad security rule
	Intended actions	Mistakes	Knowledge-based errors ■ Related to performing a novel security action for which there is no procedure or rule in place to serve as a guide
		Violations	Routine or exceptional violations ■ Security-relevant actions that are inconsistent with security policies and procedures ■ Acts of sabotage (attacks) ■ Security-relevant actions taken for malicious reasons

Modified from Reason (1990).

Human error modeling has been used in the field of reliability engineering for the purpose of mistake analysis. Human error research postulates that components of work systems contribute to human actions, accidents, or mistakes. Human error taxonomies have been used in many technical fields, such as nuclear power, air transportation, weapons systems, and manufacturing (Hollnagel, 1993), in order to classify and analyze accidents in terms of the work system components contributing to those accidents.

The Computer Science and Telecommunications Board of the National Research Council (2002) has acknowledged the distinction between "accidental" and "deliberate" causes in e-business security. Accidental causes are natural or human, but nondeliberate (e.g., human error). Deliberate causes result from conscious human choice (e.g., terrorism). Human error taxonomies often distinguish between intentional and nonintentional actions (see Table 3.2), consistent with the consideration of deliberate and accidental causes of e-business security problems. Intentional actions may result from problems with security policies or procedures or from misguided attempts to deal with unfamiliar or novel situations. Nonintentional actions can result from inappropriate workplace elements, such as poorly written rules. Table 3.2 provides a taxonomy of error types and their relationship to intentional and nonintentional actions. The application of human error taxonomies to understand accidental causes of security problems links organizational components to computer system vulnerabilities and security breaches (Carayon and Kraemer, 2002).

Human error taxonomies are directly relevant to the e-business security arena. Suboptimal work system factors can contribute to human errors in computer and information systems, and hence to vulnerabilities and security breaches. The use of human error taxonomies in the e-business security arena can facilitate both the understanding of and response to vulnerabilities and security breaches that occur as a result of accidents or mistakes in computer and information systems. They also help build improved defense mechanisms against attacks.

The design of a work system must be integrated with the components of the corresponding technical system (Trist, 1981). One problem associated with the failure to mesh these two systems can be a lack of end-user knowledge about the components of the technical system. For example, if highly technical language is used to articulate the needs and status of the technical system to nontechnical users, the result is likely to be a lack of user knowledge about the system. The technical language of computer and information systems may prove too difficult for a nontechnical user, thereby producing a knowledge gap. It can be difficult to identify the key information needs of end users, educate or train them with technical knowledge, and explain why this is important for security. Lack of end-user knowledge may be a factor that leads to error and in turn contributes to security weaknesses, vulnerabilities, and breaches.

Communication problems are obviously related to lack of security knowledge among end users. A significant security threat perceived by a technical expert (e.g., a network administrator) may be very different from what a nontechnical end user would perceive as a security threat. Nontechnical end users may also not be familiar with the technical language used to describe security-relevant situations. Hence, communication barriers may prevent technical personnel from articulating security information to nontechnical personnel. It is important not only to communicate appropriate security practices and policies to end users, but also to provide channels by which end users can communicate security-related concerns and information back to the technical experts. Furthermore, information must be provided to end users in such a way that they can meaningfully apply it to their own work and understand how it relates to the organization as a whole. Failure to accomplish these communication tasks may lead to end-user errors that contribute to security weaknesses of the organization as a whole.

Software installation is another challenging issue. Errors may occur in design, coding, implementation, and maintenance of software. From a technical point of view, software upgrades are also difficult to deploy throughout the entire technical system. Good software installation requires awareness of security holes and patches from the security community, enough knowledge of the technical system to understand whether the software installation or upgrade will fit into the overall structure, and an understanding of how the installation or upgrade will affect overall use of the system. The technical experts need to think about not only how the security of the technical system will be affected but also what kinds of issues will arise for users of the altered system. Will the change present issues in usability or new/different issues in security? Technical users must identify and deploy secure software to achieve and maintain system security, while nontechnical users must be able to use the technical system in such a way that the software installation or upgrade promotes e-business security.

In the human error research literature, there are many definitions of human error. One working definition is *a generic term to encompass all those occasions in which a planned sequence of mental or physical activities fails to achieve its intended outcome, and when these failures cannot be attributed to the intervention of some chance agency* (Reason, 1990). In the realm of e-business security, this means an action leading to an unplanned and possibly adverse outcome (e.g., a vulnerability, security breach). Many error taxonomies have been used to describe human error. This style of analysis can be useful in the e-business security arena to classify various kinds of errors according to the organizational factors that contribute to them. Understanding errors in terms of contributing factors can help to identify those organizational areas with the largest impact on overall system security.

One human error taxonomy introduced by Rasmussen (1983) distinguishes between psychological and situational variables contributing to performance levels. The error types in this model correspond to an individual operating under one of three performance levels: skill based, rule based, or knowledge based. These error types have been used in the study of organizational accidents (Reason, 1997), which are relevant to the security arena, since organizational accidents can include security vulnerabilities or breaches. In skill-based performance, the user carries out routine, highly practiced tasks with only occasional conscious checks, and a slip or lapse may occur in the event of inattention or failure of memory. Rule-based mistakes account for situations in which actions or behaviors must follow detailed procedures; rule-based mistakes include misapplications of normally good rules, the application of bad rules, and failure to apply good rules. Knowledge-based mistakes occur when the user does not have a preformulated solution to a situation or problem available and does not have sufficient knowledge or ability to come up with an appropriate solution in the absence of a preformulated procedure. Security-related human errors at the skill-, rule-, and knowledge-based performance levels are listed in Table 3.2.

It is important to note that these error types are useful primarily to understand how the elements of the work system support (or fail to support) user behavior. In this context, the term *error* is not used in the sense of blaming the individual who committed the error, but rather to shift the focus to creating a system in which users will commit fewer errors.

When thinking about a security system, end users and network administrators or information technology professionals are likely to differ in terms of their needs and technical expertise. End users may have minimal impact on actual or potential breaches in security. Firewalls, authentication systems, and access levels are typically set up to prohibit end users from obtaining root-level access and inadvertently causing a breach in security. However, end users may still contribute to vulnerabilities in the social system, for example through noncompliance with security policies and procedures.

Network administrator error can have an even greater impact on system security, simply because of the level of access granted to administrators, as shown in Table 3.3. As designers and maintainers of the system, network administrators may commit errors that can have a more serious impact on

Table 3.3. End-User Versus Network Administrator Perspectives

Perspective	Vulnerability	Asset
Network administrator	Design: A design error whereby even perfect implementation will result in a vulnerability	Computer or network logical entities ■ Account ■ Process
	Implementation: A vulnerability resulting from an error in the software or hardware implementation of a satisfactory design	■ Data
	Configuration: A vulnerability resulting from an error in the configuration of a system, such as having system accounts with default passwords, having "world write" permission for new files, or having vulnerable services enabled	Physical entities ■ Technological components components ■ Computer ■ Network ■ Internet access
End user	Usage: A vulnerability introduced by an error in using the network or system created by the above three actions	

Adapted from Howard and Longstaff (1998).

vulnerabilities and security breaches. Their contributions to computer security include monitoring new patches, hacker techniques, and vulnerabilities identified in the security community. Inappropriate maintenance of the system can result in serious consequences, as administrators are closer to the information and assets they are protecting than most end users.

3.4. USABILITY AND IMPLEMENTATION OF COMPUTER SECURITY METHODS

A variety of computer security methods are available: public-key encryption, digital signatures, passwords (see Table 3.4 for good strategies for choosing passwords), biometrics, access tokens, firewalls, intrusion detection systems, vulnerability audits, smart cards, etc. (Schneier, 2000). The 2002 CSI/FBI survey of computer crime and security shows that the most frequently used security methods are antivirus software (90%), firewalls (89%), access control (82%), intrusion detection (60%), encrypted files (58%), encrypted log in (50%), and reusable passwords (44%). Biometrics was used only by 10% of the companies surveyed. Proctor et al. (2000) argue that lack of usability is a major obstacle to the acceptance of security methods, in particular third-party authentication methods such as smart cards, fingerprints, and retinal identification.

Task analysis is a human factors technique that allows identification of the demands placed on a human being performing a certain task. In addition, a task analysis may reveal the types of errors that are likely to be most common. Proctor et al. (2000) have applied task analysis to the use of smart cards and biometric authentication devices. The task analysis of the use of smart cards led

Table 3.4. Strategies for Good Passwords

Principles	Techniques
Content of password	Choose mnemonic-based passwords
Size of password	In systems like Unix, which limits password lengths to 8 characters, users should be told to choose passwords of exactly 8 characters
	With systems that allow longer passwords, users should be encouraged to choose passwords of 10 or more characters
Entropy per character	Choose passwords that contain numbers and special characters as well as letters
Compliance	Consider enforcing password quality by system mechanisms

Yan et al., 2000.

to the identification of 15 required behavioral steps, and the task analysis of the use of a fingerprint recognition system involved 11 steps. In general, tasks are more difficult or less user friendly if they require longer task sequences.

Adams et al. (1997) conducted a Web-based questionnaire survey of 139 respondents regarding their password-related behaviors. Infrequently used passwords were associated with greater memory problems. Results also showed significant correlations between a desire to decrease security and frequent memory problems, therefore justifying the need to examine human factors and usability of security methods to maintain user support for security measures. Use of security methods such as passwords that are difficult to remember is likely to reduce user motivation and favorable attitude toward security. This study also found that 50% of the respondents wrote their passwords down in one form or another. This study thus demonstrates the importance of password memorability. A follow-up qualitative analysis of semistructured, detailed interviews with 30 users in two companies highlighted several human factors and organizational issues affecting password-related behaviors (Adams and Sasse, 1999), including the importance of compatibility between work practices and password procedures. For example, in one company, employees pointed out that individually owned passwords were not compatible with group work. This study also highlighted the lack of security knowledge and information among users. It is important to recognize that users are not necessarily opposed to security, but must understand the need for security methods and be informed of the rationale behind security mechanisms.

Whitten and Tygar (1998, 1999) studied the usability of the PGP 5.0 encryption software. They defined usability for security as follows: "Security software is usable if the people who are expected to use it (1) are reliably made aware of the security tasks they need to perform, (2) are able to figure out how to successfully perform those tasks, (3) do not make dangerous errors, and (4) are sufficiently comfortable with the interface to continue using it." The usability evaluation of PGP 5.0 consisted of two methods. First, a cognitive walk-through was conducted to identify those interface characteristics that failed to meet the usability standards listed in the definition. Second, a user test was conducted in a laboratory setting. The cognitive walk-through identified a range of usability issues, such as unclear visual metaphors, misunderstanding of the software structure (e.g., failing to recognize and understand the existence of the key server), irreversible actions, and too much information. The user test was based on test scenarios presented to 12 subjects. Another set of usability problems was identified in the user test: difficulty avoiding dangerous errors such as e-mailing secret information without encryption, difficulty encrypting e-mails, difficulty identifying the correct key for encrypting, and difficulty decrypting an e-mail message. This research demonstrates the lack of usability of

Table 3.5.   Examples of Human Factors Methods for Evaluating Computer Security Methods

Human Factors Method	Sample Application
Task analysis	Proctor et al. (2000): analysis of third-party authentication methods
Accident analysis	Carayon and Kraemer (2002): accident analysis method adapted to the investigation of a computer security breach or vulnerabilities
Cognitive walk-through	Whitten and Tygar (1998, 1999): evaluation of encryption software
User test	Whitten and Tygar (1998, 1999): evaluation of encryption software

PGP 5.0 and shows the difficulties encountered by users who are not knowledgeable in the area of encryption. Table 3.5 shows examples of human factors methods that can be used for evaluating computer security methods.

Schneiderman (1998) has proposed principles of interface design; Table 3.6 provides a description of the usability principles. Designers of computer security methods that include some form of interface design should follow Schneiderman's principles of interface design. The studies by Whitten and Tygar (1998, 1999) on the usability of an encryption software show that the software had design characteristics that violated some of Schneiderman's principles of interface design. For example, it was difficult for some users to avoid dangerous errors such as e-mailing secret information without encryption. This design feature clearly violates the fifth principle of Schneiderman. The encryption software was not designed in such a way as to avoid serious user errors. Computer security methods designed according to Schneiderman's principles are more likely to be usable and user friendly and to improve the overall system security.

The introduction of a computer security method is also likely to affect work and work processes. A work system can be described as having five elements: the *individual* performing certain *tasks* using *tools and technologies* in a specific *environment* and under *organizational conditions* (Carayon and Smith, 2000; Smith and Carayon-Sainfort, 1989). Using this model, a computer security method can be considered as a technology that could influence the other elements of the work system, including the individual, his or her tasks, other tools and technologies, the physical environment, and the organizational conditions. Let us consider passwords as an example of a security method. Imagine that an organization has issued new guidelines for passwords, such as their required length and content. It is not unusual for employees to use several different software packages and have access to different types of hardware, therefore requiring the use of several different passwords. For different *tasks*, an em-

Table 3.6.   Usability Principles for Interface Design

Principle	Description
1. Strive for consistency	■ Consistent sequence of actions in similar situations ■ Identical terminology in prompts, menus, and help screens ■ Consistent color, layout, capitalization, fonts, etc.
2. Enable frequent users to use shortcuts	■ Abbreviations, special keys, hidden commands, macro facilities
3. Offer informative feedback	■ System feedback for every user action
4. Design dialogs to yield closure	■ Sequences of actions organized into groups with a yield beginning, middle, and end
5. Offer error prevention and simple error handling	■ System design to avoid serious user errors ■ System detection of user error ■ Simple, constructive, and specific instructions for error recovery
6. Permit easy reversal of actions	■ Reversible actions
7. Support internal locus of control	■ Avoid surprising system actions, tedious sequences of data entries, inability to or difficulty in obtaining necessary information, and inability to produce the action desired
8. Reduce short-term memory load	■ Simple displays ■ Window-motion frequency to be reduced ■ Sufficient training time

Schneiderman, 1998.

ployee may have to use different passwords. The study by Adams and Sasse (1999) shows an example of a lack of fit between passwords and *organizational conditions*, as discussed above. End users complained that the password guidelines did not support the work team structure. Each individual employee had his or her own password, but the organization required employees to work in teams and share computing resources. In general, many employees may share offices, share workstations, or not have secure access to their office or workstation. This *physical environment* means that employees will have to keep their passwords in a secure, locked place or will have to remember them. Thus, when implementing a new computer security method, it is important to consider the fit (or lack thereof) between the new security method and the organization's work and work processes.

The implementation of any new computer and e-business security method should be considered a technological change and therefore should be managed like any other organizational or technological change (Eason, 1988; Haims and Carayon, 2000; Kanter, 1983). Experts have long recognized the importance of

Table 3.7.   Principles for the Management of the Implementation of Computer Security Methods

Principle	Application to Computer Security
Employee participation	Employees involved in decisions and activities related to the implementation of a computer security method
Information and communication	Employees informed about the implementation of the computer security method through various means of communication
Training and learning	Training provided to employees, and learning by employees, regarding the new computer security method
Feedback	Feedback is sought during and after the implementation of the new computer security method
Project management	Activities related to the organization and management of the implementation itself

the implementation process in achieving a successful organizational change (Carayon and Karsh, 2000; Korunka et al., 1993; Tannenbaum et al., 1996). Various principles for the successful implementation of technological change have been defined in the business and industrial engineering research literature. Table 3.7 summarizes the principles for the management of the implementation of computer security methods.

Employee participation is a key principle in the successful implementation of an organizational or technological change (Coyle-Shapiro, 1999; Korunka et al., 1993; Smith and Carayon, 1995). Both empirical research and theory demonstrate the potential benefits of participation in the workplace. These benefits include enhanced employee motivation and job satisfaction, improved performance and employee health, more rapid implementation of technological and organizational change, and more thorough diagnosis and solution of ergonomic problems (Gardell, 1977; Lawler, 1986; Noro and Imada, 1991; Wilson and Haines, 1997). The manner in which a new technology is implemented is as critical to its success as its technological capabilities (see, for example, Eason, 1982 and Smith and Carayon, 1995). End-user participation in the design and implementation of a new technology is a good way to help ensure a successful technological investment. One can distinguish between *active participation*, where the employees and the end users actively participate in the implementation of the new technology, and *passive participation,* where the employees and end users are merely informed about the new technology (Carayon and Smith, 1993). Hence, when implementing a new computer security method, employees should be involved in the decisions and/or activities related to the implementation of the new security method. At minimum, employees should be kept informed of the implementation of a new security method and, when necessary, should be trained in its use. In some instances, selected employees may be asked to participate more actively in the implementation of the new security method, for instance to identify the most efficient and effective way to design the security method or the training method.

Technological implementation should be considered an evolving process that requires considerable *learning* and adjustment (Mohrman et al., 1995). The participatory process model developed by Haims and Carayon (1998) specifies the underlying concepts of learning and adjustment: i.e., action, control, and *feedback*. The importance of feedback in managing the change process is also echoed in the literature on quality management; see, for example, the Plan-Do-Check-Act cycle proposed by Deming (1986). Feedback is known to be an important element of changing behavior (Smith and Smith, 1966). An aspect of learning in the context of technological change is the type and content of *training* (e.g., Frese et al., 1988; Gattiker, 1992). When a new computer security method is introduced, end users should be trained to understand why the security method is useful and important for the overall system security and how to use it.

Studies have examined the characteristics of technological change processes that lead to successful implementations in industrial settings. For example, Korunka and Carayon (1999) examined the implementation of information technology in 60 Austrian companies and 18 American companies. Compared with the Austrian implementations, the American implementations were characterized by a higher degree of professionalism (e.g., more use of *project management* tools) and greater participation, but at the same time by more negative effects for employees (e.g., more personnel reduction). If a new security method is introduced that potentially has a large impact on work and work processes, the implementation of this new security method should be managed like a project. Stakeholders and people who will be directly impacted by the new security method should be represented in the project management.

3.5. CONCLUSION

In this chapter, various human factors issues in computer and e-business security were reviewed. First, a taxonomy of attacker attributes and characteristics was proposed and their impact on security strategies used by companies was described. Then the concept of human error and its relationship to computer security was explained. Finally, usability and implementation of computer security methods were discussed. Much is still unknown about human factors of computer and e-business security. However, guidelines and approaches to deal with the human factors issues of computer and e-business security were provided in this chapter.

REFERENCES

Adams, A. and Sasse, M. A. (1999). Users are not the enemy, *Communications of the ACM,* 42(12), 41–46.

Adams, A., Sasse, M. A., and Lunt, P. (1997). Making passwords secure and usable, in *People & Computers XII, Proceedings of HCI'97,* Thimbleby, H., O'Conaill, B., and Thomas, P., Eds., Springer, Bristol, pp. 1–19.

Anderson, R. H., Bozek, T., Longstaff, T., Meitzler, W., Skroch, M., and Van Wyk, K., Eds. (2000). *Conference Proceedings: Research on Mitigating the Insider Threat to Information Systems #2,* Rand, Santa Monica, CA.

Bier, V. M. (1997). An overview of probabilistic risk analysis for complex engineered systems, in *Fundamentals of Risk Analysis and Risk Management,* Molak, V., Ed., CRC Press, Boca Raton, FL, pp. 67–85.

Bilar, D. (forthcoming). Quantitative Risk Analysis of Computer Networks, unpublished Ph.D. dissertation, Dartmouth College, Hanover, NH.

Brannigan, V. and Smidts, C. (1998). Performance based fire safety regulation under intentional uncertainty, *Fire and Materials,* 23(6), 341–347.

Brannigan, V., Kilpatrick, A., and Smidts, C. (2001). Human behavior and risk based fire regulation, paper presented at the Second International Symposium on Human Behavior and Fire, Massachusetts Institute of Technology, Cambridge, MA.

Carayon, P. and Karsh, B. (2000). Sociotechnical issues in the implementation of imaging technology, *Behaviour and Information Technology,* 19(4), 247–262.

Carayon, P. and Kraemer, S. (2002). Macroergonomics in WWDU: What about computer and information system security? in *Proceedings of the 6th International Scientific Conference on Work with Display Units (WWDU 2002) — World Wide Work,* Cakir, G., Ed., ERGONOMIC Institut für Arbeits- und Sozialforschung Forschungsgesellschaft mbH, Berlin, pp. 87–89.

Carayon, P. and Smith, M. J. (1993). The balance theory of job design and stress as a model for the management of technological change, paper presented at the Fourth International Congress of Industrial Engineering, Marseille, France.

Carayon, P. and Smith, M. J. (2000). Work organization and ergonomics, *Applied Ergonomics,* 31, 649–662.

Computer Science and Telecommunications Board–National Research Council (2002). *Cybersecurity Today and Tomorrow: Pay Now or Pay Later,* National Academy Press, Washington, D.C.

Coyle-Shapiro, J. A.-M. (1999). Employee participation and assessment of an organizational change intervention, *The Journal of Applied Behavioral Science,* 35(4), 439–456.

Deming, W. E. (1986). *Out of the Crisis*, Massachusetts Institute of Technology, Cambridge, MA.

Duggan, R. (2000). Insider threat — A theoretical model, paper presented at the Conference Proceedings: Research on Mitigating the Insider Threat to Information Systems #2, Santa Monica, CA.

Eason, K. (1988). *Information Technology and Organizational Change*, Taylor & Francis, London.

Eason, K. D. (1982). The process of introducing information technology, *Behaviour and Information Technology*, 1(2), 197–213.

Ezell, B., Farr, J., and Wiese, I. (2000). Infrastructure risk analysis model, *Journal of Infrastructure Systems*, 6(3), 114–117.

Frese, M., Albrecht, K., Altmann, A., Lang, J., Papstein, P., Peyerl, R., Prümper, J., Schulte-Göcking, H., Wankmüller, I., and Wendel, R. (1988). The effects of an active development of the mental model in the training process: Experimental results in a word processing system, *Behaviour and Information Technology*, 7(3), 295–304.

Gardell, B. (1977). Autonomy and participation at work, *Human Relations*, 30, 515–533.

Gattiker, U. E. (1992). Computer skills acquisition: A review and future directions for research, *Journal of Management*, 18(3), 547–574.

Haims, M. C. and Carayon, P. (1998). Theory and practice for the implementation of "in-house," continuous improvement participatory ergonomic programs, *Applied Ergonomics*, 29(6), 461–472.

Haims, M. C. and Carayon, P. (2000). Work organization interventions, in *The International Encyclopedia of Ergonomics and Human Factors*, Karwoski, E., Ed., Taylor and Francis, London, pp. 1441–1445.

Hayday, G. (2002). Online Pollster in Email "Catastrophe" Blames Human Error, Ebusiness Security, retrieved from http://www.silicon.com/public/door?6004REQEVENT=&REQINT1=55285&REQSTR1=silicon.com.

Hollnagel, E. (1993). *Human Reliability Analysis Context and Control*, Academic Press, San Diego.

Howard, J. D. and Longstaff, T. A. (1998). *A Common Language for Computer Security Incidents*, SAND98-8667, Sandia National Laboratories, Albuquerque, NM.

Hutchinson, B. and Skroch, M. (2001). Lessons learned through Sandia's cyber assessment program, paper presented at the Energy Assurance Conference, U.S. Department of Energy, Arlington, VA, December 12–13.

Kanter, R. M. (1983). *The Change Masters: Innovation and Entrepreneurship in the American Corporation*, Simon and Schuster, New York.

Khan, S. (2001). When laptops "walk away," company secrets go too, *USA Today*, March 13.

Knight, E. (2000). *Computer Vulnerabilities*, retrieved from http://downloads.securityfocus.com/library/compvulndraft.pdf.

Korunka, C. and Carayon, P. (1999). Continuous implementations of information technology: The development of an interview guide and a cross-national comparison of Austrian and American organizations, *The International Journal of Human Factors in Manufacturing*, 9(2), 165–183.

Korunka, C., Weiss, A., and Karetta, B. (1993). Effects of new technologies with special regard for the implementation process per se, *Journal of Organizational Behavior,* 14(4), 331–348.

Lawler, E. E. (1986). *High Involvement Management: Participative Strategies for Improving Organizational Performance,* Jossey-Bass, San Francisco.

Lemos, R. (2000). Western Union data heist: "Human error," *ZDNet News,* September 10 (http://news.zdnet.com/2100-9595 22-523769.html).

Longstaff, T. A., Chittister, C., Pethia, R., and Haimes, Y. Y. (2000). Are we forgetting the risks of information technology? *Computer,* 33(12), 43–51.

Martz, H. F. and Johnson, M. E. (1987). Risk analysis of terrorist attacks, *Risk Analysis,* 7(1), 35–47.

Mitnick, K. D. and Simon, W. L. (2002). *The Art of Deception — Controlling the Human Element of Security,* Wiley, Indianapolis, IN.

Mohrman, S. A., Cohen, S. G., and Mohrman, A. M. J. (1995). *Designing Team-Based Organizations: New Forms of Knowledge and Work,* Jossey-Bass, San Francisco.

Noro, K. and Imada, A. (1991). *Participatory Ergonomics,* Taylor & Francis, London.

Palmer, C. C. (2001). Ethical hacking, *IBM Systems Journal,* 40(3), 769–780.

Pate-Cornell, E. and Guikema, S. (2002). Probabilistic modeling of terrorist threats: A systems analysis approach to setting priorities among countermeasures, *Military Operations Research,* 7(4), 5–23.

Poulsen, K. (2002). *New York Times* internal network hacked: How open proxies and default passwords led to Adrian Lamo padding his rolodex with information on 3,000 op-ed writers, from William F. Buckley, Jr. to Jimmy Carter, *SecurityFocus,* February 26.

Power, R. (2002). 2002 CSI/FBI computer crime and security survey, *Computer Security Issues & Trends,* VIII(1).

Proctor, R. W., Lien, M.-C., Salvendy, G., and Schultz, E. E. (2000). A task analysis of usability in third-party authentication, *Information Security Bulletin,* April, 49–56.

Rasmussen, J. (1983). Skills, rules, knowledge: Signals, signs and symbols and other distinctions in human performance models, *IEEE Transactions: Systems, Man, and Cybernetics,* SMC-13, 257–267.

Reason, J. (1990). *Human Error,* Cambridge University Press, Cambridge, U.K.

Reason, J. (1997). *Managing the Risks of Organizational Accidents,* Ashgate Publishing Company, Brookfield, VT.

Sandia National Laboratories (2000). *Information Design Assurance Red Team (IDART),* retrieved from http://www.sandia.gov/idart.

Schneiderman, B. (1998). *Designing the User Interface — Strategies for Effective Human-Computer Interaction,* 3rd ed., Addison-Wesley, Reading, MA.

Schneier, B. (2000). *Secrets and Lies: Digital Security in a Networked World,* Wiley, New York.

Schudel, G. and Wood, B. (2000). Modeling behavior of the cyber-terrorist, paper presented at the Conference Research on Mitigating the Insider Threat to Information Systems #2, Santa Monica, CA.

Smith, K. U. and Smith, M. F. (1966). *Cybernetic Principles of Learning and Educational Design,* Holt, Rhinehart, and Winston, New York.

Smith, M. J. and Carayon, P. (1995). New technology, automation, and work organization: Stress problems and improved technology implementation strategies, *The International Journal of Human Factors in Manufacturing,* 5(1), 99–116.

Smith, M. J. and Carayon-Sainfort, P. (1989). A balance theory of job design for stress reduction, *International Journal of Industrial Ergonomics,* 4, 67–79.

Soo Hoo, K. J. (2000). Working Paper: How Much is Enough? A Risk-Management Approach to Computer Security, Consortium for Research on Information Security and Policy, Stanford University, Stanford, CA.

Stokes, J. (2000). Stock watch, *Denver Rocky Mountain News,* September 12.

Tannenbaum, S. I., Salas, E., and Cannon-Bowers, J. A. (1996). Promoting team effectiveness, in *Handbook of Work Group Psychology,* West, M. A., Ed., Wiley, New York, pp. 503–530.

Trist, E. (1981). *The Evaluation of Sociotechnical Systems,* Quality of Working Life Center, Toronto.

USA Today (2001). Silicon Valley trade-secret case ends, July 26.

U.S. Department of Justice (2001a). Clara Man Sentenced for Theft of Trade Secrets (press release), retrieved from http://www.cybercrime.gov/chang_sent.htm, December 4.

U.S. Department of Justice (2001b). Former Cisco Systems, Inc. Accountants Sentenced for Unauthorized Access to Computer Systems to Illegally Issue Almost $8 Million in Cisco Stock to Themselves (press release), retrieved from http://www.usdoj.gov:80/criminal/cybercrime/Osowski_TangSent.htm, November 26.

U.S. Department of Justice (2002). Russian Computer Hacker Sentenced to Three Years in Prison (press release), retrieved from http://www.usdoj.gov:80/criminal/cybercrime/gorshkovSent.htm, October 4.

Vijayan, J. (2000). Theft of Qualcomm chairman's laptop provides security lessons for users, *Computerworld,* retrieved from http://www.computerworld.com/hardwaretopics/hardware/desktops/story/0,10801,50710,00.html.

Whitten, A. and Tygar, J. D. (1998). Usability of Security: A Case Study, CMU-CS-98-155, School of Computer Science, Computer Science Department, Carnegie Mellon University, Pittsburgh.

Whitten, A. and Tygar, J. D. (1999). Why Johnny can't encrypt: A usability evaluation of PGP 5.0, paper presented at the 9th USENIX Security Symposium, August.

Wilson, J. R. and Haines, H. M. (1997). Participatory ergonomics, in *Handbook of Human Factors and Ergonomics,* Salvendy, G., Ed., Wiley, New York, pp. 490–513.

Wood, B. (2002a). An insider threat model for adversary simulation, paper presented at the Conference Research on Mitigating the Insider Threat to Information Systems #2, Santa Monica, CA.

Wood, B. (2002b). An insider threat model for model adversaries, paper presented at the Conference Research on Mitigating the Insider Threat to Information Systems #2, Santa Monica, CA.

Yan, J., Blackwell, A., Anderson, R., and Alasdair, G. (2000). The Memorability and Security of Passwords — Some Empirical Results, Technical Report No. 500, Cambridge University Computer Laboratory, Cambridge, England.

MANAGING RISK WITHIN SUPPLY CHAINS: USING ADAPTIVE SAFETY STOCK CALCULATIONS FOR IMPROVED INVENTORY CONTROL

Richard Boedi and Ulrich Schimpel

4.1. INTRODUCTION

Risk management in supply chain management has many different aspects and facets. Usually, it is applied where uncertainties of the demand that drives the supply chain have a noticeable influence on the effectiveness of a supply network. In order to ensure certain availabilities of raw and work-in-progress materials as well as finished products, it is inevitable to build up inventories at strategic points of a supply network, thus decreasing demand variability at, for example, manufacturing sites. Risk management has to balance the costs associated with stockouts and the various costs for managing inventories. In this respect, the problem just mentioned encompasses (1) determining where to put inventories for certain items, (2) setting appropriate service levels for these, and (3) developing a reliable method for translating a given service level and the associated costs (ordering costs, inventory holding costs, stockout costs, etc.) into a suitable replenishment policy.

Safety stock is supposed to cover uncertainties of demand during the inbound lead time of an item, that is, the time it takes from issuing an order from the warehouse to a supplier up to the arrival of the goods, as well as the uncertainties of the lead times. Here, however, the focus will be on demand uncertainties. If the safety stock level is set too high, more financial resources are bound to inventory than necessary. If, however, the safety stock level is too low, stock will run out more often and the desired serviceability may not be met. Most of the software tools used in inventory control calculate the level of safety stock for each product by assuming that daily demands are normally or Poisson distributed or by simply setting a fixed safety stock level.

However, the problem with these assumptions is that in many cases the daily demand is far from normally or Poisson distributed. In particular, this is true for special kinds of inventories, such as spare parts. In the end, this results in incorrectly calculated safety stock levels, low service levels, and nevertheless high average inventory levels. This prevents transposing risk management decisions into replenishment policies in a rigorous way. For a discussion of how different assumptions about how the demand distributions may affect the efficiency of inventory control, the reader can refer to the following selection of articles: Bagchi et al. (1983, 1984), Bookbinder and Lordahl (1989), Eppen and Martin (1988), Grange (1998), Jacobs and Wagner (1989), Lau (1989), Lau and Zaki (1982), Mentzner and Krishnan (1985), Tadikamalla (1984), and Tyworth and O'Neill (1997).

In order to overcome this problem and to improve the quality of safety stock calculations, thus enabling reliable risk management, it is indispensable to use an adapted demand distribution for every single product. The method presented in this chapter is able to calculate safety stocks more precisely by assigning an individual continuous demand distribution to each product based on either its historical or forecasted daily demand data. In addition, it allows the safety stock calculation scheme to be adjusted adaptively. A special feature of this method is the integration of a cluster technique to improve the statistics, especially for low-usage parts, and to speed up calculations considerably. The calculation speed for an inventory of about 10,000 items is on the order of one minute and is approximately linear with the number of stock items.

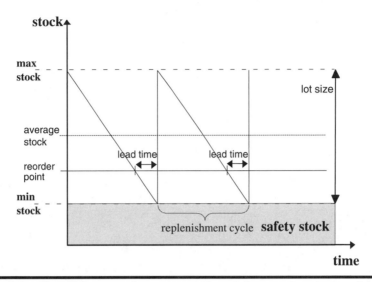

Figure 4.1.   Classical sawtooth representation of the warehousing model.

4.2. WAREHOUSING MODEL

The purpose of keeping safety stock is to cover the effects of demand and lead time variance and to ensure a prescribed availability of articles. Thus, safety stock contributes to meeting a given service level. For the sake of simplicity, we focus on the commonly used α_1-service level (α_1-SL) (Schneider, 1997), which measures the percentage of replenishment cycles without any stockout. For the definition of a replenishment cycle, see Figure 4.1.

We start with a commonly used model of a multi-item inventory system with n independent items $P_1, \ldots, P_n$, which is based on the assumptions of normally distributed daily demands and lead times (see, e.g., Müller-Merbach, 1969 or Schwarz, 1999). How these assumptions affect the service levels achieved in a real-world scenario will be presented later in this section. All axioms are supposed to be satisfied by each stock item $P = P_i$. The index usually will be dropped and μ_D written instead of μ_{D_i}, etc.

Axioms concerning demand:
(*A1*)   The demand during one time period (minute, hour, day, week, …) is a normally distributed random variable D.
(*A2*)   The average demand μ_D is constant within one replenishment cycle.

(*A3*)   The daily demands are stochastically independent.
(*A4*)   Stockout quantities are remembered.
(*A5*)   The reorder point s is nonnegative.

Axioms concerning lead time:
(*A6*)   The lead time is a normally distributed random variable Λ.
(*A7*)   The average lead time μ_Λ is constant.
(*A8*)   Only one inbound order is pending at the same time.
(*A9*)   The lead time and the daily demands are stochastically independent.

A warehousing policy for some item P_i consists of three components: the replenishment mode Σ_i, the reorder point s_i, and the lot size Q_i. We will always assume that the (s_i, S_i) replenishment mode is being used for each item P_i, that is, whenever the stock level a_i falls below the reorder point s_i, a replenishment order of size $S_i = Q_i + (s_i - a_i)$ is issued (see Scarf, 1960). Since we are only interested in the calculation of the safety stock level B_i, we proceed by assuming that the lot size Q_i is already calculated based on, say, a (deterministic) economic order quantity model. Note that since $B_i = s_i - \Lambda_i \cdot D_i$, it does not matter whether we calculate the reorder point s_i or the safety stock level B_i.

Fix some item $P = P_i$ and write $B = B_i$. As the lead time and the daily demands are stochastic variables here, the calculation of safety stock B consists of two components. The first component B_D covers the demand fluctuation during the lead time, and the other component B_Λ covers the lead time fluctuation. Because of axiom (*A9*), safety stock B can be decomposed as:

$$B = \sqrt{B_D^2 + B_\Lambda^2}$$

In order to cover the fluctuation in demand for *one* day with respect to a given α_1-SL of $b \in [0,1)$, safety stock B_D is expressed by:

$$B_D = f(b) \cdot \mu_D \cdot \sigma_D^*$$

Here, f is the quantile function of the standard normal distribution and σ_D^* is the coefficient of variance of the demands D. Because of (*A3*), the safety stock covering the demand's variance during the lead time Λ is determined by:

$$B_D = f(b) \cdot \mu_D \cdot \sigma_D^* \cdot \sqrt{\Lambda}$$

Similarly, safety stock B_Λ is expressed by:

$$B_\Lambda = f(b) \cdot \mu_D \cdot \sigma_\Lambda$$

with σ_Λ being the standard deviation of the inbound lead time Λ. Putting the formulas together, the total safety stock B is given by (Schwarz, 1999):

$$B = \sqrt{B_D^2 + B_\Lambda^2} = f(b) \cdot \mu_D \cdot \sqrt{(\sigma_D^*)^2 \cdot \Lambda + \sigma_\Lambda^2} \qquad (4.1)$$

4.3. SIMULATION RESULTS

Using Equation 4.1 to calculate the safety stock levels, we set up a simulation where we used an economic order quantity–driven (s, S) replenishment policy taking the (randomized) transactional data (most of them capturing about one year of demand) of 10 real-world warehouses spread among various different industries and purposes to generate the demand. The number of articles in these warehouses ranged from around 2500 to more than 120,000. The simulation was run on the basis of daily demands. The simulated time scale spanned 2000 days in order to get statistically sound results. We started our simulation with the maximum stocking levels S_i for every article P_i. The average inbound lead time Λ_i was set to half of the replenishment cycle time. The lead time variance was set to 10% of the lead time itself. We have chosen a common service level p for each P_i. In order to investigate the relationship between the given service level p and the actual distribution of the achieved service levels, we considered five simulation runs using different global service levels p of 50, 80, 90, 95, and 98%. Of course, for a 50% service level, no safety stock needs to be allocated. This scenario has just been added to see the different performance for **Norm** and **Emp** in the absence of safety stock. For each simulated day d_n, the following steps have been performed for each stock item P_i separately:

1. Determine the demand for day d_n. This is done by either taking a normal distribution with average and variance determined by the historical demand data (case **Emp**) or by using the randomized daily demands themselves (case **Emp**).
2. Check whether there are any incoming replenishment deliveries and, if so, add the delivered quantity to the actual stock level.
3. Subtract the demand as calculated in step 1 from the actual stock level. If the actual stock level is negative, a stockout occurred. In this case, the negative stock level is kept and we will start the next day with this negative stock level. This means that we keep a backlog of the demand that could not have been satisfied immediately.
4. Check whether the actual stock level a_i of item P_i is equal to or less than the reorder point s_i. If so, a replenishment order of quantity $S_i - a_i$ is sent

out. This order will arrive exactly after the given lead time Λ_i at the warehouse.

5. Update the current α_1-SL.

In Table 4.1, the average service levels achieved using the daily demand data coming from transaction databases (**Emp**) are compared to the case where normally distributed demands were used to drive the simulation (**Norm**).

It is apparent from Table 4.1 that, especially for high service levels p, we have a high deviation from the desired service levels p for case **Emp**. For a service level of $p = 98\%$, we only get an average achieved service level of 94.9% with a variation that is more than 12 times as high as for **Norm**. For convenience, we have plotted the data of the table for the service levels of 90 and 98% in Figure 4.2a and Figure 4.2b, respectively.

The warehouse that showed the worst result (warehouse 7) holds spare parts inventory. This, however, was to be expected, because spare parts usually show a high variability of demand coupled with a low average consumption. Looking closer at the results of warehouse 7, it turns out that the distribution of service levels for each item is very inhomogeneous. First of all, what distribution of service levels do we have to expect? Let us first consider case **Norm**, where we assume that the daily demands are normally distributed. Then we can use Equation 4.1 to calculate the safety stock levels correctly. Using these safety stock levels, the probability of a replenishment cycle with a stockout is just the predetermined service level p. Hence, we can regard the outcome of a replenishment cycle for stock item P_i (i.e., whether or not a stockout occurred) as a Bernoulli experiment $b_i(p)$ of success probability p. This means that the stochastic variable $b_i(p) = 1$ if no stockout occurred during a replenishment cycle and $b_i(p) = 0$ otherwise. Measuring the α_1-SL for a series of n replenishment cycles corresponds to looking at the sum $B_n(p) = [b_i(p) + \ldots + b_i(p)]/n$, which, by the central limit theorem, tends to a normally distributed stochastic variable with mean p and variance $p(1 - p)$. Thus, in a simulation of sufficiently long horizon, we would expect to see a normal distribution with a mean value of p. Indeed, this is shown in Figure 4.3a. Note that the rightmost peak represents the integral of the right-hand tail of the normal distribution and hence is to be expected. Now, if the resulting service level distribution fails to be approximately normally distributed, we infer that the Bernoulli experiments $b_1(p_1), \ldots, b_n(p_n)$ had in fact different success probabilities $p_1, \ldots, p_n$. Hence, we can use the deviation of a simulated service level distribution from the normal distribution as a quality measure of the process that translates a given service level to a safety stock level. Indeed, looking at Figure 4.3b, which shows the results of the simulation of case **Emp**, we see a service level distribution that is in no way close to a normal distribution. More than 20% of the stock items had a service level of

Table 4.1. Simulation Results Comparing Average Service Levels Achieved Using Normally Distributed Demands (Norm) Versus Randomized Transactional Data (Emp)

Desired Service Level		WH1	WH2	WH3	WH4	WH5	WH6	WH7	WH8	WH9	WH10	Avg.	Abs. Sigma	Rel. Sigma
50%	Norm	53.0%	44.8%	54.9%	49.5%	49.1%	52.0%	54.0%	55.3%	59.5%	48.9%	52.1%	0.03957	1.00
	Emp	66.5%	55.3%	71.6%	59.5%	59.1%	67.7%	61.3%	75.7%	79.7%	66.0%	66.2%	0.07363	1.86
80%	Norm	82.0%	74.8%	83.2%	79.4%	79.4%	81.2%	82.3%	83.8%	86.9%	79.8%	81.3%	0.03073	1.00
	Emp	84.6%	77.5%	86.0%	80.9%	79.4%	83.4%	74.6%	88.3%	89.6%	84.1%	82.8%	0.04500	1.46
90%	Norm	91.1%	87.3%	91.6%	89.5%	89.6%	90.2%	91.2%	92.1%	93.0%	90.6%	90.6%	0.01512	1.00
	Emp	90.4%	85.4%	90.5%	87.8%	86.4%	89.2%	79.6%	92.1%	92.4%	87.6%	88.1%	0.03599	2.38
95%	Norm	96.1%	94.0%	96.0%	95.1%	95.0%	96.0%	95.8%	96.0%	96.6%	95.3%	95.6%	0.00709	1.00
	Emp	94.0%	90.8%	93.5%	92.0%	90.9%	93.5%	83.1%	94.4%	95.2%	92.9%	92.0%	0.03274	4.62
98%	Norm	98.7%	97.8%	98.5%	98.2%	98.3%	98.5%	98.6%	98.4%	98.5%	98.3%	98.4%	0.00240	1.00
	Emp	96.6%	95.0%	95.8%	95.3%	94.6%	95.9%	86.3%	97.0%	96.7%	95.9%	94.9%	0.02959	12.33

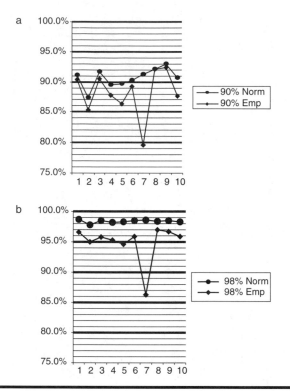

Figure 4.2.   Simulation results for (a) 90% and (b) 98% service level.

less than 60% during the simulation (**Emp**), and more than 18% of the stock items had no stockout during the simulation.

Although the achieved average service levels for the warehouses other than warehouse 7 were closer to the predetermined service levels, the achieved service level distributions were more or less the same as for warehouse 7. As a consequence, we think that the situation we face when using empirical demand data is unacceptable, and consequently we have to take more care about the actual demand distributions. This leads us to the following revision of our warehousing model.

4.4. WAREHOUSING MODEL REVISITED

As the simulation results of the previous section suggest, the nonnormality of demands causes very unpredictable service levels in practice. Thus, it is not

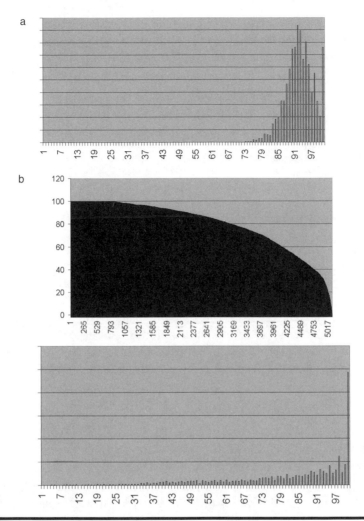

Figure 4.3. (a) Service level distribution for simulation (**Norm**). (b) Service level distribution for each item coming from simulation (**Emp**).

sufficient to make f dependent only on b, because the quantile $f(b)$ of the normalized normal distribution does not estimate the safety stock proportion with sufficient accuracy. In order to improve the initial model, we therefore replace axiom (*A2*) with the modified axiom:

(*A2**)   The demand during one time period is a real, nonnegative, *continuous, not necessarily normally* distributed random variable D.

In the following sections, we will show how Equation 4.1 has to be changed in order to reflect axiom *(A2*)*, and we will explain a method for estimating the distribution of the random variable *D*.

4.5. ADAPTIVE SAFETY STOCK CALCULATIONS

Having replaced axiom *(A2)* by *(A2*)*, thereby dropping the assumption of normally distributed demands, the following question arises: How do we have to change the equation

$$B = \sqrt{B_D^2 + B_\Lambda^2} = f(b) \cdot \mu_D \cdot \sqrt{(\sigma_D^*)^2 \cdot \Lambda + \sigma_\Lambda^2}$$

for the safety stock level *B* in order to support axiom *(A2*)* instead of *(A2)*?

Using the individual quantile function $f(b, D)$ would obviously be the best solution in this situation, since it exactly models axiom *(A2*)*. The problem is that we do not know D_i for each stock item P_i. In most real-world cases, the only information available is the historical demand D_H coming from the transaction data. In order to avoid the introduction of additional variables, we will use the same notion for a random variable and its underlying distribution. In the following, we propose a method for estimating the demand distributions D_i based on the set of all historical demand distributions D_H. The method of calculating the estimates $D_M = D_{M,i}$ is split into four processes.

We start with the historical demand time series (i.e., the transaction data) of each item *P*. The first process generates for each *P* a normalized discrete demand distribution from its historical demand time series, as shown in Figure 4.4.

Figure 4.5 illustrates the second process, which collects these distributions, clusters this collection by means of similar-looking distributions, and finds an optimal discrete probability distribution for each cluster that represents all members of a cluster. The purpose of clustering the data is twofold. First, it enhances the quality of the succeeding steps by enlarging the amount of data that is being analyzed. This is important especially for slow-moving or sporadic items. Second, the preceding steps need only be performed on the clusters' representatives, thus reducing the computation time considerably. The second process will be explained in depth in the next section.

The task of the third process, shown in Figure 4.6, is to assign some continuous probability *C* distribution to each distribution *R* that represents a cluster such that *R* can be regarded with a high probability as a sample of *C* and to adjust some of the parameters of *C* for each member of the cluster to yield the desired continuous distribution D_M. This model distribution D_M is then taken

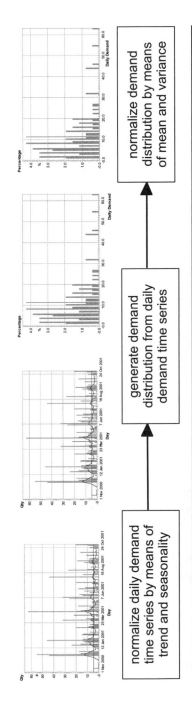

Figure 4.4. Normalization process of historical demand.

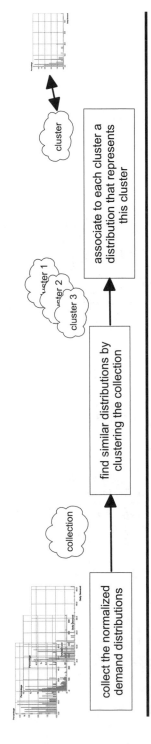

Figure 4.5. Clustering process.

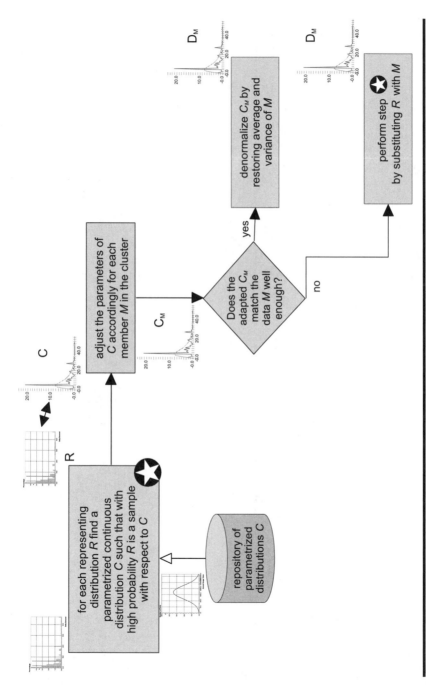

Figure 4.6. Finding a continuous probability distribution that serves as an estimate of the demand distribution for all stock items of a cluster.

as an estimate for the demand distribution D for each stock item P of the cluster that is being represented by R.

In the last process, the safety stock level for each stock item P is calculated individually based on the associated continuous distribution $D_{M,P}$ that has been found by the previous process. There is one thing we did not mention for the sake of simplicity. In the inventory data we investigated, we saw a large portion of stock items for which there was no demand at all for most of the time periods. This resulted in a high peak in the demand distributions at position 0. The clustering process was dominated by the size of this peak, and the rest of the demand distribution did not influence the clustering sufficiently. To overcome this problem, we rescaled the zero peak and the rest of the distribution to reduce the influence of the zero peak and restricted process 3 to the positive part of the demand distribution (i.e., the distribution $D_{M,P}$ is in fact an estimate of the distribution of positive demands). Consequently, we have to replace Equation 4.1, which relates the safety stock level B to the α_1-service level SL(P, B) of item P, by:

$$ SL(P, B) = \sum_{k=1}^{\Lambda} \Delta_{M,P}\left(\frac{B}{\sqrt{k}} + \mu_D \frac{\Lambda}{k} \right) p_k + p_0 \qquad (4.2) $$

where $\Delta_{M,P}(x) = \int_{-\infty}^{x} D_{M,P}(t)dt$, p_0 is the probability that there is no demand at all during the lead time Λ, and p_k is the probability that there will be some demand on exactly k days of the inbound lead time L for P. Equation 4.2 splits up the different cases as follows: no demand during the lead time, one day of demand during the lead time, demand every day during the lead. This splitting is achieved by taking the convolution of Equation 4.1 and the binomial distribution b(Λ, p_0), which eventually yields Equation 4.2. As we want to calculate the safety stock level B from a given service level SL(P, B), we have to invert Equation 4.2. This can be done rather easily using a standard iteration scheme, as SL(P, B) happens to be a continuous, convex function in B.

In summary, to each item P of a given inventory we have assigned an individual continuous demand distribution $D_{M,P}$, which serves as an estimate for the real demand distribution D. Based on that distribution, we have shown how to calculate the safety stock level of P.

4.6. KOHONEN CLUSTERING

The key to finding an individual continuous demand distribution for each item P_i is to cluster the discrete distributions that originate from the daily demands of the items $\{P_1, ..., P_n\}$. One solution could be to calculate and compare distances of any kind between the demand distributions of all possible pairs of articles. However, this does not solve the problem of identifying clusters and consumes a lot of time and resources. The latter aspect is especially crucial in the context of bigger warehouses holding many thousands of stock items. To manage the clustering of the demand distributions as described in process 2 of Section 4.4, we use a Kohonen type of algorithm (see Kohonen, 2001).

The Kohonen algorithm (KA) (Kohonen, 2001) uses a set of representatives (also called *centers*) in order to form clusters. Each representative gives rise to exactly one cluster, so that we end up with the same number of clusters and centers. Each center represents the subset of the data — discrete normalized demand distributions of the items in our case — to which it is closest. By using the word "closest," we have implicitly assumed that we are working in a (sub)metric space, where we can measure the distance between two discrete probability distributions. We now provide some formal definitions to facilitate the explanation of our clustering algorithm.

Definition (submetric space). A space (X, d) is called *submetric* if $X \neq \varnothing$ and if the *distance* d: $X \times X \rightarrow R_{\geq 0}$ between two points x and y satisfies $d(x, y) = 0$ if and only if $x = y$.

Note. Distances of submetric spaces do not have to be symmetric, nor do they have to comply with the triangle inequality.

Example. Let

$$X = \left\{ x \in R^n \mid \sum_{i=1}^{n} x_i = 1, \ x_i \geq 0 \right\}$$

and

$$d(x, y) = -\sum_{i=1}^{n} x_i \log \frac{y_i}{x_i} \text{ with } x, y \in X$$

This space is a submetric space called the *n-dimensional Kullback-Leibler space* (KL space) *for discrete values* (Kullback and Leibler, 1951), which will be used throughout this section. As the coordinates of every point in the KL space are nonnegative and add up to 1, the KL space is predestined to handle discrete probability distributions. Each of the n dimensions of the KL space represents a single range of the normalized demand quantities (e.g., the range between 150 and 225 items), and its value represents the corresponding probability. Thus, one point in the KL space exactly determines a discrete distribution. The distance d weights the "log expression" with the probabilities of x_i. In this way, the values of y at high values of the distribution of x are stressed.

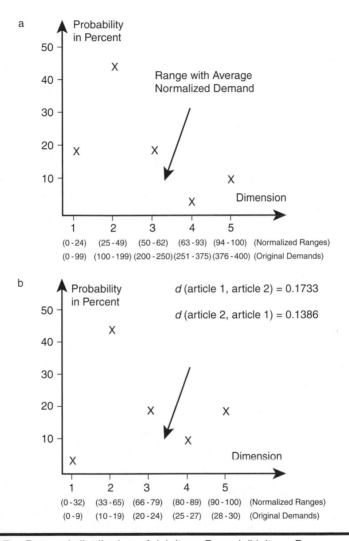

Figure 4.7. Demand distribution of (a) item P_1 and (b) item P_2.

This makes sense because a high value represents a high probability of a certain order's quantity. See Figure 4.7 for some examples. By using the symmetrical distance measure defined by $d * (x, y) = \min[d(x, y), d(y, x)]$, it is easy to see that we can turn the KL space into a metric space. But since the resulting clusterings when using the symmetric distance instead of the nonsymmetric one showed inferior quality most of the time, we do not consider symmetric KL spaces here.

Both distributions are quite similar, and the distances between them are rather small. Another item P_3 having the same distribution as item P_1 but with interchanged probabilities in dimensions 2 and 4 would have a far greater distance $d(P_1, P_3) = 0.8789$.

Definition (centers and data). Let (X, d) be a submetric space. Let A, $\mathfrak{R}$ $\subseteq X$ be nonempty. A is regarded as the set of *data*. For $r \in \mathfrak{R}$, let $C_r := \{a \in A \mid \forall s \in \mathfrak{R} : d(a, s) \geq d(a, r)\}$. In our case, the data are the set of all normalized discrete demand distributions of the items $P_1, ..., P_n$. $\mathfrak{R}$ is the *set of representatives* or the *set of centers*, and C_r is the *cluster* represented by the center r. Both the quintuple $(X, d, A, \mathfrak{R}, \Psi)$ and the set $\Psi = \{C_r \mid r \in \mathfrak{R}\}$ are called *clustering* of A. The *quality* of the clustering is measured by the reciprocal average distance between all points of data and its closest representative(s):

$$q(\Psi) = \cfrac{1}{\cfrac{1}{\sum_{r \in \mathfrak{R}} |C_r|} \cdot \sum_{r \in \mathfrak{R}} \sum_{a \in C_r} d(a, r)}$$

Note: Centers can be regarded as fictional items having a demand distribution that best represents their associated items (cluster) (see Figure 4.8).

Definition (topological clustering). A clustering $(X, d, A, \mathfrak{R}, \Psi)$ is called *topological clustering* if a system of neighborhoods $U = \{U_r \subseteq \mathfrak{R} \mid r \in \mathfrak{R} \wedge r \in U_r \wedge |U_r| > 1\}$ is defined on $\mathfrak{R}$. The set U_r is called *neighborhood* of the center r and assigns to each $r \in \mathfrak{R}$ at least one other center $s \in \mathfrak{R}\setminus\{r\}$. We write $(X, d, A, \mathfrak{R}, \Psi, U)$ for a topological clustering.

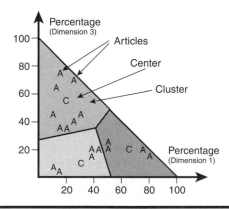

Figure 4.8. Projection of a three-dimensional KL space with items (A) and centers (C).

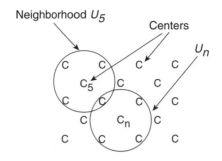

Figure 4.9. Possible neighborhoods of two centers.

Example. Lining the centers up, the neighborhood U_r could look as shown in Figure 4.9.

An approved technique for generating high-quality clusterings with reasonable costs with respect to CPU time and memory size is the Kohonen algorithm. It can be understood as a series of clusterings $T_n = (X, d, A, \Re_n, \Psi_n, U)$, also called *époques*. Whereas the set A of data remains unchanged throughout the chain of époques, the centers move within the KL space, and their associated clusters are being recalculated within each step. We use an enhanced version of the original Kohonen algorithm as described by Kohonen (2001), to which we have added two features, namely the so-called *conscience* introduced by Desieno (1989) and a modification of our own called *engulfing*. Our Kohonen algorithm works as follows:

A. **Initialization phase**

   In this first phase, we set the initial positions of the centers and the initial movement speed m_c for the centers. As it turns out, the initial positions of the centers did not influence the final clustering much, nor did they affect the speed of convergence. Moreover, as our studies indicate, the number of clusters should be approximately half of the dimension of the KL space that is being used. In our experiments, we have been using a 100-dimensional KL space together with 49 centers.

B. **Iteration phase**

   Given époque T_n, we reach the next époque T_{n+1} by performing the following steps once for each (randomly chosen) element $a \in A$.

   B1. *Movement of centers and their neighbors*

   For each element a, we take the center c closest to a. Then the center c is moved according to the mapping $c \to m_c \cdot (a - c) + c$ on a straight line toward a. All neighbors c' of center c are moved as well by the mapping $c' \to m_c' \cdot m_c \cdot (a - c') + c'$, where

$$m'_c = \min\left(1; e^{\frac{-d(c',c)}{d(a,c)}}\right)$$

B2. *Deactivation and activation of centers*

The clustering is intended to be a balanced representation of set A, that is, the size of all clusters should be about the same. In order to encourage this behavior, the quota $z_c = |C_c| \cdot |A|^{-1}$ is introduced, which expresses the percentage of elements to which the center r happened to be closest. In a balanced clustering, all quotas z_c have to lie within some given (narrow) range (m_l, m_u). Whenever at least one of the quotas z_c is smaller than m_l, the centers c' having the highest quota are deactivated if their quota equals or exceeds m_u. If, on the other hand, all quotas z_c satisfy $z_c \geq m_l$, the deactivated center with the smallest quota is activated again. Moreover, a center is reactivated if its quota drops below the upper margin m_u. This technique is called *conscience* and was first introduced by Desieno (1989).

B3. *Engulfing centers*

Sometimes a center t meets the condition $z_t \geq m_l$ for its quota z_t and moreover represents its cluster C_t with a very small average distance:

$$d_t = \frac{1}{|C_t|} \cdot \sum_{a \in C_t} d(a, t)$$

This suggests a cluster of a high quality $q(C_t)$. Deactivating center t because it happens to have the highest quota z_t or moving t away from its current position because of some neighborhood effect should be avoided in this situation. Giving center t the option of moving to an optimal position within C_t seems to be more appropriate. Hence, in this case, if we exclude t from all neighborhood effects and prevent t from being deactivated, center t will stay close to cluster C_t with high probability. This behavior is expressed by saying that center t is being *engulfed* by C_t. However, the neighbors of t are not excluded from the neighborhood U_t. Thus, they will still be able to move toward cluster C_t in order to discover finer substructures within C_t, if there are any. Center t remains engulfed as long as it represents enough articles, which is ensured by requiring $z_t \geq m_l$ and d_t to be sufficiently small.

B4. *Cluster determination*

Once all elements $a \in A$ have been processed in steps B1 to B3, the clustering $\Psi = \{C_t \mid r \in \mathfrak{R}\}$ is determined by assigning each $a \in A$ to some cluster C_t such that $d(a, t) \leq d(a, r)$ holds for any $r \in \mathfrak{R}$.

B5. *Adaptation of movement speed and calculation of quotas*

The movement speed m_c is decreased by setting $m_c = 0.9 \cdot m_c$. The quotas z_c are calculated as $z_c = \mid C_c \mid \cdot \mid A \mid^{-1}$. However, the quotas of the elements $a \in A$ might be influenced by engulfed centers, especially if they conjoin a major part of the data. Therefore, the articles in C_t are neglected when it comes to calculating the quota for centers that are not engulfed.

C. **Closing phase**

In the last phase, the quality $q(\Psi_n)$ of the final clustering T_n is calculated.

4.7. CLUSTERING RESULTS

In this section, we give some sample centers and some of their associated data. We tested the clustering method for 10 different inventories introduced in Section 4.2. It turned out that for each of these inventories there was always a very significant and characteristic cluster that belonged to an engulfed center having only two peaks and no other significantly positive values (see Figure 4.12). The size of such an engulfed cluster was between 10 and 15% of the entire inventory. One of the peaks results from the high value of the dimension representing zero demand. The other peak describes one other demand quantity. Inspection of this cluster shows that it conjoins articles mostly with very sporadic demand of the same quantity. This phenomenon is very prominent for the spare parts inventories, where such a cluster holds almost all of the very slow-moving items (about one pick per year). As indicated in the top chart in Figure 4.12, a Laplace distribution could be chosen to represent the center as well as all elements of its cluster. More than 95% of the items of this cluster looked very similar to the one shown in the middle chart of Figure 4.10.

Another typical, although much smaller, cluster that showed up for all our inventories contained articles with very frequent demands and many different pick quantities. This case is illustrated in Figure 4.11. It can be seen that although the distributions of this cluster are different, they all share common features, such as a 30% probability of zero demand; a high probability of demand within the normalized range (0,20); some, but not much, demand within the range (20,60); and almost no demand during the remaining interval. As

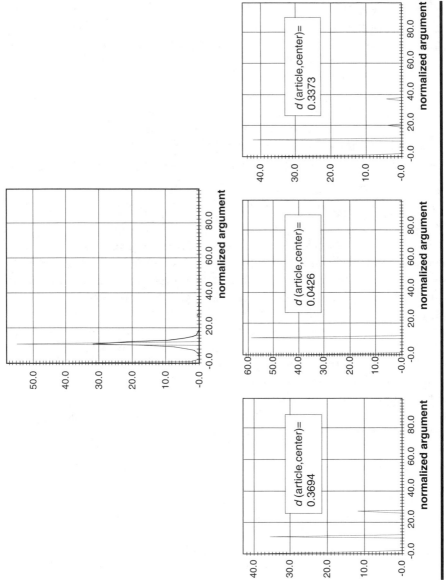

Figure 4.10. Engulfed center (top) with three of its matched articles (bottom).

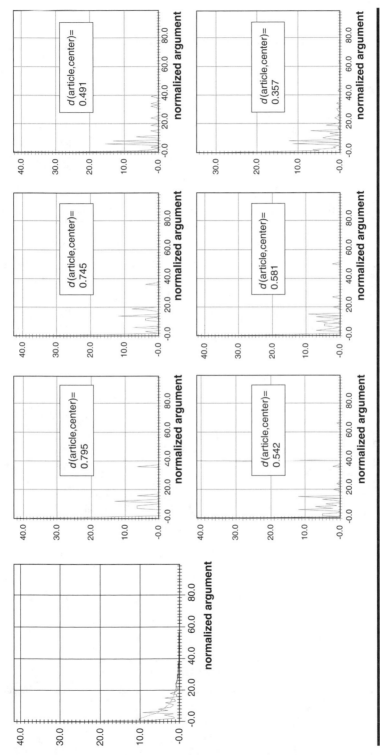

Figure 4.11. Center (left) representing articles with highly varying demand quantities.

indicated in the chart on the left in Figure 4.11, it is convenient to use an exponential distribution for the center as well as for all items within its cluster.

4.8. SIMULATION RESULTS

In order to test our adaptive method for calculating safety stocks, we used the data of the 10 inventories and ran the simulation as described in Section 4.2. Again, we used randomized transaction data for generating the demand for each article of the inventory, as in the case **Emp**. We added to Table 4.1 another line for each service level labeled by **Opt**, which shows the results when using the method for calculating safety stocks as described above. Table 4.2 shows these additional results.

Returning to our spare parts inventory of warehouse 7, the results we obtained for this inventory improved significantly when we used our adaptive method for calculating safety stock levels, as shown in the top chart in Figure 4.12. For convenience and the sake of comparison, the bottom chart in Figure 4.12 once again shows the results of warehouse 7 derived from simulation (**Emp**). Not only was the achieved average service level raised from 86.3% to

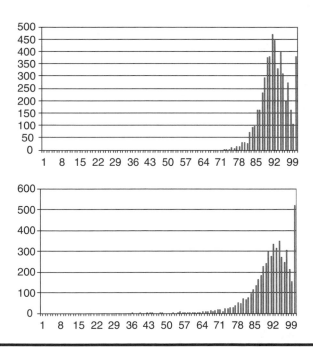

Figure 4.12. Service level distributions for (**Norm**) and (**Opt**).

Table 4.2. Simulation Results Comparing Average α_1-SLs Achieved with the Traditional Approach (Emp) or Calculating Safety Stock Levels Versus Our Adaptive Method (Opt)

Desired Service Level		WH1	WH2	WH3	WH4	WH5	WH6	WH7	WH8	WH9	WH10	Avg.	Abs. Sigma	Rel. Sigma
50%	Norm	53.0%	44.8%	54.9%	49.5%	49.1%	52.0%	54.0%	55.3%	59.5%	48.9%	52.1%	0.03957	1.00
	Emp	66.5%	55.3%	71.6%	59.5%	59.1%	67.7%	61.3%	75.7%	79.7%	66.0%	66.2%	0.07363	1.86
80%	Norm	82.0%	74.8%	83.2%	79.4%	79.4%	81.2%	82.3%	83.8%	86.9%	79.8%	81.3%	0.03073	1.00
	Emp	84.6%	77.5%	86.0%	80.9%	79.4%	83.4%	74.6%	88.3%	89.6%	84.1%	82.8%	0.04500	1.46
	Opt	78.4%	77.3%	78.0%	81.4%	76.3%	78.1%	78.8%	82.6%	85.0%	79.7%	79.6%	0.02539	0.83
90%	Norm	91.1%	87.3%	91.6%	89.5%	89.6%	90.2%	91.2%	92.1%	93.0%	90.6%	90.6%	0.01512	1.00
	Emp	90.4%	85.4%	90.5%	87.8%	86.4%	89.2%	79.6%	92.1%	92.4%	87.6%	88.1%	0.03599	2.38
	Opt	90.0%	89.6%	91.0%	91.9%	88.6%	86.7%	90.1%	92.0%	94.6%	91.3%	90.6%	0.02028	1.34
95%	Norm	96.1%	94.0%	96.0%	95.1%	95.0%	96.0%	95.8%	96.0%	96.6%	95.3%	95.6%	0.00709	1.00
	Emp	94.0%	90.8%	93.5%	92.0%	90.9%	93.5%	83.1%	94.4%	95.2%	92.9%	92.0%	0.03274	4.62
	Opt	95.3%	94.8%	95.9%	95.9%	94.5%	94.3%	95.3%	95.3%	97.3%	95.9%	95.5%	0.00821	1.16
98%	Norm	98.7%	97.8%	98.5%	98.2%	98.3%	98.5%	98.6%	98.4%	98.5%	98.3%	98.4%	0.00240	1.00
	Emp	96.6%	95.0%	95.8%	95.3%	94.6%	95.9%	86.3%	97.0%	96.7%	95.9%	94.9%	0.02959	12.33
	Opt	98.0%	97.7%	98.6%	98.3%	97.7%	97.1%	98.1%	98.3%	98.9%	98.5%	98.1%	0.00496	2.07

98.1%, but the distribution of the service levels also happens to be normally distributed (a chi-square test showed a significance level of 99.98%), reducing the service level variability from 12.33 times compared to (**Norm**) down to 2.07.

REFERENCES

Bagchi, U., Hayya, J., and Ord, K. (1983). The Hermite distribution as a model of demand during lead time for slow moving items, *Decision Sciences*, 14, 447–466.

Bagchi, U., Hayya, J., and Ord, K., (1984). Concepts, theory and techniques: Modeling demand during lead, *Decision Sciences*, 15, 157–176.

Bookbinder, J. H. and Lordahl, A. E. (1989). Estimation of inventory re-order levels using the bootstrap statistical procedure, *IIE Transactions*, 21, 302–312.

Desieno, D. (1989). Adding a conscience to competitive learning, in *Proceedings of IEEE International Conference on Neural Networks*, Vol. 1, IEEE, San Diego, pp. 117–124.

Eppen, G. D. and Martin, R. K. (1988). Determining safety stock in the presence of stochastic lead time and demand, *Management Science*, 34, 1380–1390.

Grange, F. (1998). Challenges in modeling demand for inventory optimization of slow-moving items, in *Proceedings of the 1998 Winter Simulation Conference*, Medeiros, D. J. et al., Eds., ACM Press, Washington, D.C., pp. 1211-1227.

Harris, T. (1997). Optimized inventory management, *Production and Inventory Management Journal*, 38, 22–25.

Jacobs, R. A. and Wagner, H. M. (1989). Reducing inventory systems costs by using robust demand estimators, *Management Science*, 35, 771–787.

Kohonen, T. (2001). *Self-Organizing Maps*, 3rd ed., *Springer Series in Information Sciences*, Vol. 30, Springer, Berlin.

Kullback, S. and Leibler, R. A. (1951). On information and sufficiency, *Annals of Mathematical Statistics*, 22, 79–86.

Lau, H. S. (1989). Toward an inventory control system under nonnormal demand and lead-time uncertainty, *Journal of Business Logistics*, 10, 89–103.

Lau, H. S. and Zaki, A. (1982). The sensitivity of inventory decisions to the shape of lead time demand distribution, *IIE Transactions*, 13, 265–271.

Mentzer, J. T. and Krishnan, R. (1985). The effect of the assumption of normality on inventory control/customer service, *Journal of Business Logistics*, 6, 101–119.

Müller-Merbach, H. (1969). *Operations Research*, Verlag Franz Vahlen, Berlin.

Scarf, H. (1960). The optimality of (s,S) policies in the dynamic inventory problem, in *Mathematical Methods in the Social Science*, Arrow, K. and Suppes, P., Eds., Stanford University Press, Stanford, CA.

Schneider, H. (1997). *Servicegrade in Lagerhaltungsmodellen*, Günter Marchal und Hans-Jochen Matzenbacher Wissenschaftsverlag, Berlin.

Schwarz, M. (1999). *Die K-Kurven-Methode und Sicherheitsbestände*, Diplomarbeit, Universität Hamburg, Germany.

Tadikamalla, P. (1984). A comparison of several approximations to the lead time demand distribution, *Omega,* 12, 575–581.

Tyworth, J. E. and O'Neill, L. (1997). Robustness of the normal approximation of lead-time demand in a distribution setting, *Naval Research Logistics,* 44, 165–186.

SECURING YOUR E-BUSINESS BY MANAGING THE INHERENT IT SECURITY RISKS

Andreas Wespi

5.1. INTRODUCTION

Technology is revolutionizing the way we do business. Information technology (IT) allows us to make most business transactions electronically, and the Internet has rendered access to information more widespread and cheaper. However, technology also poses impediments to the overall acceptance of e-business. For one thing, today's IT infrastructures are prone to numerous problems. Incidents in which information is irrevocably lost or hackers manage to steal confidential information are reported daily. It seems that the problems encountered in e-business are quite similar to those that already existed in traditional business; it is nothing new that information can be lost or divulged to unauthorized persons. However, as will be described in Section 5.2, the fact that many systems may contain the same vulnerability and a single attack can reach many targets simultaneously poses higher risks to today's e-business environments.

Irrespective of the many differences between traditional and e-business, it appears that risk management is needed in both cases to cultivate an awareness of the problems related to an underlying business infrastructure. However, given the speed with which e-business transactions are made, managing the risks related to an e-business infrastructure appears to be more difficult and to require new solutions.

IT infrastructures are prone to the risk of failures. Expressed in dependability terminology, a failure is an event that occurs when the delivered service deviates from the correct service (Powell and Stroud, 2003). We differentiate here between accidental, or nonmalicious, deliberate faults and deliberately malicious faults that can cause a system to fail. A failed disk drive, for example, belongs to the first category, whereas a hacker attack belongs to the second. While we have quite a good understanding of how to deal with accidental faults (disk RAID systems are widely used, for example), dealing with malicious faults still poses many unresolved problems. We will concentrate here on the latter type of faults and focus on IT security risk management.

Security risk management is a widely used term that covers many different tasks. To group these tasks, let us adopt the terms *static* and *dynamic* security risk management. Static security risk management addresses architectural issues, whereas dynamic security risk management deals with security issues at the time they occur. This chapter focuses on dynamic security risk management for two reasons. First, static security risk management has become common practice. Second, as will be shown in Section 5.2, not all security risks can be foreseen and therefore must be addressed as they occur.

The chapter is structured as follows. Section 5.2 presents some of the most severe security threats and gives some reasons why they are difficult to eliminate. Section 5.3 outlines the principles of static risk management. Section 5.4 presents the basics of intrusion detection, a key technology for dynamic security risk management. Dynamic security risk management, with its advantages and limitations, is discussed in Section 5.5. Conclusions are drawn in Section 5.6.

5.2. SECURITY THREATS

Computer crime is an ever-growing problem. Numerous studies have concluded that the losses of productivity, customer confidence, and competitive advantage caused by security breaches constitute substantial costs. Take, for example, the major findings of the 2003 Computer Crime and Security Survey, which is the eighth annual survey conducted by the Computer Security Institute (CSI) in cooperation with the San Francisco Federal Bureau of Investigation's (FBI) Computer Intrusion Squad (CSI and FBI, 2003). Based on responses from practitioners in U.S. corporations, government agencies, financial institutions, medical institutions, and universities, the findings of the 2003 Computer Crime and Security Survey confirm that the threat from computer crime and other information security breaches continues unabated.

The key findings of the report show the vital importance of being aware of security breaches and that security breaches can result in substantial financial losses:

- Attacks were reported by 92% of respondents.
- Overall financial losses sustained by 530 respondents totaled $201,797,340. A total of 75% of organizations acknowledged financial losses, although only 47% could quantify them.
- As in prior years, theft of proprietary information caused the greatest financial loss. As much as $70,195,900 was lost, with the average reported loss approximately $2.7 million.
- In a shift from previous years, the second most expensive computer crime reported by respondents was denial of service, which cost $65,643,300, an increase of 250% from the loss of $18,370,500 reported in 2002.
- Computer crime threats come both from within and outside of the electronic perimeter, confirming the observations made in previous years. For example, 45% of respondents detected unauthorized access by insiders.

According to a Gartner report (Gartner, 2003), 2003 was the first year in which more than 5% of IT budgets was spent on security. This figure means that security spending grew at a compound annual rate of 28% since 2001. In comparison, IT budgets grew at a compound annual rate of only 6% over the same period.

This indicates that, on the one hand, organizations are aware of security threats and are taking measures to address them. On the other hand, these measures are evidently insufficient to protect organizations from substantial losses, as indicated in the 2003 CSI/FBI survey. One can presume that organizations do a poor job of securing their computing infrastructure. However, one can also conclude that securing a computing infrastructure is an intrinsically difficult problem with no easy solution.

Without claiming completeness, let us examine in the following four subsections some reasons why security risks persist.

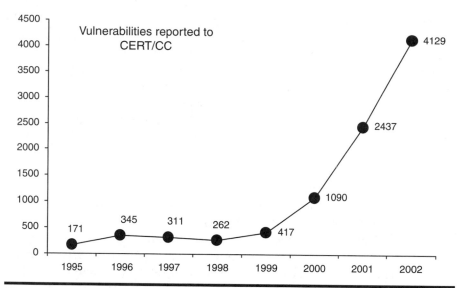

Figure 5.1. Number of vulnerabilities reported to CERT/CC between 1995 and 2002.

5.2.1. Increasing Vulnerabilities

The CERT® Coordination Center (CERT/CC) is a center of Internet security expertise located at the Software Engineering Institute, a federally funded research and development center operated by Carnegie Mellon University. Among other activities, the CERT/CC publishes statistics about vulnerabilities found in products and reported to the CERT/CC. As shown in Figure 5.1, the number of reported vulnerabilities has grown exponentially over the past years. In 2002, an average of 11 vulnerabilities was reported per day. Thanks to the statistics published by the CERT/CC, a large community is aware of this problem. However, despite many initiatives by software vendors to secure their products, secure software development appears to remain a difficult undertaking.

5.2.2. Poorly Designed Software

Quite often, software developers are interested mainly in new functionality and enhanced performance, but do not pay much attention to security aspects. As a consequence, many security problems are due to poor engineering. Of the many known security vulnerabilities, the buffer overflow problem is the most common (Cowan et al., 2000). Despite a long history of understanding how to write secure programs (Bishop, 1986), vulnerable programs continue to emerge on a regular basis. In particular, the widely used C language is a notorious source of many buffer overflow vulnerabilities. Although the most common security mistakes would be easy to avoid, software developers seem to make the very same mistakes again and again.

5.2.3. Attack Sophistication Versus Intruder Technical Knowledge

As reported by Lipson (2000), hacker attacks have become increasingly sophisticated. In the early 1980s, for example, simple password-guessing attacks were quite popular. In the meantime, hackers have a rich portfolio of attacks at their disposal. Furthermore, they use various advanced techniques to analyze programs systematically for weaknesses to exploit.

Another observation is that it is becoming increasingly simple to execute an attack. Well-known attack tools can be downloaded from the Internet, allowing virtually anyone to attack another system. Persons who use such tools despite their lack of a deep technical background are called *script kiddies*. Script kiddies can be just as dangerous as "real" hackers because quite often they have little understanding of the potentially harmful consequences of the tools they use.

5.2.4. Vulnerabilities Left Unfixed

Intuitively one would assume that intrusions into computer systems as a result of exploiting a specific vulnerability show a common pattern. Before the vulnerability is known, no intrusions are observed. Once the hacker community discovers the vulnerability, however, the number of intrusions increases as the news of the vulnerability spreads. This trend continues until a patch is released, after which the number of intrusions decreases quite quickly.

Based on data collected by CERT/CC, Arbaugh et al. (2000) investigated whether the assumed behavior corresponds to the observed one. To interpret their findings, let us examine one of their examples.

In a phf incident, attackers exploited an implementation vulnerability that is quite easy to fix. The phf program extends the functionality of Web servers and provides a Web-based interface to a database that usually contains personnel information. The program works by constructing a command line based on user input. However, the authors failed to filter out malicious user input that eventually allows the user to execute arbitrary commands on the Web server.

The vulnerability was first reported on Bugtraq, a well-known mailing list to discuss computer vulnerabilities, on February 5, 1996. Patches became available within a few weeks. However, in November 1998, more than two and a half years after the vulnerability was first detected, intrusions exploiting this vulnerability were still being reported to CERT/CC. It is also worth mentioning that the vast majority of these intrusions were committed after a script to exploit the phf vulnerability had become available and was being used by script kiddies.

Arbaugh et al. list similar examples of overwhelming evidence that many computer systems either are not patched or are patched only after long delays. This means that computer systems are prone not only to new types of attacks but also — and to a large extent — to attacks that are well known and could easily have been thwarted.

5.2.5. Summary

IT infrastructures are prone to security risks. Although this is widely known, it is apparently difficult to eliminate this problem. Despite the increasing number of vulnerabilities, software developers continue to make the same or similar mistakes. Attack tools exist that allow virtually anyone to perform hacker attacks, and system administrators are quite often not sufficiently effective in patching their systems. All these and many other factors need to be taken into account by an IT security risk management system. We have seen the importance of an IT security risk management system. Security risks persist, and the challenge is to be aware of and mitigate them as much as possible.

5.3. STATIC IT SECURITY RISK MANAGEMENT

There are two information sources for risk management. The source of static information is the information available about the IT infrastructure itself. Properties of machines, networks, processes, and users are examples of static information. The source of dynamic information is the recorded information concerning the use of the IT infrastructure. This information is recorded, for example, in log files written by applications or operating systems. Both types of information are important for assessing the risks to which an IT infrastructure is prone. Static information is used primarily for planning purposes and enables the system architect to address security issues at an early stage. Dynamic information is used to identify and counteract short-term security problems such as hacker attacks. Based on the information source used, we differentiate between static and dynamic risk management, respectively.

The risk management process itself can be split into various subprocesses. Let us adopt the schema presented by Bauknecht (2000) to describe the risk management process in terms of four components, namely:

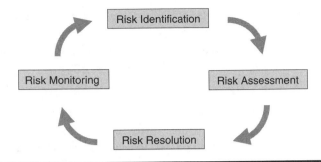

Figure 5.2. Risk management cycle (Bauknecht, 2000).

- Risk identification
- Risk assessment
- Risk resolution
- Risk monitoring

The interdependency of these four components (i.e., the risk management cycle) is depicted in Figure 5.2.

Traditionally, IT security risk management has been a static process, in that risks related to the IT infrastructure are investigated. Sections 5.3.1 to 5.3.4 examine static security risk management based on the four risk management components listed above. Section 5.5 introduces the novel concept of dynamic security risk management or security risks related to processes that make use of the IT infrastructure.

5.3.1. Risk Identification

Knowing the security-critical components is a key prerequisite for building a system with adequate security. Numerous examples of IT risks are described in Section 5.2. In addition, there are security risks inherent to the architecture and the management of an IT infrastructure. Three examples follow:

- Merely relying on a firewall as a single security measure to protect an enterprise constitutes a security risk. The firewall itself may harbor a security vulnerability, and if this vulnerability is exploited, the entire enterprise is no longer protected.
- Business processes implemented on protocols that are known to suffer from security problems is another form of security risk. The telnet and ftp protocols, for example, send passwords in clear text. This makes it

rather easy for an attacker to intercept passwords and use them for his or her own purposes.

■ Not having a patch management system in place that automatically detects unpatched machines is a security risk because it leaves machines vulnerable to known attacks.

The first example cites single points of failures in the system architecture to avoid. The second example identifies security risks in applications, and the third highlights a problem related to an administrative process. There are many more examples of similar IT security risks.

Identifying all the security risks in an enterprise is a challenging task. However, many risks can be detected by analyzing the IT infrastructure and how it is managed. The analysis is usually based on known problems encountered in the past or in a related environment. From that perspective, static security IT risk management and general IT risk management are quite similar. They deal with foreseeable problems.

5.3.2. Risk Assessment

Once a security risk has been identified, the degree of danger it poses must be assessed. Several factors influence the severity of a security risk. Such factors include the importance of the business processes impacted by a security failure, the number of users affected, and the estimated costs to recover from a related incident. The severity of a security risk is relative. For example, a missing security patch on a business-critical machine may constitute a greater risk than an unpatched user machine. It follows that to assess the severity of a security risk, one must have a good understanding of the IT infrastructure and the business processes running on it.

5.3.3. Risk Resolution

A risk assessment specifies which risks can be tolerated and which risks have to be eliminated. Ideally, all identified security problems are fixed. However, this is not always easy to achieve. The following are some examples of problems encountered in the risk resolution process:

■ Installing a security patch may cause a legacy application to no longer run properly.
■ Eliminating a security risk may involve major architectural changes that are expensive in terms of both money and time.
■ There is a trade-off between usability and security. The more tools available on a machine and the more features activated, the more usable

a machine may be but the more likely it is that a security vulnerability exists in one of the installed tools.

As these examples show, it is not always possible to minimize all risks. However, knowing the risks and having them documented is a significant step toward that goal.

5.3.4. Risk Monitoring

To ensure minimal security risks, continuous risk monitoring is essential. Today's IT infrastructures can be rather complex and hence difficult to administer. Operators are human beings, and humans make mistakes. Therefore, risk monitoring is an important factor in keeping IT security risks low. IT security risk monitoring comprises several activities, such as the following two examples:

- A so-called security or vulnerability scanner is run regularly to identify back-level services that have not been patched or services that pose a security risk per se because, for example, passwords are exchanged in clear text or users are not authenticated.
- Regular checks for machine reconfigurations are made. In particular, configuration changes on security-critical machines have to be checked carefully.

Ideally, the risk monitoring is performed by an independent organization that is not involved in the system administration process.

5.3.5. Summary

Static IT security risk management is widely conducted and quite well understood, although it suffers from a few limitations. Experience shows that some security risks are unknown and unpredictable. It is therefore difficult to consider all these risks in the static risk management process or to design an IT architecture that is immune to all unknown risks. Therefore, approaches are needed that address security risks as they occur. Such an approach is discussed in the next section.

5.4. INTRUSION DETECTION

The concepts of dynamic IT security risk management are closely linked to intrusion detection, a technology that aims at automatically detecting attacks —

successful and unsuccessful — on computer systems and networks. Before examining how intrusion detection relates to dynamic IT security risk management, let us recall what intrusion detection is and how it works.

The idea of applying not only preventive but also detective measures to a computer system is not new. First proposals for building a so-called intrusion detection system (IDS) were made as early as 1980 (Anderson, 1980). IDSs have received considerable attention during the past few years. The increasing number of computer security incidents (Gross, 1997; Howard, 1997) has certainly contributed to this interest. As a result, many commercial products as well as research prototypes and freeware products have been developed. IDSs now reside even on desktop computers, and it is widely agreed that an IDS is a mandatory security tool.

There are many ways to build an IDS. To compare the various intrusion detection concepts and techniques, Debar et al. (1999) have proposed an IDS taxonomy. Let us adopt an extended and refined version of this taxonomy (Debar et al., 2000) to classify various intrusion detection methods and discuss their advantages and disadvantages.

There are five main criteria to classify IDSs (Figure 5.3):

- The *detection method* describes how IDSs analyze their input data.
- The *audit source* location categorizes IDSs based on the type of input data they analyze.
- The *behavior on detection* method describes the response of the intrusion detection system to detected attacks.
- The *detection paradigm* describes whether IDSs analyze states or transitions.
- The *usage frequency* categorizes IDSs based on whether they offer real-time continuous monitoring or whether they are run periodically.

The five criteria are discussed in Sections 5.4.1 to 5.4.5.

5.4.1. Detection Method

We differentiate between *knowledge-based* and *behavior-based* IDSs. Knowledge-based IDSs, also called misuse detection systems (Jagannathan et al., 1993; Kumar and Spafford, 1994), are the most widely used IDSs. They exploit knowledge accumulated about specific vulnerabilities and the attacks exploiting them and maintain so-called signatures of known attacks. Alarms are raised when a signature of an attack is detected in the audit data monitored by the IDS. On the other hand, this also means that any action that is not explicitly recog-

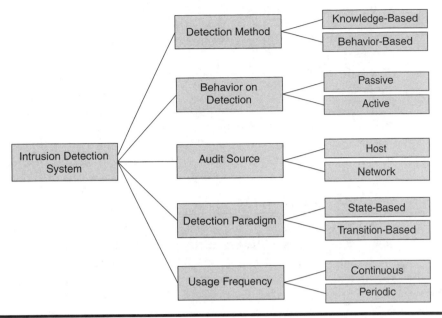

Figure 5.3. Characteristics of intrusion detection systems (Debar et al., 2000).

nized as an attack is considered acceptable. Knowledge-based IDSs have many similarities with antivirus systems.

Knowledge-based systems should generate, at least in theory, no false alarms because they do exactly what they are instructed to do. Furthermore, the alarm messages are meaningful, allowing the security officer to understand the problem and to take preventive or corrective action. Most commercial IDSs are knowledge based.

Behavior-based IDSs have no *a priori* knowledge about attacks. They look for significant deviations from the normal or expected user or system behavior and flag such occurrences as suspicious and therefore a sign of a possible attack. Typically, one differentiates between a training and a detection phase. In the training phase, the model of normal or expected behavior is learned. In the detection phase, the current activity is compared with the learned normal behavior, and an alarm is raised when a significant deviation is encountered. The expected behavior can be defined thanks to some extensive training of the system (Debar et al., 1992; Jagannathan et al., 1993) or by other more systematic approaches such as those proposed by Wespi and Debar (1999) and Wespi et al. (2000). Behavior-based systems have the important advantage that they do not require a database of attack signatures that has to be kept up to date.

5.4.2. Audit Source Location

Typically, two families of audit sources are considered for intrusion detection:

- **Host-based** IDSs perform their analyses on data collected from a host. The host audit sources are numerous. It is fairly common to see systems using accounting data, C2 security audit files, or application log files such as Web server or firewall log entries.
- **Network-based** IDSs sniff packets from the network in a nonintrusive manner and perform their analyses on the packet header and payload.

5.4.3. Behavior on Detection

IDSs are either *passive* or *active*. Passive IDSs issue an alarm when an attack is detected but apply no countermeasures to thwart the attack. It is the task of the security officer to initiate the appropriate countermeasure. Active systems, on the other hand, are able to stop attacks in progress and thus to avoid any further harm. The spectrum of active responses is broad. Cutting TCP connections; reconfiguring routers, switches, and firewalls; stopping vulnerable services; and modifying configuration files are some examples of active responses.

Most IDSs are passive because nobody wants to risk taking a wrong active response based on a false alarm. Even worse, there is also the danger that an attacker could misuse the active response mechanism to launch a countermeasure against a third, innocent party.

Recently, intrusion prevention systems (IPSs) have become popular, and vendors claim that they are superior to IDSs. Unfortunately, the term IPS is not well defined and leaves room for interpretation. There are basically two interpretations of intrusion prevention:

- Every measure that helps to secure a system and protect it from intrusions can be considered an IDS.
- Intrusion prevention is tightly coupled to intrusion detection. This means that, after successful detection of an attack, the system can launch some preventive action to keep the attack from succeeding.

In order for an IPS to be effective, it is essential that the attack be detected before it reaches its target. A network-based IDS that drops malicious packets before they reach their target hosts is an example of an IPS. However, it has to be mentioned that intrusion prevention is a relative term. An attack that was successful against a first target can be prevented from being (successfully) run against other targets by applying an active response. If this attack is blocked and further distribution hindered, one can speak of intrusion prevention even though the attack was already successful.

5.4.4. Detection Paradigm

There are two paradigms in intrusion detection engines. The first class of intrusion detection engines looks at states and the second one at transitions between states. It is simple to imagine that an attack will change the state of the system under attack. Before the attack, the system is in a normal state; after the attack, it is in a failure state.

- **State-based** systems detect that a given system has reached a failure state (or a state that is likely to lead to a failure).
- **Transition-based** systems recognize elements that are known to trigger a transition from the normal to a failure state.

5.4.5. Usage Frequency

With respect to their usage frequency, IDSs can be classified as being either periodic or continuous.

- **Periodic** IDSs periodically take a snapshot of the environment and analyze this snapshot, looking for vulnerable software, configuration errors, etc. The system compares the various snapshots and, by doing so, can detect that an attack has successfully been carried out against the system and, for example, left a back door open.
- **Continuous** IDSs monitor the actions that happen in the system. Continuous monitoring implies real-time analysis of network packets and audit file entries, and it provides an up-to-date assessment of the security of the system.

5.4.6. Summary

There are many ways to build an IDS. However, as experience shows, there is no single IDS that can detect every kind of attack. Therefore, a combination of IDSs that have different characteristics is expected to increase the chances of successful attack detection. Combining heterogeneous IDSs and correlating their output are topics that are currently under investigation by the intrusion detection community.

Table 5.1. Relation Between Dynamic IT Security Risk Management and Intrusion Detection

Risk Management Discipline	IDS Characteristic
Risk identification	Detection method
Risk assessment	Detection method
Risk resolution	Behavior on detection
Risk monitoring	Audit source
Detection paradigm	
Usage frequency	

5.5. DYNAMIC IT SECURITY RISK MANAGEMENT

Dynamic IT security risk management deals with security problems that are difficult to foresee or too costly to protect against in the first place. Critical situations are identified, assessed, and resolved in real time. A key technology for the real-time detection of security problems is intrusion detection, as described in the previous section. In this section, we will investigate what intrusion detection can contribute to dynamic IT security risk management. We especially want to examine the advantages and disadvantages one must be aware of when trying to address short-term risks that are difficult to foresee and therefore have to be dealt with as they occur. The discussion is based to a large extent on Dacier (2001).

Let us investigate dynamic IT security risk management with respect to the four disciplines introduced in Section 5.3 and show their relationship to the five IDS characteristics discussed in Section 5.5. Table 5.1 summarizes this relationship.

5.5.1. Risk Identification

The identification of risks in dynamic IT security management systems is related to the detection of attacks. A detected attack is an obvious sign that the system is exposed to a security risk. Ideally, an IDS can detect all kinds of attacks very reliably and accurately. Unfortunately, IDSs are not perfect and may misinterpret observed activities. What can be detected by an IDS is closely linked to the detection method. Let us examine the advantages and disadvantages of knowledge- and behavior-based IDSs to determine what can be expected from a dynamic IT security management system.

The quality of knowledge-based IDSs is closely linked to the completeness and accuracy of the signatures they use. However, keeping the signature base up to date and hence being able to detect the newest attacks is a difficult problem:

- New vulnerabilities are reported on a daily basis, as seen in Section 5.2.1. It is difficult to keep up with this pace and have the newest signatures ready shortly after vulnerabilities and corresponding attacks are reported. Furthermore, many of the reported vulnerabilities can be exploited in different ways. Quite often, a single signature per reported vulnerability is not enough. Therefore, keeping the IDS signature base up to date is a difficult and challenging process.

- Taking into account that the same vulnerability can be exploited in different ways and knowing that attacks can be varied, some IDSs try to devise so-called generalized signatures. A generalized signature is expected to detect several attacks or at least several variations of the same attack. An example of a generalized signature is the search for long arguments as symptoms of buffer overflow attacks. However, as experience shows, generalized signatures quite often trigger an alarm even when normal traffic is observed, thus resulting in false alarms.

- Certain types of attacks require detailed analysis. However, for performance reasons, the detailed analysis is quite often replaced with a simplified one. This is yet another reason why IDSs are prone to generate false alarms.

- There are several known techniques that allow attackers to evade detection by an IDS. If the attacker knows which IDS is installed, he or she may be able to craft the attack in a way that will let it go undetected.

Despite their drawbacks, knowledge-based IDSs can detect many attacks very reliably and accurately. Furthermore, the way knowledge-based systems work is easy to understand, and some IDSs enable users to write their own signatures, thus addressing environment-specific security risks.

Behavior-based IDSs address some of the limitations inherent to knowledge-based IDSs. Behavior-based IDSs do not have to maintain a signature base, and furthermore, they are able to detect new attacks. However, behavior-based IDSs also suffer from a few limitations:

- A deviation from the expected normal behavior is not necessarily an indication of a security problem. A misconfiguration or a failing device may be the cause of such an observation. This means that alarms generated by a behavior-based IDS should not always be interpreted as a security problem, but merely as an unusual situation that warrants further investigation.

- The alarms of a behavior-based IDS are rather difficult to interpret because a behavior-based IDS merely tells the user that something is different, but not *what* is different. Therefore, the investigation of such alarm messages can prove to be a very difficult task.

- Behavior-based IDSs are said to look for significant deviations from normal behavior. However, there is no clear definition of what "significant" means. Furthermore, an attacker can delay an attack in a way that at any point in time only small deviations from the normal behavior are observed. This means that there are also evasion techniques for behavior-based IDSs.
- System behavior may change over time. Behavior-based IDS have to adapt themselves to the changing environment and learn the normal behavior in the real environment. If such an approach is chosen, there is a risk that malicious users can teach the system, in a stealthy way, to recognize their attacks as normal behavior.

It would be wrong to assume that IDSs can detect all kinds of attacks. However, they do provide valuable information that is the basis for identifying short-term security risks.

5.5.2. Risk Assessment

Depending on the detection method used, there are two ways to assess the risk of a detected attack. A knowledge-based IDS may have assigned to each attack signature a severity value that can be considered a measure of the danger of the attack. For example, attacks that allow the attacker to gain system administrator privileges may be assigned a higher severity value than attacks that "only" result in gaining normal user privileges. Severity of attack may also be determined based on how long the attack has already been known. However, as shown in Section 5.2.4, such a measure is difficult to devise.

In behavior-based IDSs, the deviation of the observed behavior is quite often expressed as a numerical term. The greater this term, the more dangerous the attack.

In both cases, the risk assessment is a generic one and does not consider the local environment in which the attack is observed. Usually an IDS does not know the role of an attacked machine. For example, it does not know whether the attacked machine is a business-critical machine. This information is usually a result of the static risk analysis. Therefore, an interesting approach is to combine the knowledge gained in the static risk analysis with the observations made in the dynamic risk analysis.

5.5.3. Risk Resolution

In static risk management, risk resolution is a manual process. In dynamic risk management systems, quite often there is insufficient time to address an identified risk because a prompt reaction is needed to prevent any further harm.

Passive IDSs, by definition, do not actively protect a system. The only thing they can do is raise an alarm. It is up to a human being to look at the alert and decide what to do. This creates several operational problems, such as ensuring the availability of the security officer, the reliability of his or her judgment, and the existence of a clear policy to decide which countermeasure to apply under which conditions.

Active IDSs, on the other hand, can automatically launch well-defined actions when an attack is detected. The main advantage of these systems is that they force users to formally define these countermeasures. However, when defining automated countermeasures, one has to keep in mind that an IDS can generate false alarms and that launching a countermeasure based on a false alarm can have negative consequences as well. For example, disabling business-relevant services may result in decreased productivity and revenue.

5.5.4. Risk Monitoring

Attacks can be made against any system component at any time. This poses several challenges for the risk-monitoring process in dynamic security risk management. The following IDS characteristics are relevant for dynamic security risk monitoring: the audit source location, the detection paradigm, and usage frequency.

5.5.4.1. Audit Source

Dynamic security management involves monitoring the system and network activities and looking for signs of security threats. As described in Section 5.4.2, there are several places where the system and network activities can be monitored.

If one relies on host-based monitoring, then, ideally, the activities on all hosts are monitored. One also has to decide which log files to monitor. For optimal protection, as many system events as possible should be recorded and made available for security risk analysis. It must be noted that the system-event-gathering process can have a serious impact on performance. Furthermore, if events are analyzed locally on the host where they are collected, further performance degradation is encountered.

If the costs of deployment and performance are an issue, it is possible to activate host-based monitoring only on selected machines. For example, one may choose to monitor only those machines that have been identified by the static security management process as critical to overall security, or if an infrastructure is known to be vulnerable to certain kinds of attacks, one may choose to monitor only those activities that are relevant to detecting attacks that attempt to exploit these vulnerabilities.

Network-based IDSs are widely used because they run on a separate, dedicated machine and thus are relatively easy to deploy. The key advantage of network-based monitoring is that a single machine can monitor communication between many other machines. However, network-based monitoring has certain drawbacks. As network bandwidth increases, performance issues make it increasingly difficult to have a single observation point for an entire network. To address this drawback, network-based IDSs quite often use generalized signatures and heuristics so that one signature can be used to detect not only a single but several attacks. However, the limitation of this approach is that normal traffic is quite often misclassified as an attack. Therefore, network-based systems are known to generate hundreds or even thousands of false alarms per day (Julisch, 2000).

Many network protocols have some inherent ambiguities that make it difficult for the IDS to predict how the receiver of a network packet will interpret it. Several tools are available on the Internet that allow an attacker to fool a network-based IDS.

Whereas static risk management provides hints as to where the security-critical components are installed and thus an IDS should be placed, one can also consider the opposite. As a result of static security management, the IT infrastructure may be set up in a way that makes it easier to deploy intrusion detection.

5.5.4.2. Detection Paradigm

State-based IDSs only detect attacks that have already succeeded, at least partially. This might represent a major drawback in some environments. In situations where users are concerned about the availability of the computing systems, the fact that the network has been partially compromised might not be a problem as long as it is possible to get rid of the attacker. However, if confidentiality is a requirement, even a partial break-in can be disastrous. As opposed to availability, confidentiality is a property that, once compromised, cannot be restored.

Transition-based IDSs, on the contrary, can identify attacks while they are taking place. Therefore, they can block attacks (if the IDS is also active) before the system is compromised. However, it is very difficult for transition-based IDSs to decide whether the detected attack will be or already has been successful. Therefore, the output of a transition-based IDS can be very verbose. This might not be a problem for users interested in knowing about all security-related events (e.g., all the port scans launched against their systems). However, it might be a problem for systems where dozens of scans take place per hour. In the latter case, the noise generated by these systems is likely to hide more serious attacks.

5.5.4.3. Usage Frequency

Periodic IDSs may not fulfill the requirements of a dynamic IT security risk management system, especially if there is a long period between the snapshots that are analyzed. One reason is that once a host has been compromised, its output may no longer be trusted. Therefore, if a periodic IDS is checking a hacked machine, there is no assurance that the intrusion will be detected. On the contrary, a clever attacker could reconfigure the system in such a way that, seen from the outside, it appears to be safe and secure.

Continuous IDSs are a key component of a dynamic IT security risk management system. They are a prerequisite for detecting short-term security risks and for taking appropriate actions in such cases.

5.6. CONCLUSIONS

IT infrastructures face many security threats. Experience shows that it is not possible or feasible to build secure systems. Security risk management ensures an awareness of security risks and the ability to react to them when they occur.

We have examined the terms static and dynamic security risk management. Static security risk management uses as input all available information about applications, machines, networks, and users and how they relate to each other. Dynamic security risk management is concerned with all information produced in real time about the behavior of the system. This information may allow short-term risks to be identified that cannot be identified with the static approach.

Intrusion detection has been introduced as an interesting technology for dynamic security risk management. We have examined the various characteristics of IDSs and considered their advantages and disadvantages with respect to dynamic security risk management. All in all, intrusion detection offers many features that help to build an efficient and powerful dynamic security risk management system.

Static and dynamic risk management can benefit from each other. Dynamic risk management may detect risks that cannot be detected by static risk management, and dynamic risk management can acquire useful information from the static management system, which allows it to more accurately assess a risk and react to it in a more effective manner.

REFERENCES

Anderson, J. P. (1980). Computer Security Threat Monitoring and Surveillance, Technical Report, James P. Anderson Co., Fort Washington, PA, April.

Arbaugh, W. A., Fithen, W. L., and McHugh, J. (2000). Windows of vulnerability: A case study analysis, *IEEE Computer*, 33, 52–59, December.

Bauknecht, K. (2000). *Lecture in Information Security*, ETH Zurich.

Bishop, M. (1986). How to write a setuid program, *:login;*, 12(1), January/February.

Computer Security Institute and Federal Bureau of Investigation (2003). 2003 Computer Crime and Security Survey.

Cowan, C., Wagle, P., Pu, C., Beattie, S., and Walpole, J. (2000). Buffer overflows: Attacks and defenses for the vulnerability of the decade, DARPA Information Survivability Conference and Expo (DISCEX), Hilton Head Island, SC, January.

Dacier, M. (2001). Intrusion detection: State-of-the-art and current problems with deployment, *Compsec 2001*, London, October.

Debar, H., Becker, M., and Siboni, D. (1992). A neural network component for an intrusion detection system, in *Proc. IEEE Computer Society Symposium on Research in Security and Privacy, Oakland, CA*, pp. 240–250.

Debar, H., Dacier, M., and Wespi, A. (1999). Towards a taxonomy of intrusion detection systems, *Computer Networks*, 31, 805–822.

Debar, H., Dacier, M., and Wespi, A. (2000). A revised taxonomy for intrusion-detection systems, *Annales des Télécommunications*, 55, 361–378.

Gartner, Inc. (2003). *Security Spending on the Rise* (http://thewhir.com/marketwatch/gar060303.cfm).

Gross, A. H. (1997). Analyzing Computer Intrusions, Ph.D. thesis, University of California, San Diego Supercomputer Center, San Diego.

Howard, J. D. (1997). An Analysis of Security Incidents on the Internet, Ph.D. thesis, Carnegie Mellon University, Engineering and Public Policy, Pittsburgh.

Jagannathan, R., Lunt, T., Anderson, D., Dodd, C., Gilham, F., Jalali, C., Javitz, H., Neumann, P., Tamaru, A., and Valdes, A. (1993). System Design Document: Next-Generation Intrusion Detection Expert System (NIDES), Technical Report A007/A008/A009/A011/A012/A014, SRI International, Menlo Park, CA.

Julisch, K. (2000). Dealing with false positives in intrusion detection, presented at Recent Advances in Intrusion Detection, Third International Workshop, RAID2000, Toulouse (http://www.raid-ymposium.org/raid2000/Materials/Abstracts/50/Julisch_foils_RAID2000.pdf).

Kumar, S. and Spafford, E. (1994). A pattern matching model for misuse intrusion detection, in *Proceedings of the 17th National Computer Security Conference*, pp. 11–21.

Lipson, H. F. (2000). Survivability — A new security paradigm for protecting highly distributed mission-critical systems, IFIP WG 10.4, Summer 2000 Meeting, June/July.

Powell, D. and Stroud, R., Eds. (2003). Conceptual Model and Architecture of MAFTIA, Project IST-1999-11583, Malicious and Accidental Fault Tolerance of Internet Applications, Deliverable D21.

Wespi, A. and Debar, H. (1999). Building an intrusion-detection system to detect suspicious process behaviour, *RAID 99, Workshop on Recent Advances in Intrusion Detection, West Lafayette, IN.*

Wespi, A., Dacier, M., and Debar, H. (2000). Intrusion detection using variable-length audit trail patterns, in *Recent Advances in Intrusion Detection*, Debar, H., Mé, L., and Wu, S. F., Eds., *Lecture Notes in Computer Science*, Vol. 1907, Springer, Berlin, pp. 110–129.

A PREDICTIVE MODEL FOR E-BANK OPERATIONAL RISK MANAGEMENT

Marcelo Cruz

6.1. INTRODUCTION

The term "operational risk" in the financial industry was probably used for the first time in 1995. This was as a result of the infamous bankruptcy of Barings Bank in which a trader brought down the venerable bank by hiding futures and derivatives positions in the Asian markets. This event raised the awareness of financial institutions to this risk type, which could not be classified as either credit or market risk and which until then had not been properly appreciated, despite the considerable impact that it might have on results. As a result, from 1995 until today there has been a rapidly growing recognition of the importance of operational risk in banks.* A survey conducted by the British Bankers Association in 2000 showed that banks estimated that their risks are divided into credit (60%), market and liquidity (15%), and operational risk (25%). This is

---

* Although the focus here is on banks, the term "bank" will be used hereafter to denote financial institutions in general, including banks, investment firms, insurers etc.

an approximation, as no financial institution has yet derived a credible and reliable measure for its global operational risks. It is important to highlight that at the time of the Barings event, banks did not acknowledge this risk category explicitly, with the result that they have belatedly come to recognize these risks in their risk management framework/processes.

In terms of a formal definition, operational risk has been defined by the Basel Committee as *the risk of direct or indirect loss resulting from inadequate or failed internal processes, people and systems or from external events*; operational risk, therefore, is related to losses arising from operational errors of any sort that affect the earnings stream of a bank.

The sudden interest within the financial industry in the area of operational risk might be surprising to those in other industries. However, banks are, in general, primarily focused on the revenue side of their activities in fields such as trading assets, structuring complex operations, issuing bonds and stocks etc., and there appears to be a secondary interest in the cost of processing for such operations. (A small soap manufacturer, for example, would understand exactly its marginal costs and the impact of any change in these on its results.) Banks have a historical disregard for the cost side, and the results were simply the effect of the complex financial transactions without considering errors or even the costs involved in such transactions.

As banks are learning to appreciate the importance of the cost side of their operations in their overall result and risk measurement framework, more operational data are becoming available for modeling exercises. A methodology is presented in this chapter to enable estimation of the level of operational risk* in an e-bank;** this is relatively generic so that it can be easily adapted to any type of e-business. The method presented here values an e-bank using real options theory and estimates the operational risk initially through numerical techniques and then through an analytical multifactor model.

In terms of the chapter organization, Section 6.2 describes the operational loss database modeling structure. The following section gives a brief summary of the real options valuation framework. Section 6.4 gives an example of how the framework presented in the previous section can be used to measure operational risk in an e-bank. Section 6.5 presents an analytical method for a predictive model for evaluating the level of operational risk.

---

* The use of the term "level of operational risk" should be taken to mean the level of some proxy for operational risk; in general, this is represented by losses and expressed in monetary terms.

** An e-bank is a virtual bank, that is, a bank that maintains contact with customers (including operations) basically through the Internet.

6.2. MODELING AN OPERATIONAL RISK DATABASE

The task of collecting information for operational risk measurement and management is more challenging than in the areas of credit or market risks. Given the relative indifference toward rigid controls on costs, banks do not generally collect or hold information about their internal control environment in a systematic manner, and therefore, the design and implementation of an appropriate infrastructure to collate these loss events and indicators might be costly and take several years to accomplish.

Operational risk is jointly a function of, first, the internal control environment of an institution (over which it has some degree of control), rather than solely past losses, which are the evidence of operational risk, and, second, the external environment. While the observed losses serve to inform management where the major risks lie, the control environment is much more of a leading indicator as to where the major operational risks might lie in an organization.

The data model proposed here has several layers, the first being a loss data collection exercise (i.e., the impact of operational losses on the results). The loss data are not enough to form a complete understanding of how operational risk manifests itself; additionally, the internal control environment must be understood to get a handle on the level of operational risk. In order to model the control environment, some quantitative factors, termed control environment factors and key control indicators, must be identified, in addition to any qualitative ones, which will help us to understand the inputs and the outputs. Figure 6.1 depicts the data model proposed here for operational risk.

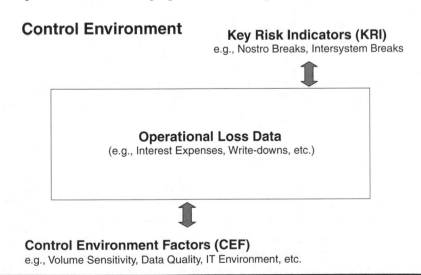

Control Environment

Key Risk Indicators (KRI)
e.g., Nostro Breaks, Intersystem Breaks

Operational Loss Data
(e.g., Interest Expenses, Write-downs, etc.)

Control Environment Factors (CEF)
e.g., Volume Sensitivity, Data Quality, IT Environment, etc.

Figure 6.1. Operational risk data model.

Table 6.1.   Classification Scheme for Operational Risk Losses

Event-Type Category (Level 1)	Definition	Categories (Level 2)
Internal fraud	Losses due to acts of a type intended to defraud, misappropriate property, or circumvent regulations, the law, or company policy, excluding diversity/discrimination events, which involve at least one internal party	Unauthorized activity, theft and fraud
External fraud	Losses due to acts of a type intended to defraud, misappropriate property, or circumvent the law, by a third party	Theft and fraud, systems security
Employment practices and workplace safety	Losses arising from acts inconsistent with employment; health or safety laws or agreements from payment of personal injury claims or from diversity/discrimination events	Employee relations, safe environment, diversity, and discrimination
Clients, products, and business practices	Losses arising from an unintentional or negligent failure to meet a professional obligation to specific clients or from the nature or design of a product	Suitability, disclosure and fiduciary, improper business or market practice, product flaws, selection, sponsorship and exposure, advisory activities
Damage to physical assets	Losses arising from loss of or damage to physical assets from natural disasters or other events	Disasters and other events
Business disruption and system failures	Losses arising from disruption of business or system failures	System

Source: BIS, Basel Committee for Banking Supervision.

6.2.1. Operational Loss Data

The losses attributable to manifestations of operational risk are obviously very important as they represent the direct impact on the results of an institution. The causes of these losses may be categorized in a number of ways. Table 6.1 was produced by the Basel Committee as a suggestion of how the manifestation of operational risk can be split among event types inside a financial institution into several different levels (shown here up to the second level).

Table 6.2.   Examples of Control Environment Factors

Business Environment	Factor	Description
Systems	System downtime System slow time System stability (...)	Number of minutes that a system is off-line Number of minutes that a system is slow Number of lines changed in a program
People/organization	Employees Employee experience (...)	Number of employees Average number of months of experience
Data flow and integrity	Data quality (...)	Ratio of transactions with wrong data inputs to total transactions
Volume sensitivity	Transactions (...)	Number of transactions
Control gaps	Ratio of processes under control (...)	Processes under control-audit/total processes
External environment	Counterparty errors Number of changes in regulations	Number of errors caused by counterparties Number of changes in pertinent regulation over a period of time
(...)	(...)	trparties

6.2.2. Control Environment Factors

Another important input to any model is control environment factors, which are primarily quantitative and used as a proxy for the quality of the systems and controls in a business. For example, in order to report the quality of the processing systems of a bank, two representative factors of the quality of the control environment might be system downtime (the number of minutes that a system stayed off-line) and system slow time (the number of minutes that a system was overloaded and consequently running slowly). These factors will be used later in conjunction with loss data in Section 6.5. Table 6.2 provides a few examples of control environment factors.

6.2.3. Key Risk Indicators

The identification of errors, in terms of both where and how they occur, is termed key risk indicators (or alternatively key performance indicators). Key risk indicators may indicate the location and level of operational risk within an organization even without knowing the number and size of resulting losses.

Taking transaction processing as an example, if the number of breaks in the "Nostro" account is increasing, this might indicate that one of the processes has problems. A financial institution should identify such indicators in its operations in order to gauge performance.

6.3. REAL OPTIONS

A real option is a right, but not an obligation, to undertake an action in relation to an investment or situation (e.g., deferring, expanding, contracting, or abandoning a process) at a predetermined cost (the exercise price), for a predetermined period of time (the life of the option). The framework for considering real options is derived from that for financial options and is, in general, applied to real-life situations.

Research in this field was initiated when Myers (1977) realized that part of the value of a firm is accounted for by the present value of options to make further investments on (possibly) favorable terms. Real options theory* addresses the issue that investment valuation based on static discounted cash flow tends to overlook the value of decision flexibility. What Myers proposed is that a firm in a position to exploit potentially lucrative business opportunities is worth more than one not in a similar position.

Under traditional investment analysis, using the net present value or any other technique based on discounted cash flows, the impact of risk is always on the downside, as the presence of risk depresses the value of an investment. Real options theory recognizes that the level of risk in an organization may be actively influenced through managerial flexibility, and the action of taking on more risk may become a central instrument for value creation. Consequently, in such circumstances, increased risk may actually increase the value of an investment opportunity. By considering the innovative view that the opportunity for management to actively increase the level of risk is a key element in valuing an investment, one can proceed to incorporate other types of corporate real options that capture the inherent value of active management of the risk factor.

The determinants of risk, termed risk factors, may be categorized in a number of different ways, but it is simplest to do so under the headings of credit, market, and operational risks. It is desirable to understand fully the role of each risk factor in giving rise to the various forms of risk and, especially in the context of real options, to what extent there is some degree of managerial ability to

---

* Real options theory has become the subject of increasing interest among academics and practitioners recently. Further details may be found in Copeland and Antikarov (2001) and Trigeorgis (1999).

influence it. As an example of a risk factor in the area of operational risk, the level of fixed costs in an organization is one such input. An operating structure characterized by a prevalence of fixed costs will be rigid and difficult to modify when production levels or market conditions change. Keeping other factors equal, the degree of cost structure rigidity substantially conditions the effect that changes in volume might have on operating results. Management decisions such as hiring or dismissing employees or buying a better operating system might be informed using real options theory.

For example, high fixed costs, as might be caused by a large number of wrongly processed transactions (potentially giving rise to high losses), would tend to render many corporate decisions difficult to reverse and will often imply significant reconversion costs. Given that, there is value to the possibility of delaying a project's implementation under such a level of uncertainty (operational risk level) and conditioning such decisions on a favorable state of the risk factors.

In the next section, it will be shown how the real options valuation framework can play a role not just in valuing an e-business but also in estimating risk. Cruz (2002) surveys the use of real options in evaluating strategy and business risks as well.

6.4. ESTIMATING THE LEVEL OF OPERATIONAL RISK IN AN E-BANK

One of the key challenges facing new businesses is the evaluation of the potential market for their products and services and the attendant risks involved in the business. The challenge is especially pertinent in totally new markets such as virtual banks, brokerages, or financial institutions (hereafter termed generically e-banks). Given these circumstances, the theory of real options has been playing an important role in the valuation of these new e-businesses and also in estimating their risk.

The decision as to which real options model should be included in the modeling process and when it might be exercised is also critical. The outlook is highly uncertain, especially for start-up companies in a relatively immature marketplace: in addition to the usual market potential issues, there are doubts related to the effectiveness of the technology behind the e-bank, acceptance by customers, appropriate level of operational framework, etc.

Another challenge is that, because these e-banks are proposing to operate in a relatively new area, often little historical information of particular applicability to a specific sector or company is available. Perhaps most pertinently, external operational loss data are very scarce (if at all available) and the relevance of such data across seemingly similar organizations in a new business may be open to question.

Despite all these shortcomings, it is possible to estimate the level of risks in these ventures using mathematical techniques. In this chapter, we will show an example of the use of real options theory to estimate the level of operational risk in an e-bank. We first need to build a risk architecture for the e-bank stating which factors are important and would affect the bank's revenues, costs, and market position. Figure 6.2 shows a simple risk architecture for an e-bank.

In the structural design of the e-bank business, future cash flows may be seen as being contingent on a number of risk factors that may be categorized, in this instance, under the headings of operational, market, and credit risks. As the objective here is to quantify the level of operational risk involved in the venture, the operational risk factors have been split into four subtypes: systems, security, transaction processing, and settlement. This list is not meant to be definitive and other factors might also be included, depending on the level of detail required.

Given a limited upper bound on the number of clients that may be served at a given time, the materialization of operational risk will affect the actual number of clients served and, therefore, impact the cash flows realized, thereby causing volatility in earnings. Similarly, the same operational factors may adversely affect the ability of management to react to evolving market conditions such as an unexpected increase in the number of possible clients if a competitor exits this line of business.

Operational risk may be considered the main risk an e-bank faces, in contrast to the traditional bricks-and-mortar bank where credit risk is in general predominant. In the general business model for e-banks, market risk may be more appropriately considered to be demand risk from the market for its products/services rather than the risk of bearing financial instruments. Credit risk should be negligible or even nonexistent, depending on the business model chosen.

In the risk architecture shown above, the future cash flows depend on the reaction of management to the particular materialization of any uncertainty. Consequently, all types of uncertainty should be considered under a number of future business conditions to evaluate how a particular factor would impact the earnings. After all the risk factors have been mapped in this way, the calculations can be done by Monte Carlo simulation or even by using more sophisticated techniques such as stochastic dynamic programming.

The net cash flows of an e-bank may be generally represented by:

$$\text{Net cash flow} = \text{Revenues} - \text{Costs} = \left(\sum_{\text{products}} \text{Margin} * \text{Sales} \right)$$

$$- (\text{Fixed operating costs} + \text{Variable costs})$$

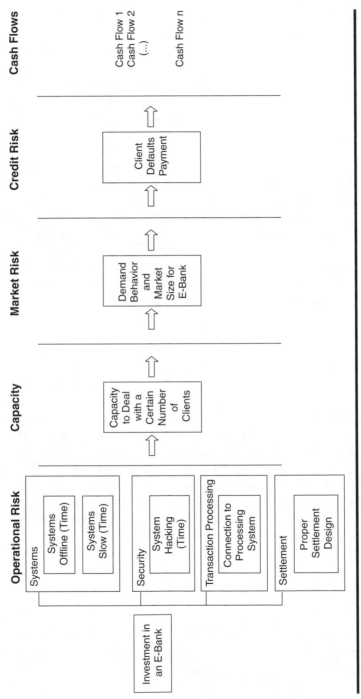

Figure 6.2.   Risk architecture for an e-bank venture.

Operational risk will affect the revenue side (e.g., in that it might limit the number of clients served in a given period), but primarily the variable costs (e.g., in requiring that process[es] be repeated or that compensation be paid to third parties).

Given that, the value V of an e-bank might be represented by:

$$V = \sum_{\text{factors}} \text{Net cash flows } (C, M, \alpha)$$

where C is the credit risk, M is the market risk, α is the operational risk, and the cash flows are a function of the risk factors (which may themselves be classified under one of the three major risk types).

Consequently, the net cash flows (and V) are stated as a function of the three major risks. Any change in the risk environment would influence the value of the e-bank.

Developing the analysis in relation to operational risk specifically, the level of operational risk may be represented by the variation in value due to changes in net cash flows caused by the relevant risk factors:

$$\alpha = \Delta V (\Theta_n)$$

where the formula above can be interpreted as the level of operational risk (α) represented by changes in value (ΔV) of the cash flows, which in turn are a function of a set of n operational risk factors (Θ). The estimation of the operational risk figure can be performed numerically, for example by Monte Carlo simulation, where these operational risk factors would be stressed and the impact in the results would be felt using an appropriate number of simulations.* In this case, we define the level of operational risk as the volatility around the value of the e-bank caused by fluctuations in these operational risk factors.

An analytical approach to considering the impact of incorporating these factors is to link them to the losses in a given period of time by invoking a multifactor model, as shown in the next section.

6.5. MULTIFACTOR MODELS TO PREDICT OPERATIONAL RISK

A pure value at risk (VaR) approach is one in which historical losses are used to generate estimates of future losses within specified confidence intervals. For

---

* Most modeling exercises generate between 10,000 and 100,000 scenarios.

operational risk, it would be important and informative to relate directly the inputs (i.e., the control environment factors and/or indicators) to the output (i.e., the observed losses [or the VaR figures]) to attempt to understand their causal relationship. Analogously, in VaR approaches for market risk, there are several risk factors that may be isolated to assist in the decomposition of the VaR figure into its underlying drivers, such as the short- and long-term interest rates, inflation, GDP growth, etc. By understanding the effect of, for example, macroeconomic variables such as money supply level(s), interest rates, and inflation on the fixed income products, we might analyze whether a change in the inflation forecast would affect the final VaR figure.

Similarly, it would be of value to do the same when considering operational risk. There is a shift in emphasis in VaR modeling to operational risk relative to market risk, as most of the factors that influence the latter are internal to the bank and managed by the bank. In order to relate the observable outputs to the inputs (which should be manageable to some degree), we might seek to develop causal models that explain the influence of certain variables on the results.

One approach, based on causal modeling, is to propose that the losses (or VaR) are linear with respect to the inputs and use a multifactor model to relate them. The factors are chosen as defined in the previous sections. Any factor representing an input variable may be used, and its importance to the analysis can even be tested by factor or principal component analysis.

The form of the model is given by:

$$\alpha_t = \beta_t + \beta_{1_t} X_{1_t} + \dots + \beta_{n_t} X_{n_t} + \varepsilon_t$$

where α_t represents the level of operational risk VaR (or operational losses) in the bank at time t in a particular business unit or area, X_{n_t} represents the control environment factors, and β are the estimated scaling parameters at the same point in time.

It is important to realize that for this model to be most effective, the loss events due to operational risk should be attributed to the operating period at which the materialization of operational risk triggered the loss: in general, operational losses manifest themselves some appreciable time after the failure occurred. In a causal model such as this, it is very important that the state of the control environment is measured at the time that the error/failing occurred so that the modeling process can use the most accurate level of the inputs, leading to a more "true" model. Consider, for example, a processing system that crashes for a material length of time and consequently results in some unsettled transactions which, in turn, give rise to interest claims by the counterparties, quite possibly paid on different days. If we wish to identify accurately the state of the control environment when the original error occurred, it will be necessary

Date	Losses	System Downtime	Number of Employees	Number of Transactions	Data Quality
2-Sep-02	42,043.83	2	13	1,115	93%
3-Sep-02	34,732.14	1	14	1,250	95%
4-Sep-02	20,725.78	0	14	999	96%
5-Sep-02	14,195.16	0	15	1,012	98%
6-Sep-02	2,213,891.54	20	11	1,512	65%
9-Sep-02	31,654.90	1	14	1,076	94%
10-Sep-02	39,948.60	1.5	13	1,003	95%
11-Sep-02	11,901.87	0	15	855	99%
12-Sep-02	—	0	15	915	700%
13-Sep-02	112,169.21	4	12	1,590	78%
16-Sep-02	80,816.23	3	13	1,390	90%
17-Sep-02	—	0	15	891	100%
18-Sep-02	65,053.57	2	13	1,422	91%
19-Sep-02	114,862.81	4	12	1,615	75%
20-Sep-02	—	0	15	920	100%
23-Sep-02	51,006.72	2	13	1,412	90%
24-Sep-02	24,770.00	1	15	1,215	95%
25-Sep-02	35,232.53	1	15	1,111	93%
26-Sep-02	35,285.33	1	15	1,115	93%
27-Sep-02	16,460.19	0	15	997	97%

Figure 6.3. Transaction processing data set.

to identify the relevant time; this is, of course, dependent upon appropriate systems being in place to enable us to recognize that all of the resulting claims had the same root cause. Pursuing the losses individually might be misleading.

A numerical example will help to clarify the point. Consider the hypothetical data in Figure 6.3 in which four control environment factors to explain the losses are specified:

- System downtime (measured in minutes per day)
- Employees (number of employees in the back office on a given day)
- The total number of transactions that day
- Data quality (in reality, a key performance indicator: the ratio of the number of transactions with no input errors from the front office to the total number of transactions on a given day)

Using simple OLS estimation, the multifactor model in this case may be given by:

$$\text{Losses} = 1108 + 135.9 * \text{System downtime} + 49.7 \text{ Employees}$$
$$+ 221.02 * \text{Transactions} + 578.1 * \text{Data quality} + \varepsilon$$

The ANOVA can be seen in Table 6.3.

The "goodness of fit" of the model in this case is extremely high, over 99%,* meaning that we can trust in the model with a very high degree of confidence. This extremely high fit will probably not happen frequently, but we have reasons to believe that there is a very high extent of linear correlation between these variables (input) and losses (output).

By knowing the coefficients in the equation (i.e., the sensitivity of the operational losses to fluctuations in these variables), we may price individual units of the variables. For instance, the cost of one more minute of system downtime in a day is $135,910.45, and therefore, any decision that leads to an improvement of the processing systems might use such figures as a starting point.

If, for example, we were to consider that all variables took their mean level in the period (i.e., 2.18 minutes downtime, 1170 transactions, and 14 employees a day), an improvement of 1% in the mean data quality factor (from 92% to 93%) would result in a decrease in losses of $5780.90. As would be expected by considering the mean values, the decreased volatility (i.e., variability) of the input variables results in improved performance, as there would be less risk present in the system; the decrease seen is, however, an approximation, as the coefficients in the equation above are conditioned on the original data set.

The wider application of these types of model may be seen in the following case. Suppose that the management of an e-bank were to decide to increase the daily volume of transactions by 30% due to the profitability of the products traded. Consequently, the board would also like to see an assessment of the likely impact on the level of operational risk as a result of pursuing this course of action, but with the overriding constraint that there is to be no increase in the number of employees in this area (in effect, the exercise of a discretionary option by senior management).

An increase of 30% in the daily volume of transactions over the period sees the mean increase to 1521. Using the above model, we realize that, keeping all other variables constant, the additional losses would be significant, $77,579.34 on a daily basis, obtained from the equation above. As senior management has decreed that no employees can be hired, management with control over processes involved in handling transactions must find ways to improve the quality

---

* This good fit can be explained by the short period that the data set covers (i.e., 20 observations). Based on practical experience, more realistic long-run numbers would generally be in the range of 75 to 90%, which is still relatively high.

Table 6.3. ANOVA Table

Summary Output

Regression Statistics

Multiple R	99.651%
R square	99.304%
Adjusted R square	99.118%
Standard error	45,785.94
Observations	20

ANOVA

	df	SS	MS	F	Significance F
Regression	4	4.48463E+12	1.12116E+12	534.8133074	5.59373E-16
Residual	15	31445290155	2096352677		
Total	19	4.51607E+12			

	Coefficients	Standard Error	t Stat	P-value	Lower 95%	Upper 95%	Lower 95.0%	Upper 95.0%
Intercept	(1,108,992.08)	543484.5594	-2.040521771	0.059307281	-2267402.705	49418.55378	-2267402.705	49418.55378
System downtime	135,910.45	5830.735382	23.30931554	3.39554E-13	123482.5249	148338.3767	123482.5249	148338.3767
No. employees	49,712.13	17739.10049	2.802404203	0.013394591	11902.10885	87522.15069	11902.10885	87522.15069
No. transactions	(221.02)	106.2911473	-2.079418268	0.055146767	-447.5781105	5.530603461	-447.5781105	5.530603461
Data quality	578,089.20	442238.0696	1.307190033	0.210832372	-364519.5149	1520697.909	-364519.5149	1520697.909

of operations without hiring. This could be achieved, for example, by improving the data quality factor, which is only 92%. If internal quality programs were to be developed and the quality of the input were increased to a mean level of 95%, there would be no net impact arising from this desired growth in the number of transactions. Such models, which are widely available in many other industries, are a novelty in the financial industry and are set to make a difference in how they manage operations and the subsequent operational risks involved.

6.6. CONCLUSION

The relatively recent growth of interest in the area of operational risk in financial institutions has led to an increased focus on the operational aspects of providing financial services, especially in relation to cost and the consequences of errors/failures. As a consequence, more sophisticated methodologies are being developed to measure operational risk and predict the consequences of operational events *a priori*; these are now complementing models already used in the revenue-generating areas to produce a more holistic view of operational risk in financial institutions.

REFERENCES

Copeland, T. and Antikarov, V. (2001). *Real Options: A Practitioners' Guide,* Texere LLC, New York.

Cruz, M. (2002). *Modeling, Measuring and Hedging Operational Risk,* John Wiley & Sons, Hoboken, NJ.

Myers, S. C. (1977). Determinants of corporate borrowing, *Journal of Financial Economics,* 5, 147–175.

Trigeorgis, L. (1999). *Real Options and Business Strategy,* Risk Books, London.

PREDICTIVE DATA MINING FOR PROJECT PORTFOLIO RISK MANAGEMENT

Abderrahim Labbi and Michel Cuendet

7.1. INTRODUCTION

In the ever-changing e-business environment, project design, delivery, and management is usually a highly complex and risky process due to the very dynamic and uncertain nature of business requirements, customer expectations, and technology, among other complexity drivers. Therefore, project performance and health tracking, prediction, and management require adaptive decision support tools that integrate various business data and suggest appropriate response actions in a *sense-and-respond* manner (Haeckel, 1999). To track and manage project health effectively, one needs to collect and analyze up-to-date information about various aspects of a project and identify possible deviations (trends) from initial and/or expected plans. Advanced data analysis techniques can provide valuable input for informed prediction of future project health by identifying emerging trends (patterns). The project manager can then respond proactively to early warnings in the project life cycle.

However, to design such adaptive management systems, a number of requirements have to be met. First, one must gather and consolidate as much

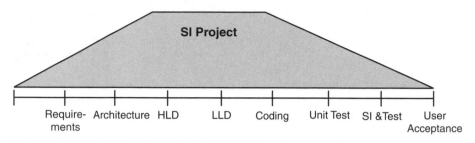

Figure 7.1. Typical phases of a system integration (SI) project.

historical data as possible on various aspects of current and previous projects. Then, using data analysis models and domain knowledge provided by subject matter experts, one has to derive appropriate process metrics and rules to serve as a baseline for:

- Quantification of project quality and performance
- Identification of emerging trends
- Prediction of future project health and financials

In a typical system integration project scenario for example (see Figure 7.1), such metrics and rules would be determined by a combination of several factors stemming from the project financials, quality assurance reports, milestones, system integration and test data, customer satisfaction reviews, etc. These factors, if appropriately combined, can strongly help to quantify both current and future positions of a project in terms of financial expectations, project quality, and management.

7.2. DATA MINING PROCESS

Key to the adaptive approach is the data mining process. This three-step approach is briefly described below and illustrated in Figure 7.2. These steps represent a systematic approach to the data integration and analysis processes that is relevant to the issues addressed. The overall process consists of data consolidation, project portfolio segmentation, and portfolio performance estimation.

7.2.1. Data Consolidation

Several data sources are usually required to build such a learning system. Data reports on project financials, quality assurance, risk assessment, and customer

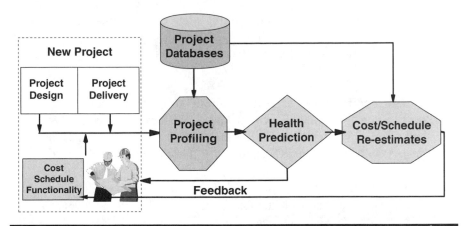

Figure 7.2.   Data mining system for project portfolio management.

interviews (ratings), among other information sources, should be gathered and consolidated. This task is usually time and resource consuming, which can be exacerbated by poor quality of the data, but it usually pays off in the longer run if carefully carried out.

7.2.2. Project Portfolio Segmentation

The consolidated data are analyzed in order to identify subsets (referred to below as project risk groups) of projects which show, or have shown, similar health characteristics (features). The similarity is based on some given metrics (e.g., cost overrun, quality, rating, etc.). Such segmentation can be very useful for project profiling in its early phases (e.g., project scoping and project design). Building few project profiles can strongly help to determine specific prerequisites to be fulfilled by a given proposal before moving forward in the project development cycle.

Given the results of the segmentation process, the different portfolios are analyzed in order to identify statistically relevant causes of healthy/troubled behavior. In this step, data mining techniques are used to determine salient project features which, when combined, produce the observed project health patterns.

It is important to note here that analyses should be run on data for both healthy (successful) and troubled projects in order to have an objective baseline for performance measures. Such a procedure would keep one from spotting false patterns or root causes that would be biased by troubled project data and would not have a real impact on project health management.

For instance, an analysis using historical data could produce probabilistic decision rules that predict the likelihood and/or the severity of project trouble. For illustration purposes, the following decision rule is the kind of probabilistic patterns that can be inferred:

> IF a system integration project has a total cost estimate between $2 million and $4 million, is within line of business A, and involves technologies B, C, and D, THEN there is a 0.8 probability that the project will experience a cost overrun after 18 months.

In this study, boosting techniques were used to build the predictive system. Such techniques, together with the experimental methodology developed, are described in more detail in Section 7.3.

7.2.3. Estimation of Portfolio Financial Performance

After deriving the probabilistic rules which potentially characterize future project health rating, the question we want to answer is: What does an expected project health estimate mean in terms of budget overrun? In other words, what is the expected financial impact of the health rating of a single project or of a portfolio of projects? To answer this question, our approach combines probabilistic rules for health prediction and a Monte Carlo simulation. The simulation engine takes as input a probability distribution over possible future health ratings of a given project and then uses historical data to estimate a probability distribution of the project cost at completion. This step is described in Section 7.5.

7.3. DECISION TREES FOR PROJECT CLASSIFICATION

Building predictive decision trees for classification is a widely studied subject in the machine learning literature. The general problem of building a classification tree from a set of data (observations) can be formally stated as follows: We are given a set of N *examples* or *instances* of projects described by a number of attributes (or features). These attributes can be real-valued numbers (e.g., project cost) or nominal descriptors (e.g., project manager). The attribute values characterizing an instance are grouped in the input vector x. Each instance is affected to a class, described by the *label* y (e.g., project health). The set of all possible attributes is noted X and the set of labels Y. In the first part of this work, we only consider the two-class or binary problem, where the labels can only take values in $Y = \{-1; +1\}$. The examples are noted $z = (x, y)$ and they constitute the *training set Z*.

The goal of a classification algorithm is the following: Given a number of project examples $z = (x, y)$ (referred to as a training set), one wants to be able to predict the labels y (e.g., health) of new projects for which only descriptors x are known. For this purpose, the algorithm builds a predictive model, referred to below as hypothesis $H(x)$, such that the *training error*

$$E^{train} = \frac{1}{N} \sum_{i=1}^{N} I[H(x_i) \neq y_i]$$

is minimal. Here $I(.)$ stands for the indicator function.

The hypothesis minimizing the training error should also minimize the prediction error on any set of examples not used in the learning process. To assess this in practice, a fraction of the available data is often kept out of the training set to constitute a *test set* on which the *generalization error* or *test error* can be evaluated.

There are many types of classification algorithms, including neural networks, nearest-neighbor algorithms, support vector machines, and decision trees (Hastie et al., 2001). In this work, the focus is only on decision trees, a brief description of which is given.

Figure 7.3 shows a plot of a simple decision tree with two decision nodes (rectangles) and three prediction leaves (ellipses). The tree defines a binary classification rule, which maps instances of the form $x = (a, b)$ into one of the two classes denoted by -1 or $+1$. According to the results of the tests performed at each decision node, an instance is mapped into a path along the tree from the root to one of the leaves.

The use of a decision tree to classify an instance is straightforward, but the construction of the optimal tree from the data is the challenging part. Usually, the algorithms proceed iteratively, starting at the root of the tree and adding one decision node at a time. The optimal split is found by an extensive search over all possible splits, and the decision rule minimizing or maximizing a given

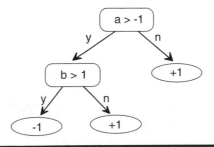

Figure 7.3.   Example of a decision tree for a binary classification problem.

criterion is kept. The most commonly used criteria are the Gini index (Breiman et al., 1983) and the information gain ratio (Quinlan, 1998).

In this work, either of those two criteria is used to build decision trees. Another construction rule is used that optimizes the trees for use with *boosting*. Furthermore, we will in fact only build one-level decision trees, known as stumps (Iba and Langley, 1992), which relieves us from the problem of *pruning*.

Pruning refers to the limitation of the final size of the tree. It is often required that the iterative splitting stop when a minimum number of instances is reached in a leaf node. Even with this constraint, the trees obtained by repeating the Gini or information gain technique are quite complex, with long and uneven paths. The pruning of the decision tree is done by replacing an entire subtree by a leaf node, thus canceling all further splits. The replacement takes place if the expected error rate in the subtree is greater than in the single leaf.

7.4. BOOSTING TECHNIQUES

In the previous section, a way to build a tree classifier directly from the data was discussed. However, the generalization accuracy of such a classifier is usually limited. One can wonder whether there is a way to improve this accuracy, for example by combining different decision trees. More generally, can a "weak" learning algorithm that performs just slightly better than random guessing be boosted (through combination) into an arbitrarily accurate "strong" learning algorithm? The technique of boosting answers this question. The term boosting, coined by Freund and Schapire (1996) in a milestone paper, introduced a concept that relies on two main intuitive ideas:

■ Averaging the predictions of several weak learners to get a more accurate hypothesis (predictor)
■ Letting the weak learners focus on "hard-to-learn" examples

We will see shortly how these two benefits are efficiently combined in the AdaBoost algorithm. The challenge is how to compute weights for the averaging of the weak learners and how to make the weak learners focus on hard examples. The boosting algorithm operates iteratively. An example is called "hard" if it has not been classified correctly by the previous weak learners. This can be specified to the next weak learner in two ways. Selective resampling of the training set can be used, but the best way is to attribute weights to the examples, especially if their number is limited.

The first versions of AdaBoost were constructed based only on the two intuitive ideas above and gave surprisingly good experimental results. For example, the generalization error was observed to continue to decrease even after the training error had reached zero. When used with decision trees, AdaBoost seemed to solve the problem of pruning by unraveling the unnecessary complexity. It also showed remarkable results with weak learners as simple as a single decision node (*stumps*) (Mitchell, 1999).

Several justifications for this appeared later in the literature. First, the theory of margins (Allwein et al., 2000) shed some light on these outstanding capabilities. Theoretical convergence bounds on the training and generalization errors were derived (Schapire and Singer, 1999). AdaBoost was proved to iteratively minimize a loss functional over all possible weak hypotheses, and it also turned out to be grounded in game theory as well as in statistical learning theory (Freund and Schapire, 1999b; Friedman et al., 1998). Extensive work is still in progress in a number of research groups to settle the theoretical framework of AdaBoost and to find even more powerful refinements.

7.4.1. AdaBoost Algorithm

In this paragraph, the original AdaBoost algorithm is reproduced as it was proposed by Freund and Schapire (1996) and refined in subsequent papers by the same authors and others (Freund and Schapire, 1999a; Schapire and Singer, 1999). The algorithm is given a training set of N examples $Z = \{z_i = (x_i, y_i), i = 1, \ldots, N\}$. On this set, AdaBoost maintains a weight distribution

$$W = \left\{ w(z_i) \; \middle| \; \sum_{i=1}^{N} w(z_i) = 1 \right\}$$

It is assumed that we have at hand a weak learning algorithm that guarantees a weighted training error $\varepsilon < 1/2$ for any weights distribution.

AdaBoost
Initialize: $w(z_i) = 1/N$ for all $i = 1 \ldots N$.

Do for $t = 1 \ldots T$:
1. Train the weak learner with the weighted training set $\{Z, W\}$. Obtain hypothesis $h_t(x) \in \{-1, 1\}$.
2. Calculate the weighted training error of h_t:

$$\varepsilon_t = \sum_{i=1}^{N} w_t(z_i) I[h_t(x_i) \neq y_i] \qquad (7.1)$$

3. Set the voting weight:

$$a_t = \frac{1}{2} \ln \frac{1 - \varepsilon_t}{\varepsilon_t} \qquad (7.2)$$

4. Update the weights:

$$w_{t+1}(z_i) = \frac{w_t(z_i) \exp[-y_i a_t h_t(x_i)]}{Z_t} \qquad (7.3)$$

where Z_t is a normalization constant such that

$$\sum_{i=1}^{N} w_{t+1}(z_i) = 1$$

Output: Final hypothesis

$$H(x) = \sum_{t=1}^{T} a_t h_t(x)$$

Cuendet and Labbi (2001) consider some improved versions of AdaBoost. Namely, this version only accepts Boolean hypotheses from the weak learner, whereas versions dealing with real-valued hypotheses show better performance. A multiclass AdaBoost version of the above algorithm to deal with multilabel classification problems instead of binary ones has also been derived.

7.5. BOOSTING PROJECT RISK ASSESSMENT

In this section, some experimental results obtained using boosting techniques for multiclass prediction are shown. The results for several variations of the original AdaBoost algorithm described above are presented. These variations were introduced and discussed in further detail in a separate study (Labbi and Cuendet, 2001).

To test the effectiveness of the boosting algorithm, our study focused on a project management database, which contains data entries describing various types of projects. Each entry is represented by a set of attributes that describe project demographics, financials, management, performance, etc. Among the attributes are the performance attributes one would like to estimate *a priori* so that preemptive management actions can be taken before a project encounters problems. Our prediction tasks here focus on the health of projects, but other parameters can also be predicted similarly.

The labels are the health ratings (similar to ratings of a balanced scorecard system), which are usually described by an ordered set such as {1; 2; 3; 4} or {A; B; C; D}.

The boosting methods tested here are the following (see Labbi and Cuendet [2001] for details of these algorithms):

- Plain stumps adapted to the multilabel case
- Two versions of the *favoring stumps* method
- Alternating decision trees adapted to the multilabel case

All four methods in Figure 7.4 show very similar results. The ADT reaches a minimum generalization error slightly before the plain stumps. We can say that these two methods perform 1% better on average than the favoring stumps method. This is, however, a slight difference compared to the confidence interval of 5%. An improved version of the favored stumps in the lower right-hand graph in Figure 7.4 seems to reduce the training error better than with the regular criterion. This leads, however, to an insignificant generalization improvement. The most striking feature of this lower right-hand graph is the high starting point of the boosting process (60% error rate) and the subsequent instability during the first 10 iterations.

7.5.1. Attribute Global Contribution

It is interesting from a data mining point of view to determine on which attributes the predicted labels depend the most strongly. This allows one, for example, to identify the most important risk factors. A good measure of the attribute relevance is how often in the boosting process the weak learner chooses this attribute, as well as its contribution to the final hypothesis. At a given boosting step, the confidence level of a weak hypothesis — and thus its weight in the final hypothesis — is expressed by the amplitude $|h_t(x_i)|$.

Let us consider a given attribute x, and let N be the number of examples in the training set. Let t_x represent the steps where attribute x was chosen. We define the *absolute contribution* of x, C_x^{abs}, as:

$$C_x^{\mathrm{abs}} = \frac{1}{N} \sum_{i=1}^{N} \sum_{t_x} |h_t(x_i)|$$

C_x^{abs} is the magnitude of the weak hypothesis averaged over all examples and summed over all t_x. It happens, however, that, at least for some values of the

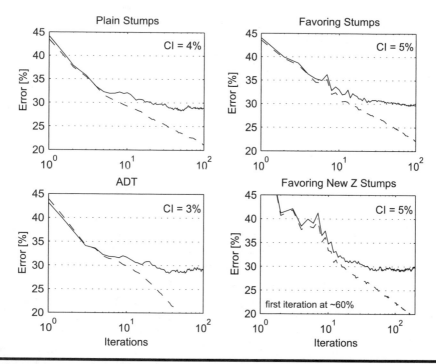

Figure 7.4. Four different boosting methods applied to the multilabel project data. The dashed line is the classification error on the training data set, and the solid line is the error on the test set, both averaged over 20 trials. The confidence intervals (CI) are also shown.

attribute, the weak hypotheses are contradictory in the voting process (i.e., they have opposite signs). In this case, their effective contribution is less, because they do not add up to a large value of $H(x_i)$. Thus C_x^{abs} is overestimated. Therefore, we introduce the *balanced contribution* of attribute x:

$$C_x^{bal} = \frac{1}{N} \sum_{i=1}^{N} \left| \sum_{t_x} h_t(x_i) \right|$$

This time we first make all the weak hypotheses of t_x vote together and get the partial final hypothesis based on attribute x. This partial hypothesis is then averaged over the N examples. In the regions where the $h_t(x_i)$ are contradictory, $\left| \sum h_t(x_i) \right|$ is smaller than $\sum |h_t(x_i)|$ (Figure 7.5). Thus $C_x^{bal} \leq C_x^{abs}$, and C_x^{bal} is a more objective measure of the contribution of the attribute x.

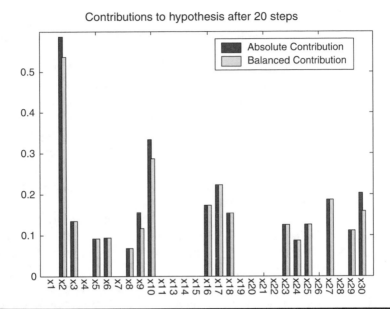

Figure 7.5. Contribution levels C_x^{abs} and C_x^{bal} of various project attributes to the prediction of project health label. These contribution levels allow one to identify the attributes (or risk factors) that have a significant impact on project health.

7.6. MONTE CARLO SIMULATION

7.6.1. Framework

For the project financial analysis study, we primarily focus on project cost and project contingency. Project cost variation is defined as the difference between approved and actual costs of the project. Using our project database, we can easily compute these entities. Similarly, contingency is defined as the percentage of the project costs that is set as a reserve budget to mitigate possible adverse events the project might face. The amount of reserved contingency is proportional to the size (total cost) of the project and the probability and severity of potential risks.

Using the database, we have defined a simple model that efficiently approximates variations in cost and contingency in the following way:

$$\Delta\text{Cost} = a(1 - \delta)AP_{\text{Cost}}$$

$$\Delta\text{Contingency} = (1 - \delta)(1 - AP_{\text{Contingency}})$$

(7.4)

The factors (a, δ) are estimated from historical data and capture the functional dependency between the planned project cost (AP_{Cost}) and contingency $(AP_{Contingency})$ and their variations.

Given historical data about a large set of projects, the second step in the proposed process is to analyze the whole set of projects and segment it into subgroups $\{G_1, G_2, ..., G_k\}$, where projects in each group (referred to below as risk groups) share certain characteristics (e.g., quality, health, etc.). In each risk group, the risk factors (a, δ) have probability distributions, which are estimated from the data. A natural task is then to characterize the membership of each project to any of these groups. This means, on the one hand, finding the most informative project features which allow one to discriminate between the different groups and, on the other hand, finding probabilistic decision rules that combine these features and assign group membership probabilities to each project. This is achieved by using a predictive modeling algorithm based on *boosted decision trees,* as described above. This allows us to estimate group membership probabilities $(p_1, p_2, ..., p_k)$ for any given project P.

In the next step of the process, we estimate the expected variation in cost and contingency for a new project P given its characteristics and its group membership probabilities $(p_1, p_2, ..., p_k)$. For cost variation, for instance, this is given by:

$$E[\Delta Cost(P)] = \sum_{j=1}^{k} \Delta Cost[P | P \in G_j] p_j \qquad (7.5)$$

where $\Delta Cost[P | P \in G_j]$ is the expected cost variation for project P, given that it belongs to risk group G_j. This is defined as:

$$\Delta Cost[P | P \in G_j] = \int_{G_j} \Delta Cost \cdot g_{a_j}(a_j) g_{d_j}(\delta_j) da_j \cdot d\delta_j$$

where $g_{a_j}(a)$ and $g_{d_j}(\delta)$ are probability density functions of factors a_j and δ_j estimated from data of projects in risk group G_j.

Equation 7.5 can be used to evaluate different cost and risk mitigation scenarios by estimating (using Equation 7.4) the expected variations in costs and contingency. The estimates can be used by the business manager to either adapt the initial plans or set up a new reserved contingency to mitigate underlying risks specific to some project risk groups.

The above-described analysis is concerned with assessing cost and contingency of a single project. A natural extension is to consider the analysis of project portfolios. This can be highly valuable in business environments where one cannot afford to take only low-risk projects but still wants to ensure some level of overall cost, risk, and value. Portfolio management techniques allow the manager to consider optimal mixes of various project profiles by carefully picking up appropriate proportions of projects from each risk group (i.e., by diversifying the portfolio structure).

Given a set Q of ongoing projects and a set P of new projects to be assessed, and using the estimates of individual projects computed earlier in Equation 7.5, the overall (cumulative) estimates for the portfolio cost variation $\Delta\text{Cost}(Q, P)$ is given by:

$$
\begin{aligned}
E[\Delta\text{Cost}] &= E[\Delta\text{Cost}(Q)] + E[\Delta\text{Cost}(P)]) \\
&= E[\Delta\text{Cost}(Q)] + \sum_i E[\Delta\text{Cost}(P_i)] \\
&= E[\Delta\text{Cost}(Q)] + \sum_i \sum_j \Delta\text{Cost}[P_i \,|\, P_i \in G_j] p(P_i \in G_j)
\end{aligned}
$$

For the ongoing projects Q, $E[\Delta\text{Cost}(Q)]$ is fixed, while $E[\Delta\text{Cost}(P)]$ varies with characteristics of projects $\{P_1, P_2, ..., P_n\}$. Such variation is reflected in the estimates of $\Delta\text{Cost}[P_i \,|\, P_i \in G_j]$ and of $p(P_i \in G_j)$.

Therefore, if we want to ensure some cost distribution over the overall portfolio, we would need to assess the new projects $\{P_1, P_2, ..., P_n\}$ and make a selection in such a way that the overall portfolio expected cost is distributed according to some desired distribution and the overall variation is within some bounds with some probability. Therefore, we use a Monte Carlo simulation process which uses prior project information to assign project probabilities p_k of membership to each group G_k and estimates the expected portfolio cost and contingency variations by sampling from each group's (a_k, δ_k) distribution proportionally to probabilities p_k.

7.6.2. Monte Carlo Algorithm

Input: A project P described by a set of features similar to those of other projects in the historical project database.

Initialize:
1. Draw two random numbers from project ΔCost and project ΔContingency distributions (if not fixed *a priori*). These can be easily estimated from historical data.

2. Estimate the probabilities $\{p_1, p_2, ..., p_n\}$ of project P membership to groups $\{G_1, G_2, ..., G_k\}$ using the predictive model discussed above (boosted decision trees).

Repeat until stop condition reached:

3. Generate a random integer i in the interval $[1, k]$ according to probability distribution $\{p_1, p_2, ..., p_n\}$.
4. Generate two random numbers, a_i and δ_i, from distributions of a and δ, respectively, for subgroup G_i. These distributions are estimated from historical data.
5. Compute the project cost and contingency variations using Equation 7.4.

Output: Draw the distribution of $\Delta\text{Cost}(P)$ and $\Delta\text{Contingency}(P)$ and estimate expected values.

We use the above simulation algorithm to estimate the expected variations for a given project P. For a portfolio of projects, the same algorithm is used for each single project, and the expected portfolio variation is merely the aggregate of the expected project variations. However, multiple factors are to be taken into account when performing a cost analysis of new projects, many of which are beyond the scope of the present analysis. Nevertheless, appropriately designed simulation techniques can provide strong insights into how to quantitatively manage and price complex project portfolios.

The portfolio part of the analysis is very important at this step since it allows the business manager to focus on the overall target instead of on single

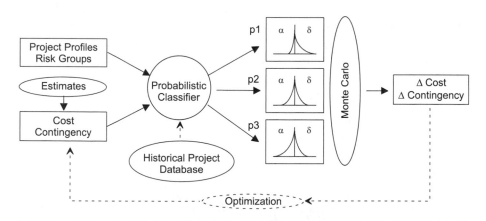

Figure 7.6. Illustration of project/portfolio cost and contingency assessment and optimization process.

projects, and therefore better assess the business performance instead of project performance.

In order to assess the validity of this predictive system (see Figure 7.6), a project portfolio database was chosen where all projects were closed (i.e., for which all the data were known, including initial and actual costs, contingency, schedules, quality, etc.). This helped in making an objective assessment of the system by comparing our predictions to what actually happened. The purpose of the test was to check the accuracy of the system's estimates versus project cost estimates provided by another system. To make the financial predictions, all available information about these projects was given to the system prior to their delivery phases. The system then delivered the expected costs at completion as well as a confidence range (standard deviation) for each project and for selected portfolios that were selected to be checked. At the end of the delivery phase of these projects (postmortem), what the system predicted was compared with what was estimated initially by another system and what actually happened at the end of the projects. Figure 7.7 shows that the expected estimate of the predictive system was within a 2% error rate of the actual cost.

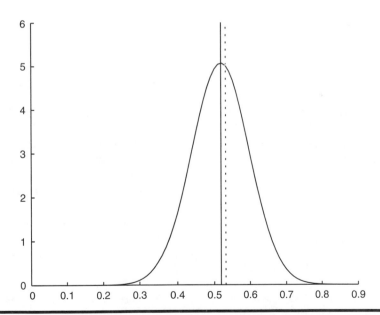

Figure 7.7. Comparison of predicted distribution (solid curve) and actual total cost (dashed vertical line) of a test project portfolio. The deviation between the average predicted portfolio total cost (solid vertical line) and the actual total cost (dashed vertical line) is around 2%.

7.7. CONCLUSION

The objective of this initial work was to show the potential of applying advanced data mining techniques in order to extract useful information to support project portfolio health management and risk assessment. Data mining techniques were used to extract the most important project characteristics and their combinations in order to segment the project portfolio into homogeneous subportfolios sharing similar features. The extracted rules provide a quantitative analysis of characteristics such as project cost and contingency. The way these characteristics combine to form similar portfolios is of great importance for the management of large portfolios of heterogeneous projects. The combination of powerful predictive modeling techniques, such as boosting, and appropriate Monte Carlo simulation allows us to derive powerful quantitative insights into the potential risks and their financial impact on portfolio health. To allow continuous improvement of such adaptive systems, special importance should be attached to gathering and maintaining additional business data sources. Significant insights could then be revealed by sophisticated data mining tools if applied appropriately.

REFERENCES

Allwein, E. L., Schapire, R. E., and Singer, Y. (2000). Reducing multiclass to binary: A unifying approach for margin classifiers, *Journal of Machine Learning Research,* 1, 113–141.

Breiman, L., Friedman, J. H., Olshen, R. A, and Stone, C. J. (1983). *CART: Classification and Regression Trees*, Wadsworth, Belmont, CA.

Cuendet, M. and Labbi, A. (2001). Some Theoretical and Practical Perspectives on Boosting Weak Predictors, IBM Research Technical Report RZ 3402, February.

Freund, Y. and Schapire, R. E. (1996). Experiments with a new boosting algorithm, in *Machine Learning: Proceedings of the Thirteenth International Conference (ICML '96)*, Bari, Italy, pp. 148–156.

Freund, Y. and Schapire R. E. (1999a). A short introduction to boosting, *Journal of the Japanese Society of Artificial Intelligence*, 14(5), 771–780.

Freund, Y. and Schapire, R. E. (1999b). Adaptive game playing using multiplicative weights, *Games and Economic Behavior*, 29, 79–103.

Friedman, J. H., Hastie, T., and Tibshirani, R. (1998). Additive Logistic Regression: A Statistical View of Boosting, Technical Report, Department of Statistics, Stanford University, Stanford, CA.

Haeckel, S. (1999). *The Adaptive Enterprise: Creating and Leading Sense and Respond Organizations*, Harvard Business School Press, Boston.

Hastie, T., Tibshirani, R., and Friedman, J. (2001). *The Elements of Statistical Learning: Data Mining, Inference, and Prediction*, Springer, New York.

Iba, W. and Langley, P. (1992). Induction of one-level decision trees, in *Proceedings of the Ninth International Machine Learning Conference, Aberdeen, Scotland*, Morgan Kaufmann, San Francisco, pp. 233–240.

Labbi, A. and Cuendet, M. (2001). Boosted Decision Trees for Risk Assessment and Pricing, IBM Research Technical Report RZ 3401, February.

Mitchell, R. A. (1999). Boosting Stumps from Positive Only Data, Technical Report UNSW-CSE-TR-9907.

Quinlan, J. R. (1998). Miniboosting decision trees (preprint), available at http://www.boosting.org/papers/Qui98.pdf.

Schapire, R. E. and Singer, Y. (1999). Improved boosting algorithms using confidence-rated predictions, *Machine Learning*, 37(3), 297–336.

ELEMENTS OF FINANCIAL RISK MANAGEMENT FOR GRID AND UTILITY COMPUTING

Chris Kenyon and Giorgos Cheliotis

8.1. INTRODUCTION

Utility models for the delivery of computation are currently appearing, driven by business needs for cost savings and increased flexibility.* Grid computing (Foster et al., 2001) is one of the technologies most in vogue for supporting this delivery, with its emphasis on open standards and support for heterogeneous and geographically dispersed platforms. However, while much attention has been paid to systems technology, there has not been a similar development in business awareness of the new environment from the point of view of financial risk. This is in strong contrast to the emphasis in conventional deregulated utilities, where risk management is seen as a core competence for the utility providers, wholesalers, and traders with an extensive literature (Pilipovic, 1997; Clewlow and Strickland, 2000; Jaillet et al., 2003).

---

* IBM "On demand computing," Sun "N1," HP "Infrastructure on tap," etc.

The aim in this chapter is to raise awareness of the importance of financial risk management for companies considering utility delivery of computation or becoming a provider, wholesaler, or trader. First, a background is provided on conventional utilities and on how computing is ordinarily seen. After establishing this background, elements important to financial risk management in utility computing are introduced. The main two elements here are delivery risk, which concerns the logical and physical design of capacity delivery, and price risk. Price risk includes availability risk, as this can be seen as just a very high price. The environment that influences and shapes these risk factors is described, as well as their importance and what can be learned from conventional utilities.

8.2. BACKGROUND: CONVENTIONAL UTILITIES AND CONVENTIONAL COMPUTING

In this section, financial risk management in conventional utilities is described. This provides a background against which to view financial risk management in conventional computing situations, which is presented next. These two situations establish reference points against which financial risk factors for grid and utility computing will be introduced.

8.2.1. Conventional Utilities

The most important conventional utility types are energy (electricity, gas, oil, coal, hydro, nuclear), communication (voice, data, fixed line, mobile), and water (drinking water, industrial-use water, wastewater). For the more developed conventional utilities (e.g., electricity or gas), financial risk management centers around the management of price risk and quantity risk.

From the point of view of financial risk management, it is also useful to segment the utility industry participants into retail users, wholesalers, and traders. Retail users generally face little or no price or quantity risks, as they typically have fixed-price variable-quantity contracts. Prices for retail users are fixed in the sense that they are known in advance with certainty, but there is often some daily or weekly variation in the price schedule. However, they face no quantity risks (e.g., when a person switches on a light, he or she always expects the required electricity to be available). Wholesale users and suppliers usually face market-determined prices and availabilities and therefore have active risk management practices. These practices quantify risks and execute strategies to mitigate those risks that the businesses do not wish to retain. Traders act to provide liquidity in utility markets where the underlying commodities are bought and sold.

In most Western countries, energy deregulation (at least for wholesale customers) is either at an advanced stage or completed, so wholesale customers do face the uncertainties of market-based prices and availabilities. However, the markets themselves can be an important source of risk. Significant problems have been encountered in the business design of some electricity markets (e.g., the United Kingdom and California), leading to their recent redesign. Deregulation in energy markets means that prices are generally available for spot contracts (immediate-use contracts) and for a range of forward contracts (i.e., reservations for later use). Again, the existence of a market does not imply that all potentially useful contracts are available in sufficient quantities when desired. Exactly which forward contracts are available depends on the particular commodity in question (gas, electricity, oil) together with the location. Gas is expensive to transport, electricity is subject to some remaining laws about interstate transmission (in most of the United States), and oil moves in tankers and pipelines. Hence, wholesalers face market risks, liquidity risks, and location risks, to name just three of the more commonly present risk factors for energy. In utility computing, these factors will also be present, but location risk will be less important, always depending on the availability of high-capacity reliable network connections between remote supply and consumption locations.

Electricity is the most common analogy used with respect to computational utilities. However, electricity is a very special commodity and utility because it embodies certain physical laws (described by Kirchoff and Maxwell) that will be respected regardless of what the market would like to happen and thus must be built in to avoid physical damage to utility system components. There is no free disposal in electricity: that is, electricity that is generated *must* go somewhere: it cannot be thrown away for free. Thus, negative real and nominal electricity prices are observed from time to time. (As an aside, negative real, but not nominal, interest rates are also observed occasionally, as in Japan in the late 1990s). Free disposal is present in computation; thus price models where prices can be negative are not required and should be avoided. This suggests that lessons from the design of electricity markets are not fully applicable, although they are very illuminating for the types of problems that can arise.

There is an enormous range of contracts used for financial risk management in conventional utilities, based on the maturity of the utility and the industries that it supports. However, the basic building blocks are the same: spot, forward, options on forwards, and swing contracts (Table 8.1). These are used as a basis from which to price any other structured contracts that wholesalers may want to hedge the financial risks resulting from the dependence of their business on a given commodity or utility.

A swing contract permits, say, five exercises over eight time periods with a maximum of two exercises at any given exercise date. It is less flexible than

Table 8.1.   Basic Commodity Contract Types

Contract	Description	Features	Sophistication	Used For
Spot	Buy now to use now	Immediacy, uncontrolled price and quantity risk	Medium	Real-time needs, fixing planning errors
Forward	Buy now to use later	Price and quantity control	Low	Base needs known in advance and with certainty
Option on forward	Buy now, decide later, use later	Price and quantity control with full flexibility	Medium	Building flexibility into plans
Swing	Buy now, decide at given number of fixed later times on limited use	Price and quantity control with limited flexibility	Medium	Building specific flexibility into plans

the same number of American-style options on forward contracts and thus cheaper. It is very common in commodity markets (e.g., gas and electricity) where only limited flexibility is required.

Electricity prices are generally set using a pooling mechanism where all supply and all demand is pooled to obtain a single price for all participants precisely to ensure an exact matching of supply and demand. Figure 8.1 gives an example. This is called a single-price auction (also used for sales of U.S. Treasury bonds since the November 2, 1998 auction). There is much literature on the details of auction formats (Krishna, 2002), but that is not the focus here. Note that supply is generally by a small number of large plants and demand is highly inelastic. In comparison, demand for computing services is intuitively more elastic, at least for batch processing.

Electricity is, outside of Scandinavian-style extensive hydro capacity, a nonstorable commodity, and this property is shared by computational utilities (capacity not used now is worthless in the next instant). This lack of inventories together with demand inelasticity implies the potential for extreme price volatility when this is not controlled by extensive use of forward contracts. However, what many electricity trading companies found out in the summers of 1999–2001 in the United States was that it was very difficult to hedge their positions because the forward markets were not deep or liquid enough. In some cases, firms have even resorted to building and buying their own generators: physical hedging. Forward contracts — reservations — are only a partial substitute for inventories. They do not change the actual amount available at any given time, so the risk of high price volatility is always present.

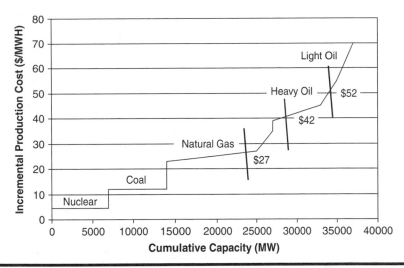

Figure 8.1. Electricity supply stack by marginal cost of production (illustrative, Florida Energy 20/20 Study Commission, 2001), and demand curves (dark lines) with resulting prices for different loads. Note that Florida does not yet have a competitive electricity market, but this has been recommended (Review of Florida's Wholesale Electricity Market, 2002).

Water is an example of a fully regulated utility with little competition. This is the case because it is viewed as a basic requirement and is so vital for both retail consumers and businesses that a market-style deregulation is simply too risky in human and political terms. However, there is the usual division, as with other utilities, into retail and wholesale use. Retail users expect water (and wastewater services) to be always available for deterministic prices, whereas wholesale users must negotiate with suppliers for long-term contracts. Computation is not at this level of wide-scale and immediate importance, so such regulation has not appeared and is not expected.

8.2.2. Conventional Computing

Conventional computing is based around boxes (i.e., hardware purchases) to satisfy given sets of business requirements that depend on the applications needed to fulfill them. What does a box look like in terms of availability, tax shield (also called depreciation), and cash flow (see Figure 8.2)? Availability is determined by downtime and maintenance. Electric equipment often becomes more reliable with age as defective parts are replaced. The end of useful life for computer hardware is often determined by incompatibility with upgrades to operating systems and the increasing relative cost of support personnel to the

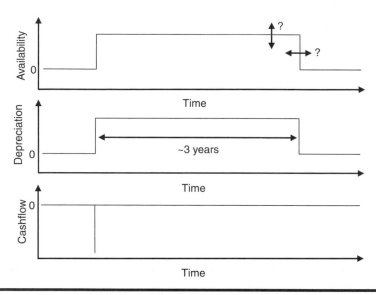

Figure 8.2. Characterization of a "box."

price per computing operation. That is, the requirements for support personnel increase with equipment life, while the power per cost becomes increasingly unattractive relative to new equipment with the same depreciation burden. Depreciation can be set against tax payments and is thus also known as a tax shield. For computer hardware, this is often three years with equal amounts in each year. Cash flow for straight purchases is just a large negative spike.

The reader should not imagine that buying boxes is completely inflexible: the computational power of a typical box is generally quite low compared with total needs, so it is possible to meet the total needs by quantity quite accurately — if these are constant. The inflexibility lies in the availability profile and cost (depreciation) of a box; these are constant for the box lifetime. Box lifetimes tend to be in the three-year range: this is one inflexibility, and the constant capacity is the other. During a box lifetime, the circuit density on new chips will typically have quadrupled, while the system personnel cost for the box will have, if anything, increased.

Information technology (IT) outsourcing, on the other hand, is basically the application of regulated-utility-type, long-term contracts to the computing needs of a company. Usually this is done with all the inflexibility that it implies; the nature of the solution has not been changed, only the identity of the computing provider.

Trying to match computing requirements with box purchases for a single set of requirements can be thought of as applying a low-pass filter to the actual computing needs; needs with a lifetime of less than a box are difficult to meet. If computing requirements are monotonic increasing, this can be done exactly (or at least w.r.t. a quantization in quantity to a box). When needs vary up and down on short time scales, matching them using boxes or conventional outsourcing contracts is simply impossible. Typically how big are these mismatches? We can get an idea from the frequently cited numbers on computer utilization: desktop, 5%; server, 35%; mainframe, 85%. This is just an indicator because we do not know whether the utilization is actually generating value or not. One way to mitigate these quantity mismatches is to buy computational capacity from external suppliers. This is common for supercomputer-type requirements but generally not practiced for other requirement areas.

While the capacity provided by boxes is inflexible, the shape of cash flow used to obtain it is not. Cash flows can be shaped either by financing companies or through the use of appropriately structured loans. The boxes themselves can be either leased long term or bought. The proper comparison of these alternatives is based on the consideration of equivalent loans and appropriate details of the tax and accounting codes. As far as a company is concerned, using a loan or a leasing company is only a matter of which gives the cheapest rate for the money. The main difference between leasing and buying is the shape of the resulting cash flow. With a purchase, there is a large negative cash flow at a single point and then a stream of depreciation allowances that can be set against tax. In leasing (or a loan), the cash flow is much more regular; in fact, the cash flow can be reshaped as desired with an appropriate financing contract structure. We will see below that cash flow shaping is important for the full exploitation of the potential flexibility of utility computing.

8.3. FINANCIAL RISK MANAGEMENT ELEMENTS IN GRID AND UTILITY COMPUTING

The conventional approach of considering risk identification, quantification, and mitigation has been adapted. Given the state of computation as a utility, most of this space will be devoted to identification and mitigation, given that data to support quantification are largely missing. Mitigation can be covered before quantification because this can address qualitative features of business design, as will be illustrated below. Before beginning, a new subclass of resources — distinct from boxes — that grid computing has highlighted will be introduced.

The greatest price risk in utility computing is simply ignorance — that is, not knowing the value of computation ("computation" is used as shorthand for boxes, networks, and storage) on the time scale at which the quantity available

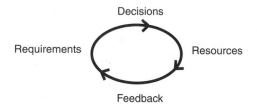

Figure 8.3.   Basic elements of the resource provisioning/requirements satisfaction loop.

can now be changed. Most companies have a good idea of their total cost of ownership (TCO) for their boxes, but no idea at all about the marginal value of a box. In fact, for almost all companies, there is no feedback loop that operates on short time scales (as compared with the lifetime of a project or a box) to validate or obtain valuations of computing resources. Figure 8.3 illustrates an information feedback loop. Information must be present on the time scale of decisions, as these are supported by the computational and business infrastructure. Given the necessity and the value of such information, it is reasonable to suppose that it will be developed. Such a mechanism by itself is not the focus of this chapter — what to do with the information is. Once prices and values can be obtained, then risks can be quantified.

The basic risks in utility computing are price and availability/demand. To some extent, all risks are price risks since availability can be rephrased in terms of prices; for example, no (timely) availability can be considered as some arbitrarily high price, and no demand can be considered as an available price of zero. However, it is useful to consider the two aspects specifically because we are concerned with scarce resources, so quantities are highly important. (This is unlike the case for many liquid stocks, or some commodities,* where quantity is relatively unimportant.) Resources are scarce in computation where there are applications that could potentially fill all available resources at some point in time. In some domains, the applications can potentially fill all resources all the time (e.g., life sciences and some energy applications such as seismic imaging). Hence the need for flexible and dynamic prioritization schemes (prices).

Because utility computing is still developing and has an initial resemblance to regulated utilities (despite its *potential* for deregulation), it is necessary to go into depth with respect to where price mechanisms will exist and how they will work. Recall also the price-quantity curves used in electricity markets:

---

* Quantity is important for at least one index commodity, Brent Crude, where the actual supply is quite limited and hence the price is potentially susceptible to manipulation by individual market participants.

value is not uniquely defined; prices are those values where two (or more) parties actually agree to a transaction. Given that there are no large-scale requirements that all transactions pass through a single pool (the case with electricity), it is possible to have several prices or price discovery mechanisms operating within an infrastructure. Additionally, the main subject of these price discovery mechanisms will be forward prices (i.e., reservations). How these interact is a function of the delivery architecture, as we shall see.

Prior to the existence of a public market for computation as a commodity — still many years away — companies need price discovery mechanisms whether they are on the delivery side or on the consumption side in order to assign resources to needs efficiently. There is a tension between having a single or a small number of providers, perhaps with long-term contracts, and having a price discovery mechanism. This paradox must be resolved for the full technical and economic potential of utility computing to be achieved. Again this interacts strongly with the delivery setup (i.e., number of providers, number of users, contention resolution mechanisms, prices, contract structures). There is space for significant development of appropriate concepts here, which this chapter also aims to stimulate.

Wholesale users of any utility are familiar with the limits imposed by suppliers. A recent example was the carrier hotel phenomenon aimed at providing a communications-carrier-neutral environment for selling hosting space. This was often physical space for racks with HVAC and physical security rather than Web hosting where computational capacity is made available. Operators of these carrier hotels forecast very high power requirements (megawatts). Local electricity suppliers required the operators to bear the (downside) risk of new power generation facilities and additional high-voltage power lines to serve these facilities. (In practice, the value proposition of carrier hotels has been overestimated and many went bankrupt.)

8.3.1. Delivery Risk Factors

Figure 8.4 describes the different delivery scenarios for utility computation. Each has a different distribution of delivery risks affecting execution, price, and availability.

8.3.1.1. Single Entity

In this scenario, all of a company's computational resources are accessed in a unitary manner with a common transparent price discovery mechanism (i.e., all participants have equal access to price information). Prices are available for both reservations (forwards) and immediate use (spots).

Delivery Scenario	Description/Variations
	Single Entity: Base Scenario This envisages that the resources within an entity form a unitary computing on-demand utility. *Variations:* ■ Exchange methods between budget entities within company
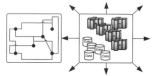	**Entity + Provider** Here some resources are available from an external provider that serves many customer companies. The company may also be running a computing-on-demand facility combining internal resources. *Variations:* ■ Many providers ■ Sale to provider ■ Combination methods between external and internal sources and control within
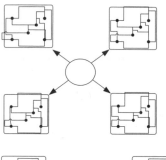	**Group of Entities** All the variants derive from how resources are shared among the group and whether there is even a group or merely many bilateral arrangements. *Variations:* ■ Exchange methods within group ■ Combination methods between external and internal sources
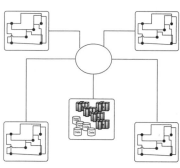	**Group + Provider** The difference between this scenario and "company + provider" is that there is an explicit sharing agreement between the members of the group and a relationship between that sharing arrangement and the provider, which may or may not be explicit. *Variations:* ■ Many providers ■ Exchange methods within group ■ Combination methods between external and internal sources ■ Combination between group resources and provider

Figure 8.4. Delivery scenarios for utility computing.

There are many variations within this scenario depending on whether and how resale is permitted. For example, must all sales go via the central price mechanism or are side deals permitted? Who guarantees trades, individual participants or the IT department? Who monitors the system to prevent excessive gaming of it? (It is unreasonable to assume that there will be no gaming given its presence in commercial commodity markets; regulators are only interested when it becomes excessive.) Clearly, if the central mechanism is not well designed, human ingenuity will immediately create a parallel "gray market" for resources. Equally, a further consequence of poor design will be that users go back to buying boxes and having private resources that the central price mechanism never sees. Basically, poor system design will lead to its practical irrelevance whatever the theoretical benefits of a central clearing point. These comments are also applicable to the other scenarios discussed.

8.3.1.2. Entity + Provider

The main difference here is the existence of the provider (i.e., an external utility) as an alternative supplier to the internal computational resources of the company. Typically, a single external utility will interact with the company as a whole according to a long-term contract. All the usual long-term contracts in Table 8.1 have predefined prices for specific quantities. That is, the long-term provider commits to prices and quantities (which may be defined by specific and even time-varying functions) in advance. The long-term contract is not a commitment to a dynamic price *mechanism*. This makes price discovery potentially highly inefficient; hence the use of a dual system: an internal dynamic mechanism with an external static mechanism. Basically, the internal prices can be used to discover whether the external provider's resources are financially attractive at any given point. There is certainly a cost associated with their availability, but there is also a need to obtain a short-term valuation of resources.

So far, no external resource provider in IT has (to the knowledge of the authors) committed itself to a price discovery mechanism — unlike the case for, say, electricity. This is an example of the aforementioned tension between long-term contracts and short-term fluctuations in needs. Long-term contracts can be quantity flexible, with price as a function of quantity, but this is a very blunt instrument with which to discover price. This statement requires some explanation because it may appear that a single price-quantity curve is quite sufficient for price discovery. The problem with a long-term contract is precisely this provision of only *one* price-quantity curve over a long period (i.e., a constant price for a given total quantity). However, the opportunity cost of that quantity

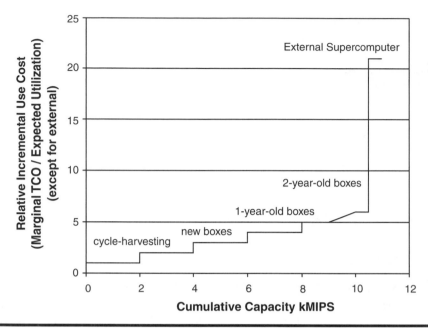

Figure 8.5. Hypothetical marginal cost of computation by (marginal TCO/expected utilization) assuming utility setup for single-entity delivery. Note that the curve is almost flat relative to conventional external resources. Roughly 10% of TCO is hardware cost; hardware speed doubles every 18 months. TCO for cycle harvesting is dominated by license and personnel costs.

will vary, possibly considerably, over this time. For example, processing overnight may be much more valuable than processing during the day for some groups (because results are then available for analysis during working hours). Note that two other factors must be added to clarify this argument. First, there may be sufficient demand (ignoring price) to fill all available capacity. Second, for running computers, the marginal cost for computation is almost zero (power cost difference between "on" and "on and computing" is very low compared to TCO for a box). A supply stack similar to that in Figure 8.1 but for computation in a single-entity delivery setting is shown in Figure 8.5 based on marginal TCO/expected utilization. This marginal cost metric is used because these factors are the most important ones. They are present for electricity generators, but the marginal fuel costs are far greater, and so are the ones that are modeled. This is only a first approximation for a good marginal cost model, and again, this is an active area for research. An important thing to note is that as markets switch from regulated to competitive, prices switch from monopoly based to cost/performance based. Thus, as utility computing becomes effectively competitive, these sorts of supply stacks will start to dominate the industry and pricing arrangements.

Typically there is no provision in long-term contracts for local reservations (forward contracts) on short time scales, which seriously inhibits the move to utility style use within a company. These limitations of long-term contracts are *potentially* resolvable, but in the meantime hybrid schemes as described here will be effective.

8.3.1.3. Group of Entities

Here a (closed) group of companies share resources on a price basis; that is, they use a common clearinghouse of price information to allocate resources. This is very similar to how conventional commodity exchanges work in that the major risks are borne by the participants in a symmetric manner. The variations in this scenario depend on how exactly prices are set: whether the central clearinghouse provides only information or whether it also provides a price-setting mechanism. There is also the question of whether the central clearinghouse can take positions in resources and whether it has any resources under its direct control, say a buffer of a given percentage of the total quantity for liquidity.

There is enormous potential for conflicts of interest in this situation, and essentially this is the basic business driver: the resolution through prices of conflicting requests for resources. Note that resources are both bought and sold by all participants. Because of this basic business driver, it may be useful to have some overall long-term agreement between the parties about the degree of participation. Extensive modeling is also indicated to judge how such a system would work in practice and to reveal potential gaming strategies. However, this is likely to always be better than the alternative of all the companies working independently because of the greater potential pool of resources available to each. The warnings in this section are directed primarily at setting the expectations of the participants to realistic levels concerning what such collaboration can produce.

With a group of entities rather than a single entity, although it may appear that the situation is very similar, there is now the risk of counterparty default with a potentially less well-defined authority to survey matters. Within a single company, swift resolution is potentially possible in ways that are beyond the scope of a loose collection of collaborating companies. There is significant scope here for misset expectations that require exploration.

With this situation, there is also the possibility that the central clearinghouse acts as a profit center and aims to make as much profit as possible from the contributing entities while offering prices that are competitive with what each company could do individually. These profits could then be redistributed to the contributing companies, say in proportion to their individual investments in TCO terms.

8.3.1.4. Group + Provider

This final scenario generalizes the previous three. Again, there may be many providers, but the key factor of this scenario is the use of price discovery mechanisms within the group as a means to select when to use resources from the external provider(s) in order to circumvent the rigidity inherent in most long-term utility-like contracts.

The organization of the group and the mechanism of interaction between the group and the provider constitute the variations on the basic idea. It may even be the case that the provider takes over the running and maintenance of all the computational resources, but the price to use and other responsibilities (e.g., for cost recovery) remain with the owners.

8.3.2. Price Risk Factors

8.3.2.1. Spot Prices

The main risks are always price and availability/demand. Depending on the delivery method, there may be several prices available or, to be more exact, there may be several price-quantity curves on offer from different sources: entities, group members, external providers, etc. It may be up to individual entities to synthesize the composite spot price-quantity curve that is actually available to them, or there may be a central clearinghouse that is assigned this task with agreement of all the parties. However, given that computation is nonstorable, high price volatility can be expected in the sport market. Additionally, although marginal TCO price-quantity curves may be very flat, providers that expect available capacity to be exhausted may simply price to "what the market will bear," as happens in all competitive markets. (This is, of course, precisely when they become noncompetitive!) The design of supply bids is both an art and a science to obtain maximum advantage.

8.3.2.2. Forward Prices

Forwards can be arranged by multiple bilateral deals or, alternatively, again through a central clearinghouse. Whatever the method, forward contracts will always be bought at different times, so there is no simple way to ensure a single price — even if it was desirable — for all purchases of capacity for a given date. Single prices (everyone pays the same) for spot purchases are possible by using a clearinghouse, as in electricity (single-price auction for multiple identical items).

One way of constructing forward prices could be to simply use the same price-quantity curves as for spot pricing. The effect would be similar to using a discriminatory version of the standard single-price auction. In bond markets, where both auction methods have been tried for spot purchases, the evidence is mixed (Sunnevag, 2001) as to whether in practice this results in significant material differences in expected revenue. Using discriminatory auctions directly could have some negative effects in that early purchases would be rewarded, thus encouraging purchase even when there was no certainty of use. In addition, for delivery setups where there are many entities and providers, the price-quantity supply curve would not necessarily be fixed. This is even true for the single-entity case given that gradual changes in total capacity can be expected based on changing business needs as forecast by the IT department and as suggested by feedback through spot and forward prices. However, approximate simple solutions for forward price mechanisms are certainly possible, although this is currently an open area for research.

8.3.2.3. Prices for Options on Forwards

Options on forwards are a basic building block for flexible contracts on nonstorable commodities. Because of nonstorability, forward contracts are primary tradables; that is, they cannot be priced from spot contracts using arbitrage arguments. (Note also that transaction costs are expected to be relatively low in a computational utility.) Options on forwards can be priced as usual by arbitrage arguments (comparison with a combination of a forward contract and a riskless security), provided so-called "ruthless" exercise is assumed (Jaillet et al., 2003). That is, the option will always be exercised for maximum financial advantage. This can also be used as the basis for pricing swing options. Ruthless exercise is questionable in practice for consumption commodities, gas in particular. It will be interesting to see how such pricing develops for computation. It may be that exercise will be ruthless in systems that are always fully utilized (which may occur in life sciences, energy, etc.).

8.3.2.4. Cash Flow Risk

Utility delivery of services can enable businesses to have huge spikes in use capacity to meet huge business opportunities. This can produce short-term cash flows that are unacceptable from an operational point of view even though the business opportunities are highly attractive. However, financing can flatten back the resulting cash flow spikes to something more acceptable from an accounting point of view. Thus, financing and utility delivery of infrastructure capability play complementary roles. Cash flow shaping has always been a basic value proposition of financing in utility computing and has long been recognized by the leading IT players (e.g., HP Financing, IBM Global Financing, GE Capital). This shaping comes at a cost, which in turn adds to the complexity of risk management for utility computing.

8.3.2.5. Volatility Risk

Fundamentally, computational resources (which is used as a shorthand for computation, storage and network) are capacity-type resources and hence nonstorable. This has been stated several times in this chapter because it is such a fundamental characteristic of grid/utility computing. What this means is the potential for very high spot-price volatilities, as seen in wholesale electricity markets in Australia, California, and Texas in the past few years. This has been studied in detail (especially California, see page 22 of California Independent System Operator Market Design 2002 Project [2002]: "Root Causes of California's Electricity Crisis"), and it is worth spending a little time on understanding the causes of this volatility because there is a lot that can be learned from these examples. It would be very rash to assume that these *cannot* be present in commercial computational utilities.

Table 8.2 summarizes these root causes and gives the equivalents, where present, for grid/utility computing. Clearly, these risks will be more or less present depending on the delivery method for computation, listed in Figure 8.4. Regrettably, it is difficult to argue that *any* of these risks will *not* be present in commercial grid/utilities. Fortunately, we do have the electricity market experience of failure together with the recommended remedies (Comprehensive Market Redesign, Design Concepts, 2002) to assist in the design of computational utilities.

8.3.2.6. Correlation Risk

Successful (i.e., profitable) provision of utility computing depends on scale and a lack of correlation between individual computational demands. Execution and delivery risks are always present, but the ability to offer computational utilities competitively depends very simply on aggregating (de)correlated loads. Understanding the drivers of correlation and methods to control the effects of correlation is vital for the provider. How big is big enough? "Enough" means that the prices are acceptable to buyers and profitable for the provider. Given loads and a correlation structure, we can answer this exactly. However, will all the potential participants join in? Will the provider be able to induce the participants

Table 8.2. Price Volatility Risk: Root Causes of California's Electricity Market Crisis (California Independent System Operator Market Design 2002 Project, 2002) and Equivalent Risks for Grid/Utility Computing

Electricity Market Failure Root Causes	Grid/Utility Computing Equivalent	Comments
Tight supply conditions in system	Not enough capacity	Direct analogy
Tight supply conditions in neighboring systems	Not enough spare capacity available from external providers or from members of group	Direct analogy
Underscheduling of forward market, leading to difficult and unreliable operation	No planning	That is, underuse of reservations
Lack of demand responsiveness due to a. Limited technical capability for real-time price responsiveness b. Insufficient forward contracting for energy c. Ambiguous accountability for reasonably priced power acquisition for retail consumers	■ End users unable to react to prices because of inadequate planning and accounting systems ■ Lack of adequate process and planning tools to support users and managers ■ Poorly defined accountability for user satisfaction	Direct analogy Prices not passed along to end users to permit them to react Real-time price feedback mechanisms linked (or not) to accounting systems totally absent from almost all current internal, outsourced, or external computational systems
Exercise of market power	Same, e.g., from dependence on single external provider	Alignment of business priorities between competing business units important
Inadequate transmission capacity	■ Insufficient bandwidth ■ Insufficient control of available bandwidth ■ Lack of integration of bandwidth prices into computation and storage price to form integrated products for applications	Often overlooked Requirement depends on application mix
Inadequate market rules to ensure schedule feasibility	Lack of rules to combat gaming of system	Need immediate financial penalties for breach of contract, similar to credit derivative instruments

to decorrelate their loads? What is the cost of service failure? This can be included in contracts in a formal way, but education and acceptance are required for oversubscription to be an option that providers can really exercise. In some cases, this may be acceptable, especially when it is the existing practice in an industry/application setting.

To continue the analogy with electricity, the correlation risk suffered by those markets was temperature: a heat wave caused millions of people to turn on their air conditioners, which overloaded the power system. This was also due to inadequate previous investments, which were caused in turn by a lack of competitive (i.e., attractive for utility builders) prices and uncertainty on the regulatory front. Again, it is easy to see analogies to utility computing.

Correlation risk for utility computing will be application and location dependent. Let us take the example of a utility to support the computation of seismic imaging for oil exploration. Suppose a utility was built to serve oil companies operating in the North Sea, and then, say, the Norwegian government put out a licensing round together with raw seismic data to help companies decide what to bid for an exploration license. *All* the interested companies in the area would want to analyze the data — with their own proprietary algorithms — at the same time. Note that the quality of imaging algorithms is a business differentiator in this industry. A utility with such a geographical focus would face a very large correlation risk. An alternative utility would be one within a single multinational company: the correlation risk between *different* governments announcing licensing rounds is significantly lower — and subject to lobbying — whereas the former situation has no obvious mitigation strategy as far as the *utility* is concerned.

Correlation risk can be mitigated by careful contract design that offers incentives (i.e., lower prices) for more flexibility where control of the flexibility is given to the provider. Thus, long-deadline contracts should be less expensive than contracts where work must be performed between specific times.

8.3.2.7. Credit Risk

Credit, or counterparty, risk is present whenever there are different budget and/ or legal entities involved in a deal. This is defined as default on the timely (as specified by contract) delivery of a (computational) service on the one hand and default on the timely payment for such service on the other hand. Legal contracts internal to a company are not possible because there is only one legal entity, so risks must be secured against higher management intervention. Credit risks between different legal entities are no different in concept from computational commodities changing hands as opposed to other commodities. However, there are essential differences in that the commodities of interest —

computation — are nonstorable and also are not transported to where they are used but rather are used *in situ*. For direct transactions, there is less control possible from the purchaser's point of view and more control from the seller's point of view: if the purchaser defaults, the equipment can simply be returned to the available pool at the click of a mouse. For resale, the picture is complicated by the presence of the third party where the physical infrastructure resides. In addition, this third party may be either of the original two. These delivery factors will affect credit risks and hence prices.

Should the credit rating of the computational service be the same as that of the delivering company? Generally, no, because execution risk is mixed with the financial default risk for credit/counterparty risk in this situation. The key here is the understanding of "timely." A company may deliver something sometime, but timely delivery is vital in service industries. Even with no formal rating, prices are likely to be shaded in practice to reflect the reputation of the delivering party.

What should the credit rating of the receiving party (end user) be? This depends on how the service is being paid and the scale of the service agreements in place. In many cases with utility computing, capacity purchases will be financed (using loans or via a financing company) and the financing part will factor the creditworthiness of the receiving party into the cost of the financing.

8.4. FINANCIAL RISK MANAGEMENT EXAMPLES IN UTILITY COMPUTING

In this section, a few early industrial examples of potential interest for risk management in utility computing are examined because of high computational requirements and flexibility needs. Then some of their risk factors are outlined. Many industries that depend on computation lose money because they cannot optimally respond to dynamic changes in loads. Three of the most extreme — and real — examples are given. First the applications are summarized:

1. **Energy**: Seismic processing to image subsurface features in order to respond to licensing opportunities. Governments lease oil and gas exploration and production rights to companies in return for license fees and production charges. The recent trend is for there to be less and less time between the request for bids and the closing of the request period. This is now in the range of a few months and often less. In order to prepare bids, companies process the information made available by the government. These are often seismic studies, which are processed to make images of the subsurface that can then be examined for potentially valuable

features. Seismic data sets are generally large (on the order of terabytes) and take weeks to months to process. The processing time depends on both the size of the data sets and the processing algorithms. The more sophisticated, and potentially more accurate, methods take increasingly long times. Depending on the algorithm used, these problems can be more or less easily parallelized. The value of an oil field ranges from the billions of dollars on up. The infrastructure problem is to obtain computing capacity as needed for uncertain dates and total requirements. For super-majors, capacity requirements can potentially be handled internally, but smaller companies have no current solution.

2. **On-line gaming**: Sizing game infrastructure to meet customer numbers. Although only a tiny fraction of the current digital gaming market (which is larger than the film and video sectors combined), this has the potential for enormous growth. Growth drivers include the introduction of compelling new games (e.g., Everquest, Ultima), Internet access for consoles (present on the Xbox and adaptors available for Nintendo GameCube and Sony PlayStation 2), and adaptations of popular existing games. Everquest by Electronic Arts had about 500,000 paying subscribers at the end of 2002, and plans were announced to ship one million units of The Sims Online through October 2002. NPD Funworld* reported that two on-line titles were the best-selling games in September 2002 (The Sims Online was in first place). IDC and Jupiter both predicted roughly 50% annual compound growth over the next three years, to reach $1.5 billion in 2005. However, the responses to individual games have proved difficult to predict. The main problem for now is how to size infrastructure initially and then how to respond to changes quickly depending on specific game success with new releases.

3. **Interactive TV game shows and advertising responses**: Processing SMS messages, call-ins and Web hits. TV game shows can allow the home audience to participate by Web voting and in other interactive ways using telephones by dialing given numbers or using SMS messages with specific content. Each call generates revenue for the telephone companies that support the shows. However, the number of calls and the required processing capacity can exceed what the telephone companies support, and it is often not economical to support the peak capacity for these applications given their use for such short periods. TV and other (e.g., the Super Bowl) advertising can include Web sites where products can be found and bought. In one example,** traffic increased by a factor

---

   * http://www.npdfunworld.com.
  ** http://www.radware.com/content/press/articles/victorias.asp.

Table 8.3. Application Capacity Requirements and Temporal Characteristics for Seismic Imaging, Massively Multiplayer Games, and TV Call-in for Telephone Network Operators

	Requirements					
Application	Storage	Network	Computation	Duration	Deadline	Comments
Imaging	High	High	High	Continuous for weeks to months	Yes	Algorithms limited by computation capacity
On-line games	Low	Medium	Medium	Continuous for weeks to months	Real time	Individual sessions last hours
TV games	Low	Low	Medium	Minutes to hours	Yes	Very low requirements per message

of 1000, and in the highest interest period, only 2% of visitors could gain access. The response to such advertising has proved difficult to predict, and again, there is a direct connection between available capacity limits and missed revenue.

Table 8.3 describes the application characteristics in these three domains. Table 8.4 lists the structure of demand and correlation drivers for computational requirements. Network requirements are significant for two of these applications and computation is for all of them. Storage is a driving factor only in seismic imaging, where it dominates the utility design: a random grid would be completely unable to support an imaging application with any sort of efficiency.

Given the nature of correlation drivers in these industries, it makes sense to ask whether utilities for within-industry sharing would be better replaced by between-industry sharing. Seismic is an exception to this given the stringent design constraints required to ensure efficient operation: here the best decorrelator at first glance is within-company sharing rather than between-company sharing (aggregation). For on-line gaming support, the key is to have a sufficient set of different games, or rather games in different phases of exploitation: first release, developing, mature, and declining. It may also be useful to choose sets of games where the players are in different demographics, but this is likely to be a second-order factor until appropriate games for daytime audiences are developed and successful. TV call-ins have little possibility for decorrelation within a particular show because of the real-time, and brief, nature of the

Table 8.4. Demand and Correlation Structure of Applications for Seismic Imaging, Massively Multiplayer Games, and TV Call-in for Telephone Network Operators

Application	Demand Driver	Alternate Demand Drivers within a Single Company	Correlation Drivers for Application	Correlation Location
Imaging	RFB, licensing, development, 4D	Nondeadline imaging and reservoir simulation	All companies replying to RFB	Temporal, geographic
On-line games	New games, events within games	Older games	All players on game, reaction to game events, seasonal	Temporal
TV games	Shows	Network maintenance, billing	All viewers	Geographical/ temporal

application. However, simply arranging not to have contracts with multiple shows during the same viewing hour seems a simple and obvious decorrelation strategy.

8.5. SUMMARY AND CONCLUSIONS

In this chapter, some key elements of financial risk management for utility computing, which naturally need further development, were identified. Financial risk management is first about price and availability risks for volatile business needs on the one side and managing the conflicting needs across different parts of a company or different companies on the other (provider) side. Financial risk management is also required to quantify and mitigate the tension between long-term, utility-type contracts on the one hand and the need for flexibility to meet short-term business needs on the other. This is significantly different from the flexibility typically built into long-term outsourcing contracts because it is required on time scales that are several orders of magnitude shorter. New concepts, relative to outsourcing, are also required to manage planning across such short time scale volatility (i.e., reservations and their required price discovery mechanisms). Finally, in a further difference from conventional computing, the number of budget entities and legal entities is significantly increased in the grid/utility context.

REFERENCES

California Independent System Operator Market Design 2002 Project (2002). Comprehensive Market Design, Proposal, April 19 (http://www.caiso.com/docs/2002/04/19).

Clewlow, L. and Strickland, C. (2000). *Energy Derivatives Pricing and Risk Management*, Lacima Publications, London.

Comprehensive Market Redesign, Design Concepts (2002). California ISO, August 23 (http://www.caiso.com/docs/2002/08/23).

Florida Energy 20/20 Study Commission (2001). December, p. 27.

Foster, I., Kesselman, C., and Tuecke, S. (2001). The anatomy of the grid: Enabling scalable virtual organizations, *International Journal of High Performance Computing Applications,* 3(15), 200–222.

Jaillet, P., Ronn, E., and Tompaidis, S. (2003). Valuation of Commodity-Based Swing Options, Working Paper, University of Texas, Austin; under revision for *Management Science,* January.

Kamat, R. and Oren, S. S. (2002). Exotic options for interruptible electricity supply contracts, *Operations Research,* 50(5).

Krishna, V. (2002). *Auction Theory*, Academic Press, New York.

Pilipovic, D. (1997). *Energy Risk: Valuing and Managing Energy Derivatives*, McGraw-Hill, New York.

Raikar, S. and Ilic, M. D. (2001). Interruptible Physical Transmission Contracts for Congestion Management, Working Paper EL 01-010 WP, Laboratory for Energy and the Environment, Massachusetts Institute of Technology, Cambridge, February.

Review of Florida's Wholesale Electricity Market (2002). Report 2002-147, Committee on Regulated Industries.

Sunnevag, K. J. (2001). Auction Design for the Allocation of Multiple Units of a Homogeneous Good: Theoretical Background and Practical Experience, Working Paper, Department of Economics, University of California at Santa Barbara, June 11.

SERVICE LEVEL AGREEMENTS FOR WEB HOSTING SYSTEMS

Alan J. King and Mark S. Squillante

9.1. INTRODUCTION

In an accelerating trend, corporations of all sizes are outsourcing their information technology infrastructure to service companies. Basic services offered range from shelf-space rental, electricity, air conditioning, and network bandwidth to the provision and maintenance of servers, storage, middleware, help centers, and deskside support. These are the first steps toward a "computing utility" in which computing services are delivered "on demand" like energy, communication, transportation, and other commodity services.

The economic pressures underlying this trend are many. On the customer side, oversubscription to accommodate peak usage requirements substantially increases fixed costs, and isolated information technology departments find it difficult to match the economies of scale that service providers have in plant, equipment refresh rates, personnel skill development, and software infrastructure. On the provider side, Moore's Law improvements on cost and performance together with the steady enrichment and standardization of middleware make it possible to supply a network in which excellent computing resources can be distributed cheaply and securely. But Moore's Law also cuts the other way. The slowdown in equipment refresh rates for both hardware and software, the inexorable decrease in unit profits, and the huge fixed costs of technical leadership strongly motivate industry leaders to move to a services provision model with its steady payments and opportunity for increased profits through bundling.

The future of the computing utility is today very much in the making. There is evidence that the market may desire specialized solution offerings such as human resources, payroll, procurement, supply chain, e-mail, Web hosting, data storage, numerically intensive computing, etc., all of which may depend on predictable contracts for the underlying computing infrastructure. Commoditized computing elements together with very high global bandwidth capacity may encourage the development of exchanges like those in the energy or telecommunications industries. Finally, as the industry confronts the days of reckoning for the current wave of outsourcing agreements, competitive pressures will undoubtedly lead to industry-wide standards for service agreements.

9.1.1. Requirements for Service Contracts

Current approaches to managing contracts for computing utilities are necessarily naive, since there is very little in the way of practical experience to guide the parties. A straightforward outsourcing contract simply takes over the customer's entire computing infrastructure, including personnel, under a business case that is based on anticipated savings from labor economies and Moore's Law effects. The risks in these contracts are addressed largely by extending the contract duration and consequently postponing the day of reckoning with the customer's cost reduction and quality of service (QoS) expectations. Slightly more sophisticated agreements may contemplate the shared usage of network bandwidth, hosting facilities, and possibly service personnel.

A computing utility is more complex than an electric or a telephone utility. Peak loads are often many orders of magnitude greater than average loads. Performance of service personnel or installations also vary over many orders of magnitude for a multitude of interacting causes. Performance measurements are not standard or easily described, measured, or predicted. Even the unit of usage is not standardized. Finally, and perhaps most importantly, actual payment for services is made on behalf of users by the customer — who will require evidence that its users are being well treated. This evidence will necessarily be statistical in nature and will be averaged over long time intervals in order to develop reasonable QoS estimates.

This chapter discusses the requirements and features of a service level agreement (SLA) between the computing utility and the customer in such a complex service environment. It is a discussion that is intended to outline basic issues and models. Section 9.2 presents basic concepts of workload measurements, charging, accommodating QoS requirements, and so forth. Section 9.3 discusses issues concerning the management of portfolios of SLA contracts.

Section 9.4 is a study of the issues arising in a particular type of contract in which customers purchase a committed level of service and pay a differential rate for bursts above this level. Finally, Section 9.5 envisions an SLA in which customers may place bids for service above the base level.

9.2. SERVICE LEVEL AGREEMENTS

The computing utility and a customer enter into a contract, or SLA, that specifies properties of the QoS performance measurements and the contract incentives and billing. Typically, these are long-term agreements that include test bed measurements and phase-in periods to collect the types of data needed to develop some of the elements of the SLA. In addition, periodic monitoring and assessment must take place to adapt the infrastructure and SLA to inevitable changes in workloads over time.

The SLA specifies how the QoS measurements are to be taken, the customer's estimate of normal and peak loads, and how the customer is charged or compensated. More formally, an SLA should contain three types of provisions:

- Satisfactory versus unsatisfactory QoS measurements
- Normal versus exceptional workloads
- Notifications, actions required or allowed, and charging under various loads and QoS conditions

The first type of provision reflects the customer's desire to obtain satisfactory levels of QoS. The second type addresses the provider's need to be protected against unexpected demands on the resource pool. The third sets out the general obligations and permissions of the parties to the contract.

Provisions of the SLA will generally be defined using terms from the following three categories:

1. **QoS metric**: Utilization, response time, and/or throughput measured at various points in the service network
2. **Statistical measures**: Averages or expectations, peaks, quantiles, moments, tail probabilities, etc., together with the sample space over which such measures are calculated
3. **Financial/contractual**: Charging rates, penalties, and circumstances under which actions may be taken and/or prices and units may be changed

Examples of such provisions are the customer must be able to successfully ping the Web site 99.99% of the time, measured response times between certain network nodes must be less than three seconds 95% of the time, and so forth, where the sample space for these statistics is commonly defined as the QoS statistic's average value during each five-minute interval in the billing period, usually one month.

9.2.1. Workload Measurement

At the foundation of the SLA is the definition of the workload and its corresponding metrics and statistical measurements. At the rawest level, one can examine http logs to estimate request arrival and file size distributions as a proxy for the workload. This type of workload analysis is probably useful in forecasting utilization rates, but it very likely does not say much about the user experience, since the most obvious type of user QoS metric is the response time. In today's complex middleware environments, the detailed analysis of what level of equipment provision contributed to what part of the response time measurement is very difficult, if not impossible. Moreover, many http logs actually record the departure time rather than the arrival time for each request.

A straightforward approach that does not require middleware session modeling is to define a simple set of standard user sessions and use them to ping the system periodically. Metrics such as response times and throughput measurements can be generated. In addition, one can monitor utilization levels on key pieces of equipment (servers, routers). Correlations between utilization levels and standard user session performance statistics can be drawn over time or derived in a test bed environment. Then, provided the workload mix does not change, one can set utilization *QoS thresholds* as a proxy for response time QoS.

A combination of the simple session ping records and the equipment utilization logs may be sufficient to construct a time series of workload QoS measurements for the purposes of an SLA. Otherwise, more sophisticated methods will likely be required.

9.2.2. Charging for Resources

In the computing utility service model, the promise is that resources may be brought on-line when required to maintain a QoS. The canonical resources in this type of thinking are a rack-mounted CPU or a network-attached disk pack. But there are other types of resources involved in the computing utility. There are the various elements of the network, from the Internet itself through the network access router to the local area network and even the internal network serving the rack itself. There are service personnel of all flavors, from system administrators to Web page programmers. There are backup facilities, tape robots, the subsystems of the building housing the hosting facility itself, and so forth.

One of the key distinctions is whether the resource is "assigned" to the user or whether the resource is "shared." The natural charging unit for assigned resources is the *utilization*, the metric for the percentage of the resource actually used. The adoption of this charging unit protects the customer from paying for unused capacity, which is important when the service provider controls the assignment of resources. For shared resources, the natural charging unit is the *throughput*. Throughput is a metric for the number of bytes transmitted or the number of jobs processed.

For both styles of charging, one also must consider the QoS received. In Web hosting, the universally adopted metric is the response time. In the case of utilization charging, response time can be accommodated by imposing an upper bound on the utilization threshold — meaning that the user may not be charged for utilization levels that degrade the agreed response time. When charging is done on a per-transaction basis, then compensation may be based on the actual response time achieved.

Customers that are assigned resources actually receive a more complex service than just the usage of a particular piece of equipment for a time interval. They also benefit from a resource shared across all customers: namely, an inventory of equipment sufficient to permit customers to get resources "on demand." As with many service examples, someone renting equipment actually purchases a bundle of services. Although the charging unit is essentially related to utilization, the pricing structure will include compensation for all these services.

9.2.3. Quality-of-Service-Adjusted Charging

When the system does not satisfy the agreed QoS, then the SLA must address this in some way. One natural way to do this for throughput charging is to impose a penalty on the service provider, such as a penalty charge for each throughput unit that was handled with an unsatisfactory QoS. In the case of utilization charging, it would be more natural to handle this in terms of utilization QoS thresholds.

As noted in the previous subsection, QoS-related concerns may limit the desirable utilization to a threshold fraction that is somewhat less than 1. Scaling the utilization by this number produces a metric, the *QoS-adjusted utilization*, which takes the value 1 for "full" utilization, that is, for the highest utilization consistent with the QoS. This scaling can be tuned to reflect the different performance characteristics of different classes of equipment. The customer would be charged for no more than the QoS-adjusted utilization, or a penalty term could even be imposed for the size of the utilization violation above the QoS-adjusted threshold.

For shared resources, when the system happens to be out of compliance with the QoS, then the throughput charges may be scaled back or even converted into a penalty to the service provider. This can be viewed as a *QoS-adjusted throughput*. This makes intuitive sense to customers that sign on for a service only to find that it is busy precisely when they wish to use it.

9.2.4. Normal Versus Exceptional Workloads

Workloads in computing systems are highly variable. Workload bursts measuring many magnitudes higher than "normal" are common, and the SLA must address these circumstances. There are two aspects to this issue. The first is the provider's need to get some information from the customer about how much equipment might be required to provide the agreed QoS. The second is the customer's desire to obtain service even when the Web site is bursting above the contracted levels.

9.2.4.1. Variable Service Level Charging Schemes

Providers often structure their computing utility service charges into a committed service level charge plus a variable service charge. The customer selects a committed service level at the beginning of the month. The provider agrees to provide the committed level of service at the agreed QoS.

In a utilization charging scheme, the service level is most naturally described in terms of the number of QoS-adjusted utilization resource units. For example, the user could specify a committed service level of 100 CPU-equivalents of a certain Pentium® grade. In throughput charging schemes, the user could specify a committed service level in terms of a throughput rate.

If the customer bursts above the committed service level, then the provider agrees to provide that level of service on a "best-effort" basis. The provider may assign new resources if they are available. If not, then the load is handled on the available equipment. At the end of the month, the customer pays a variable charge based on some cumulative measurement of the workload above the committed level.

The advantage of this scheme is that it provides information to the provider concerning the customer's own quantile estimate of usage, in addition to protecting the provider from QoS charges. The disadvantage is that the customer perceives being charged a higher rate for the less desirable best-effort service.

There are many types of cumulative measurements that can be used for the variable charges. In Section 9.4, two types of measurements are compared: the peak load and the average load above the committed level. This analysis shows that the ratio between the committed and variable charging rates is important in determining the customer's choice of committed level.

In the most commonly used version of this scheme, the variable charge is related to the 95% peak. For the provider, this scheme has a natural association with the size of equipment needed to support peak bursts. However, the analysis also shows that such a scheme could result in highly volatile monthly payments. Unfortunately, the apparently fairer charging scheme (averaged usage above committed level) requires such a high ratio between the committed and the variable charging rate to achieve reasonable commitment levels that this scheme is probably unsustainable in the marketplace.

9.2.4.2. Price-Directed Allocation for Variable Service

An alternative method to allocating resources for variable, sometimes bursty, workloads is to devise a method by which customers pay variable rates for additional service above the committed level. The outcome for the customers is similar to the variable service level charging schemes, in that they have to pay a variable charge for service above the committed level, but the context is completely different since customers will be competing among themselves for the additional resources.

In the default version of this scheme, the provider keeps an inventory of excess equipment on hand and brings it into service at a fixed rate on a first-come/first-served basis.

A slightly more sophisticated version of this allocation scheme would envision two classes of service, say gold and silver, with rates that differ. Customers would indicate which service scheme they chose, and then resources would be allocated by the service provider using revenue maximization concepts. This type of system is explored in the operational chapters.

Spot markets for resources could develop in which customers bid for resources in a local market to obtain additional services. Customers could even be allowed to trade their excess committed service levels among themselves. A brief sketch of such a system is provided in Section 9.5. Finally, contracts enabling future resource reservation and possibly even options could also be envisioned.

9.3. SERVICE LEVEL AGREEMENT PORTFOLIO AND FEASIBILITY PLANNING

A Web hosting facility at any given time will have a portfolio of contracts, each with its associated revenue and resource allocation histories. Additionally, the collection of resources in the facility that supports the contract portfolio (routers, servers, disk packs, etc.) can also be viewed as a resource portfolio. One major question that arises in this portfolio perspective is whether the resource portfolio is sufficient to serve the workload of the contract portfolio over, say, the weekly cycle of user demand.

To address this question of feasibility planning, one must turn to a different class of models than those considered in the control and optimization chapters, although this class of models can certainly exploit those in the other chapters. First of all, the problem involves considerably longer time horizons, and predicting the arrival and service characteristics in the workload processes with limited uncertainty over a weekly (or longer) time horizon can be very difficult, if not impossible. Second, it can be very difficult to build a control model with uncertainty that operates over multiple time scales spanning a wide range. In this section, we propose a method to address this question that is based on robust optimization and that exploits the models and methods developed in the control and optimization chapters.

Related issues concern the addition of a new contract, any changes to existing contracts, the addition of new services, the investment in new resources to existing portfolios, and so on. The proposed approach can be employed in an analogous manner to address these related issues.

9.3.1. Forecasting

Web loads are notoriously nonstationary, bursty processes. Despite this, many commercial Web sites show predictable patterns of usage with daily, weekly, and monthly cycles (Liu et al., 2002a, 2002b, 2003). In addition, a pool of Web sites with independent sources of usage variability will be less variable in the aggregate because of laws of large numbers effects.

For planning periods of a day, week, or month, it is reasonable to divide the period into stationary epochs during which the Web sessions seem to have predictable or forecastable arrival and service statistics of the type required for operational management. During these stationary epochs, models and methods such as those in the control and optimization chapter can be used to allocate resources to the workloads.

9.3.2. Robust Allocation

If the amount of variability in the epochal workload statistics will be very large, then the error distribution of the forecast epochal workloads is an important source of uncertainty that should be incorporated into the portfolio and feasibility planning. One specific way to conveniently capture this type of uncertainty is through the robust optimization model of Bertsimas and Sim (2002), whereby one solves for a solution that is feasible in a probabilistic sense, where the probability distribution is generated by the (independent) variation of each forecast error about its forecast mean.

During each stationary epoch, one can build a model in which the allocation of servers to Web sites is a variable of optimization. More specifically, this model would provide an estimate of the profit as a function $R(I(t), L(t))$, where $L_j(t)$ denotes the forecasted workload for Web site j during epoch t and $I_{ij}(t)$ denotes the assignment of resource i to Web site j during epoch t. We must have

$$\sum_j I_{ij}(t) \le b_t \qquad (9.1)$$

where b_t is the total number of servers available during epoch t (which could also be a forecasted number). This model would be developed based on the corresponding models and methods employed as part of the operational management of the system in order to have an accurate representation of the system behavior. By further exploiting the models and methods of the control and optimization chapters for this purpose, one can determine the maximum profit estimate obtained under the optimal scheduling of the workload on the servers with this objective. If there are, say, 4 epochs in a workday and 2 epochs in each weekend day, then there would be a total of 24 such models and 24 sets of resource allocation variables to be determined. The transitions between epochs could also be handled in a similar manner.

Because the variable expense of a Web server system is negligible and fixed costs dominate, it seems reasonable to develop a plan that meets (and hopefully exceeds) a revenue target τ. Then the objective could be modeled as the surplus revenue over target, which should be maximized. More specifically, we could seek to maximize the surplus revenue over target

$$\sum_t R(I(t), L(t)) - \tau \qquad (9.2)$$

subject to this surplus being nonnegative and to the resource constraint in Equation 9.1 and the underlying constraints of the operational management all being satisfied. Of course, the solution of this optimization problem should exploit whatever properties are known for the functions $R(I(t), L(t))$, such as linearity in the case of many utilization-based scenarios and convexity in the case of many throughput-based scenarios with response time guarantees. This is a model that is similar in style to the portfolio optimization example given by Bertsimas and Sim (2002).

The advantage of the robust optimization model over more traditional stochastic programming models, as in Birge (1997), is that the resulting optimization problem only increases linearly in the number of sources of uncertainty. The interpretation of the solution is that it generates a robust allocation that maximizes the risk-adjusted expected revenue which is feasible with a certain level of confidence that can be bounded from below. This would likely suffice for the type of planning system at hand.

9.3.3. Adding a New Resource

The robust allocation model may not be feasible with sufficiently high confidence. In this case, one must allow the model to add resources. The question of how to expense the new resource must then be addressed. One possibility would be to assign an amortization schedule for the resource and require that each added resource subtract its assigned amortization from the total revenue generated by the workloads.

9.3.4. Adding a New Contract

Once the weekly plan has been made with a certain confidence, then one can address the question of whether to add an additional contract, with its forecasted workloads, to the contract portfolio. In some cases, the weekly variation of the contract will be such that it complements the existing portfolio, and so the additional revenue will come with no additional expense. Obviously, attracting such a contract will be very much in the interest of the operator, so pricing discounts might be appropriate. In other cases, the variation will require additional resources, so the operator can use the robust planning model to determine whether this additional contract will be profitable or not.

9.4. ANALYSIS OF CUSTOMER CHOICE OF COMMITTED SERVICE LEVELS

This brief section examines the service provider's behavior and revenue implications under two versions of a contractual scheme in which customers select a "committed service level" c_0 with charge $r_0 c_0$ and pay a variable charge r_1 for service levels above c_0. The service is labeled bandwidth, but it could be for any service with a variable user demand.

One version applies rate r_1 to the total usage above c_0

$$r_0 c_0 + (r_1 / T) \sum_{t=1}^{T} \{\max[0, C_t - c_0]\} \qquad (9.3)$$

where C_t is the sequence of sampled bandwidth rates, measured by sampling bandwidth usage rates every five minutes. We can call this the CB-AB pricing method.

A second version levies rate r_1 for the variable peak load, so that the monthly bill to the customer is

$$r_0 c_0 + r_1 \max[0, P_{95} - c_0] \qquad (9.4)$$

where P_{95} is the 95% quantile, measured by rank ordering the sample sequence C_t and choosing P_{95} so that it is the smallest number that is greater than 95% of the sample. Call this the CB-PB scheme. (There are many philosophical objections to this pricing method. For one thing, it makes a difference to the service provider whether the peak is narrow or wide. Nevertheless, it is in very wide usage.)

9.4.1. Modeling Customer Choice

Under both charging schemes, the customer is faced with making a choice of c_0. What information will the customer take into consideration?

The customer will have to make some assumptions about the (related) distributions of the peaks P_{95} and the paths $C = \{C_t\}$, $t = 1, ..., T$. Let F_P be the distribution function for the peak load, that is,

$$F_P(\alpha) = \Pr\{P_{95} \leq \alpha\} \qquad (9.5)$$

One may as well make the assumption that the C_t are independent and identically distributed and that the time average is equal to the space average, so that

$$(1/T) \sum_{t=1}^{T} \{\max[0, C_t - c_0]\} \approx \int \max[0, x - c_0] dF_C(x) \qquad (9.6)$$

where F_C is the distribution function for C_1.

The customer will also need to make assumptions about the self-imposed penalty d_1 for best-effort processing (slow response time, for example, or possibly no response at all). Assume that the available bandwidth is so large that there is no effective upper bound to the choice of committed bandwidth C_0.

Under the PB-CB pricing scheme, the customer's choice can be represented by solving the following optimization:

$$\min_{c_0} r_0 c_0 + \int (r_1 + d_1) \max[0, x - c_0] dF_P(x) \tag{9.7}$$

The second term is the expected monthly variable charge for loads above the committed level.

Under the CB-AB pricing scheme, the customer's choice can be represented by:

$$\min_{c_0} r_0 c_0 + \int (r_1 + d_1) \max[0, x - c_0] dF_C(x) \tag{9.8}$$

Both of these optimization problems have the same form, so we can analyze the customer choice framework under the assumption that the distribution function F could be either F_C or F_P.

The customer's choice is assumed to be unconstrained optimization. The answer is found by taking derivatives and setting equal to zero. The main observation that helps this procedure is that the derivative of the integral is equal to:

$$\frac{d}{dc_0} \int_{c_0}^{\infty} (r_1 + d_1)(x - c_0) dF(x) = \frac{d}{dc_0} (r_1 + d_1) \left[\int_{c_0}^{\infty} x dF(x) - c_0 \int_{c_0}^{\infty} dF(x) \right]$$

$$= (r_1 + d_1)[-c_0 F'(c_0) - [1 - F(c_0)]]$$

$$+ c_0 F'(c_0)]$$

$$= (r_1 + d_1)[F(c_0 - 1)] \tag{9.9}$$

It follows that c_0 should be chosen to solve:

$$0 = r_0 + (r_1 + d_1)[F(c_0) - 1] \tag{9.10}$$

The customer's choice is the familiar newsboy solution. One can show that:

$$\bar{c}_0 = \begin{cases} 0 & \text{if } d_1 < r_0 - r_1 \\ F^{-1}\left(1 - \dfrac{r_0}{(r_1 + d_1)}\right) & \text{if } d_1 \geq r_0 - r_1 \end{cases} \tag{9.11}$$

The customer's choice of c_0 is essentially the $1 - r_0/(r_1 + d_1)$ quantile estimate for the distribution F.

Let us now examine the expected revenue consequences for the service provider, assuming that each customer accurately projects their distribution. Label the customers by $j = 1, ..., J$. Each customer chooses $\bar{c}_0^j$ as in Equation 9.11 with parameter d_1^j and distribution function F_j. The expected revenue for the service provider is

$$\sum_j r_0 \bar{c}_0^j + \sum_j r_1 \int \max[0, x - \bar{c}_0^j] dF^j(x)$$

$$= \sum_j \left[r_0 \bar{c}_0^j + r_1 \int_{\bar{c}_0^j} x dF^j(x) - r_1 \bar{c}_0^j (1 - F^j(\bar{c}_0^j)) \right]$$

$$= \sum_j \left[r_0 \bar{c}_0^j + r_1 \int_{\bar{c}_0^j} x dF^j(x) - r_0 \bar{c}_0^j \left(\frac{r_1}{r_1 + d_1^j} \right) \right] \tag{9.12}$$

$$= \sum_j \frac{r_0 d_1^j}{r_1 + d_1^j} \bar{c}_0^j + r_1 \sum_j \int_{\bar{c}_0^j} x dF^j(x)$$

In Equation 9.11, the jth customer's choice of $\bar{c}_0^j$ depends on the relationship between the customer's penalty rate d_1^j for usage above the committed service level and the difference $r_0 + r_1$ between the charging rates. Note that if $d_1^j \approx 0$, then the revenue will be dominated by the second term. Let us now examine the various relationships and their consequences for the provider's revenue streams.

At one extreme, one can set $r_0 \gg r_1$. Then the customers with $d_1^j < r_0 - r_1$ have $\bar{c}_0^j = 0$, which places them in the best-effort service state all of the time. The expected revenue is

$$r_1 \sum_j \int_0 x dF^j(x) \tag{9.13}$$

In the CB-PB charging scheme, the expected revenue is r_1 times the sum of these customers' expected peaks P_{95}^j. The CB-AB revenue is r_1 times the sum of their expected usage $E\{C^j\}$.

At the other extreme, one can set $r_0 \ll r_1$. All customers will have $d_1^j > 0 > r_0 - r_1$ and hence $\bar{c}_0^j \gg 0$. The expected revenue is

$$\sum_j \left[\frac{r_0 d_1^j}{r_1 + d_1^j} \bar{c}_0^j + r_1 \int_{\bar{c}_0^j} x dF^j(x) \right] \tag{9.14}$$

Specifically, suppose that $r_0 = r_1/5$, and suppose that d_1^j is very small compared to r_1. Then the customer's newsboy choice $\bar{c}_0^j$ can be interpreted as the $1 - 1/15 = 0.80$ quantile. Then the revenue term will be dominated by:

$$r_1 \sum_j \int_{\bar{c}_0^j} x dF^j(x) \tag{9.15}$$

In the CB-PB charging scheme, this is r_1 times the conditional expected value of the P_{95} peak given that this peak is above its 80% quantile. In the CB-AB charging scheme, this can be interpreted as the conditional expected value of usage given that usage is above its 80% quantile. As d_1^j becomes more significant, the quantile level at which these conditional expectations are taken will rise, but the revenue will still be dominated by the second term.

9.4.2. Conclusions

Equations 9.13 and 9.15 highlight the fact that the two-rate contractual scheme can be interpreted as a single-rate scheme r_1 with a required quantile level $1 - r_1/r_0$. These equations also allow us to compare the different versions of the charging schemes. For the service provider, of course, it is important to be paid for the equipment outlays needed to accommodate peak demands. The scheme chosen should bear some relationship to peak demands. Which scheme, CB-PB or CB-AB, is better in this regard?

The CB-PB case purports to obtain revenue for peak demands. Therefore, in this scheme it seems that one ought to set $r_0 \gg r_1$ and obtain revenue proportional to the expected value of the sample peak P_{95} service measurement, as in Equation 9.13. The impression that CB-PB is unfair to users is quite correct in charging schemes where $r_1 > r_0$, as one can see from Equation 9.15. In this setting, the users are being charged proportional to the expected value of the peak service measurement P_{95} given that that peak is above the $1 - r_0/(r_1 + d_1)$ quantile; however, that peak will be below this level most of the time.

On the other hand, while it may seem that the CB-AB revenue might not relate to peak demands, in fact it does. If one sets $r_1 \gg r_0$, then Equation 9.15 shows that revenue will be proportional to the conditional expected value of service usage given that it is above the $1 - r_0/(r_1 + d_1)$ quantile. This will be quite similar to the P_{95} for sufficiently high ratios of r_1/r_0. However, these ratios are much higher than the market expectations (typically $r_1 \approx 1.5r_0$). One way around this is to require the customer to select a quantile level directly, instead of implicitly as in the two-rate scheme.

The example in Table 9.1 compares the two schemes. It supposes that C_1 follows a lognormal distribution with mean 100 and standard deviation 30, that

Table 9.1.   Comparison of PB and AB Charging

r_1/r_0	1	2	3	4	5	6	7	8	9	10
c_0 level	60	102	114	121	126	129	132	135	137	139
c_0 as quantile	0.09	0.524	0.677	0.756	0.803	0.836	0.859	0.877	0.891	0.909
CB-PB	149	197	220	235	244	249	252	252	250	246
CB-AB	101	124	133	138	142	145	147	149	151	153

$r_0 = 1$, that $d_1 = 0.1$, and that the sample peak distribution F_P is replaced by placing probability one at the true peak P_{95}. The table compares the amount of revenue collected by the provider under the CB-PB and CB-AB schemes.

One can see that the CB-PB charging scheme grows very rapidly as r_1 increases. Its peak value is approximately 152, which is reached around $r_1 = 8$. The CB-AB charging scheme grows much more slowly. At $r_1 = 8r_0$, it crosses the revenue for the CB-PB value. The CB-AB scheme does eventually resemble the CB-PB charges with high enough ratio r_1/r_0, but it is a much more stable curve. When one considers the volatility of the variable part of the provider's revenue, one may speculate that the CB-AB revenue is more stable. This conclusion would depend on a careful analysis of the variance of the sampled peak P_{95} versus that of the sampled conditional expectation.

9.5. CUSTOMER-DIRECTED ALLOCATION IN SERVICE LEVEL AGREEMENTS

In this section, an agreement between the provider and the clients is described in which the service level can be increased at the direction of the customer by providing an explicit bid for additional service above a base level. A simple algorithm for the host's problem of allocating resources to changing workloads is also sketched.

9.5.1. Customer-Directed Service Level Agreement

The customer-directed SLA has the following components:

1. Base service level L, representing the maximum number of servers L to be allocated to a specific class of requests based on the parameters offered by the client
2. Per-unit bid B, representing the variable rate the client agrees to pay for adding servers beyond base service level

Service up to the customer's base service level L is guaranteed. Requests that exceed L are satisfied if possible when the per-unit bid equals or exceeds the current spot market price, which is the maximum of the bids B over the set of customers requesting additional service. The host can impose a minimum variable charge M (i.e., cost + economic profit), and customers that want service beyond L must supply a bid $B \geq M$. Whether the bid is 0, M, or B, it reflects the nature of the customer:

- If the customer wants no service beyond its base level, then its implicit bid is 0.
- If the customer wants service beyond its base level, then its implicit bid is M.
- If the customer wants requests beyond its base level to be completed, then its explicit bid is B.

Finally, the provider must satisfy a basic response-time-type QoS constraint for allocated servers or pay a penalty charge. It should be noted that the contract is designed so that the customer may change B at any time.

9.5.2. Resource Allocation

The host reallocates servers by considering the revenue implications of such a move. Consider a family of servers sharing the load of one Web site. When the number of requests for a Web site causes the probability of a large response time to the customer, we say the family of servers *is going red* or enters a *critical phase*.

To complicate matters, it is not possible to reallocate a server instantaneously. To reallocate a server, one must first let its active threads die out, remove the existing environment, and install the new environment. Only then can it be reallocated to a new customer (this can take on the order of five minutes). Finding an optimal solution through dynamic programming is an extremely difficult task due to the long time horizon in this problem (24 hours) and the short intervals in which decisions are made. This leads to a problem of such large magnitude that an exact solution is impractical.

Instead, various threshold algorithms can be used to get good solutions. An example of such a scheme is given below. We will make our decisions based on three important values:

- The probability of a server family going red
- The expected cost rate C incurred from going red

■ The expected revenue rate R for providing service beyond the customer's required level

Note that C and R are both nonnegative values and cannot both be zero at the same time for a particular family of servers. This is because C is nonzero when it has gone red as a result of not providing the resources required in the SLA, whereas R is nonzero when it has gone red as a result of traffic being so high that the level of resources agreed to in the SLA is insufficient. As mentioned above, it can take about five minutes for a server being moved to come on-line in its new family. However, the server does not immediately stop contributing to its original family. One can approximate that it continues to work for approximately one-third of a five-minute interval, after which it is removed from its family. So, for two-thirds of a five-minute interval, it is not active in any family. This reflects the period in which it is shutting down and being rebooted.

We will introduce subscripts to reflect when the parameter is measured. A subscript of 1 indicates the parameter is measured 5 minutes from now, a subscript of 2 indicates 10 minutes from now, and so on. We will introduce a superscript of +1 or −1 to our parameter P to indicate the probability of going red given the addition or subtraction of a server from the family, respectively (i.e., P_1^{-1} indicates the probability of going red five minutes from now given that a server has been removed from the family). For each family of servers, we have created the following measures:

$$\text{Need} = P_1 \cdot C_1 + P_2 \cdot C_2 + (1 - P_1^{+1})R_1 + (1 - P_2^{+1})R_2 \qquad (9.16)$$

Note that due to the mutually nonzero relationship of C and R mentioned above, either the first two terms above are zero or the second two terms are zero. If the first two terms are zero, this indicates that a traffic level higher than agreed to in the SLA would result in going red, and if the last two terms are zero, this indicates the possibility of falling into a penalty situation. Thus, *need* can reflect either a possibility to make extra revenue (if action is taken) or the possibility of paying penalties (if action is not taken), depending on which terms are zero. The higher the *need* of a family is, the more money that can be lost or earned by adding a server to that family.

$$\text{Availability} = \frac{2}{3} P_{1/3}^{-1} \cdot C_{1/3} + P_1^{-1} \cdot C_1 + P_2^{-1} \cdot C_2$$
$$\qquad (9.17)$$
$$+ \frac{2}{3}(1 - P_{1/3})R_{1/3} + (1 - P_1)R_1 + (1 - P_2)R_2$$

Availability is closely related to *need*, but there are two significant differences. The first is that the superscripts reflect that we are considering removing a computer from the family, as opposed to adding one. The second difference is that there are two extra terms. These terms reflect the fact that the server will be removed from the family after one-third of the first five-minute interval. *Availability* is intended to measure the amount of penalties that will be paid or revenue lost if a server is moved from that family.

In order to decide when to take action and move a server from one family to another, we use the following heuristic:

1. Calculate the *need* and *availability* for every family of servers.
2. Compare the highest *need* value with the lowest *availability* value. If the *need* value exceeds the *availability* value, one server is taken from the family corresponding to the *availability* value and given to the family corresponding to the *need* value.
3. If a server was told to move, go back to step 1 (note that the probabilities will change as the number of servers used to make the calculations will be different). Terminate the loop if no server was told to move in the last iteration.

The above iteration loop should be performed on a frequent basis. We suggest it be done about every 15 seconds. This is only one possible heuristic, and we have yet to actually compare it in simulation with an optimal solution. However, it has the obvious advantage of requiring considerably less computation than a long-time-horizon dynamic program, which allows it to be performed very often. This allows nearly instantaneous reaction to a predicted critical situation. The P, C, and R values are obtained from forecasts provided from the router control level.

ACKNOWLEDGMENTS

The research represented in the chapter is drawn from the results of a few years of work and discussions among our colleagues in IBM Research to investigate technical issues concerning on-demand computing under SLAs. Some of the sections are based on material that has been published in the academic literature. Parts of Section 9.1 are adapted from Bichler et al. (2002). Section 9.5 is adapted from a paper that appeared in the proceedings of the annual PIMS Industrial Problem Solving Workshop (King et al., 2001). Finally, we thank Kaan Katirciouglu for his contributions to Section 9.4.

REFERENCES

Bertsimas, D. and Sim, M. (2002). The Price of Robustness, Technical Report, Massachusetts Institute of Technology, Cambridge, 2002.

Bichler, M., Kalagnanam, J., Katircioglu, K., King, A. J., Lawrence, R. D., Lee, H. S., Lin, G. Y., and Lu, Y. (2002). Applications of flexible pricing in business-to-business electronic commerce, *IBM Systems Journal*, 41(2), 287–302.

Birge, J. R. (1997). Stochastic programming computation and applications. *INFORMS Journal on Computing*, 9, 111–133.

King, A., Begen, M., Cojocaru, M., Fowler, E., Ganjali, Y., Lai, J., Lee, T., Navasca, C., and Ryan, D. (2001). Web hosting service level agreements, in *Proceedings of the Fifth PIMS Industrial Problem Solving Workshop* (http://www.pims.math.ca/publications/proceedings/).

Liu, Z., Squillante, M. S., Xia, C. H., Yu, S.-Z., Zhang, L., and Malouch, N. M. (2002a). Traffic profiling, clustering and classification for commercial Internet sites, in *Proceedings of the Tenth International Conference on Telecommunication Systems, Modeling and Analysis*, October.

Liu, Z., Squillante, M. S., Xia, C. H., Yu, S.-Z., Zhang, L., Malouch, N. M., and Dantzig P. M. (2002b). Analysis of measurement data from sporting event Web sites, in *Proceedings of the IEEE GLOBECOM Internet Performance Symposium*, November.

Liu, Z., Squillante, M. S., Xia, C. H., Yu, S.-Z., Zhang, L., and Malouch, N. M. (2003). Profile-based traffic characterization of commercial Web sites, in *Proceedings of the Eighteenth International Teletraffic Congress Conference*, August-September.

OPTIMAL CONTROL OF WEB HOSTING SYSTEMS UNDER SERVICE LEVEL AGREEMENTS

Alan J. King and Mark S. Squillante

10.1. INTRODUCTION

The operation of a Web hosting facility involves control elements and decisions spanning many time scales. The physical computing facility contains many control points with parameters that can be tuned in real time to respond to performance statistics. At one extreme, high-performance routers operate at very fine time scales and adjust their parameters accordingly. Operating system, middleware, and application software may also monitor performance and set control parameters. At somewhat coarser time scales, computer and disk farm partitions may be reassigned in response to changing workloads. Daily, weekly, monthly, and longer term forecasts may be used to schedule and plan allocation policies. At weekly and monthly time scales, the capacity of the resource elements may be reviewed and cause a utility's supply chain model to process additional orders or to obtain short-term capacity. Finally, monthly and yearly performance reporting may require changes in the basic terms and conditions of the service level agreement (SLA) and impact strategic models addressing a computing utility's profitability. The key operational point is that the overall solution must provide a unified framework that makes it possible to have various solution methods working together in a cohesive manner across a wide range of time scales in order to meet a common overall goal.

The physical computing facility includes control points at the router and server. Policies at these control points can be used to achieve quality of service (QoS) performance objectives through the allocation of resource elements, once information about the arrival and service processes is known or forecasted. The availability of such workload information is often significantly impacted by the time scale of the control points. As a specific example, routers working at very fine time scales often do not have any additional information about the arrival process beyond its current mean rate because the overhead of collecting more detailed information is too expensive at these fine time scales. More detailed workload information is typically available as one moves to coarser time scales.

The varying assignment of resource elements over time is perhaps what most comes to mind when operational models of the computing utility are discussed and marketed: Additional resource elements can be brought to accommodate situations where customer user populations create bursts of demand. Different architectures can respond to such requirements with varying abilities, from hot repartitioning of a single large mainframe-class machine to a cold restart of a rack-mounted pizza box. Reassigned resource elements are necessarily diverted from actual or potential use by other customers, so the operational models for these decisions typically must encompass a large number of potential actions and rewards.

10.1.1. Allocation of Shared Resources

The generic scenario is as follows. A dispatcher receives incoming client requests destined for different customer hosting sites and routes these requests to an appropriate downstream server element. Each server element in turn receives the client requests routed to it and schedules the execution of these requests among its resources. Both dispatchers and servers operate according to their current control policy parameters. The dispatcher observes incoming loads from the different customer hosting sites and performance statistics for the downstream server elements. Server elements are assigned to individual customer sites and often are not shared, either physically or virtually. At a relatively fine time scale, the dispatcher's role can include deciding how to adjust its control policy parameters in an optimal, or near optimal, manner subject to the existing server element assignments. Similar control policy decisions can also be made at the server elements. At coarser time scales, the role of resource allocation control policies includes deciding when to change the assignment of server elements among the different customer hosting sites. These decisions must encompass the load forecast, the system state, alternative control policies, the charging procedures, and the SLAs for the different customers.

One version of this generic scenario is the bandwidth broker in Section 10.2. Classes of customers differ in the price charged per "megabyte" carried, in the arrival rate of requests, and in the size of the request. The provisioning dispatcher, or bandwidth broker, can accept or reject the bandwidth request in order to optimize revenue subject to a capacity bound on available bandwidth. The feasibility bound on available bandwidth is a proxy for a QoS condition, in that as long as the bandwidth bound is respected, then all users experience the desired QoS. This setting is similar to Paschalidis and Tsitsiklis (2000), and the dynamic programming solution to this problem is similar to the classical revenue management models (Lippman and Stidham, 1997; McGill and van Ryzin, 1999). The main results from this analysis are: (1) different charging rates do indeed differentiate service levels achieved by customers and (2) greedy allocation policies can be near optimal in states characterized by excess capacity and states characterized by large numbers of requests in service.

Section 10.3 considers an operational model of the Web hosting facility at fine time scales that performs optimal downstream routing and server scheduling decisions for requests arriving from multiple classes of users for each of the many customer sites. The workload model encompasses state transitions for the user classes and allows general stochastic processes of the type found in practice. Revenue is calculated by charging users a price per request as in Section 10.2. The QoS conditions and profit estimates are modeled by the probability that the per-class response times are within a specified per-class bound, which is in turn bounded from above by an exact or approximate queueing-theoretic expression. In addition, requests that violate the QoS performance guarantee cause a penalty to be charged to the provider. Versions for various types of server scheduling policies among the user classes are also considered. The resulting class-constrained resource allocation problem is shown to be convex, and an efficient solution algorithm is developed. The main results from this analysis demonstrate: (1) the viability and profitability of the general class of SLA and revenue/penalty-charging models considered, (2) the effective use of stochastic bounds and approximations on per-class response time distributions given limited workload information, and (3) the efficiency of the solution methods making it possible to exploit them on-line.

Section 10.4 expands the set of resource allocation problems in the Web hosting facility of Section 10.3 to span multiple time scales. The SLA model is simplified by eliminating penalties for QoS noncompliance and by calculating the per-class revenues as functions of the per-class average server utilization rates per time interval. To meet QoS requirements, the resource allocation policies can assign more servers to the customer. (The charging scheme protects the customer from paying for overallocations.) However, when server elements are reassigned, each such change takes the server out of service for an interval that reflects the transition time. The resulting resource assignment problem is a stochastic dynamic program. The solution approach takes advantage of the fact that this simplified revenue model causes the optimal routing and scheduling model of Section 10.3 to reduce to a linear program that has a direct solution. An approximation algorithm then provides resource assignment solutions demonstrating that the dynamic programming policies are far better than standard heuristics. Conclusions somewhat similar to Section 10.2 can be drawn, namely that greedy algorithms work well in states characterized by low utilization and that the dynamic programming solution significantly differs from greedy policies when the QoS constraints are at risk of violation — especially when the request processes are characterized by a considerable probability of bursting. In particular, as a result of employing the optimal routing and scheduling policies of Section 10.3, we find that the resource reallocation problem simplifies somewhat in the sense that small changes in the various workloads have a relatively small impact on overall profit, whereas adjusting server assignments to address major workload changes becomes a primary issue in satisfying QoS performance guarantees and maximizing overall profit.

The discussion so far describes resource allocation control policies that make operational decisions to meet QoS requirements. In Sections 10.3 and 10.4, the control policies have constraints on the per-class response time QoS. Each of these settings assumes that a feasible solution exists and further assumes that the dispatcher pays penalties for out-of-compliance service; in other words, there must be a governing provision that user loads are within certain limits and that the service provider is protected from paying penalties for load levels above these limits. Moreover, when such limits are violated, the resource allocation control policies favor requests according to their importance relative to their QoS requirements and cost model.

10.2. DYNAMIC SINGLE-RESOURCE PROVISIONING

We formulate a revenue-based single-resource allocation problem for multiple service classes. To fix ideas, the resource under management is the bandwidth on the link from the hosting facility network access router to the Internet POP, although our methods and results can be applied more generally. Classes i are distinguished by the bandwidth request A_i and the rate R_i they are willing to pay for the request. The system can decide to allocate all of the bandwidth or to reject the service request. There is no best-effort service class.

The optimal policy is achieved by discrete-time dynamic programming. Theoretical and simulation results based on actual HTTP trace logs concur with conventional wisdom that as resource usage approaches 100%, head room should be reserved for premium users. A greedy policy works well at low resource usage and in states when there are a large number of departures relative to arrivals, which suggests that one may simplify the implementation of dynamic programming policies by classifying states and applying class-based rules.

We also discuss the optimal off-line solution and report the revenue gap between on-line and off-line algorithms. Performance numbers from the off-line algorithm are not attainable in practice, but they provide the ceiling on those of the on-line algorithm. We found that the gap narrows as the service capacity increases.

The rest of this section is organized as follows. Section 10.2.1 develops the discrete-time dynamic programming framework for bandwidth allocation. Section 10.2.2 describes approximation algorithms in the off-line setting. The simulation results are presented in Section 10.2.3 and implementation issues are discussed in Section 10.2.4. Finally, Section 10.2.5 contains directions for further research.

10.2.1. Formal Framework

We develop a discrete-time dynamic programming formulation for allocating bandwidth to requests from multiple service classes. The problem is formulated as a discrete-time Markov decision process on a finite horizon. The state variable is the number of requests in progress in the system.

Consider the system with known capacity *SLA*, a set of m service classes, and a finite time T when the system returns to a renewal state. Let t denote the remaining time to T (time runs backwards in this section), and assume that allocation decisions are made at discrete time intervals of length 1. Thus, there are $T + 1$ unit length time intervals. Decision stages are numbered in reverse order $t = T, T - 1, ..., 0$, indicating the time remaining to renewal. Users arrive at random times $X_1, X_2, ...$ The ith user stays connected for a random time D_i. The goal is to come up with the assignment policy that maximizes the total revenue over the time period T.

10.2.1.1. Notation

For any fixed time t (the remaining time to renewal), define:

- $\vec{N} = (n_1, n_2, \ldots, n_m)$ and $\vec{L} = l_1, l_2, \ldots, l_m)$ and are vectors denoting the numbers of requests in progress, each requiring bandwidth $\vec{A} = (A_1, A_2, \ldots, A_m)$ for the duration of the session. The SLA constraint mandates $\sum_i^m A_i n_i \leq SLA$.
- $\vec{b} = (b_1, b_2, \ldots, b_m)$ is the vector denoting the number of different classes leaving the system; $\vec{b} > 0 \Leftrightarrow b_i > 0$ for some $i = 1, \ldots, m$.
- $\vec{N} \geq \vec{b} \, (\vec{N} \geq \vec{L}) \Leftrightarrow n_i \geq b_i (n_i \geq L_i)$, for all $i = 1, \ldots, m$.
- p_{it} denotes the probability of a request from a service class i arriving during the time interval $[t, t - 1)$.
- $q_{\vec{b}t}$ denotes the probability that $\vec{b}$ customers depart the system at time t.
- R_i denotes the revenue per unit time for the allocated bandwidth for class i.

10.2.1.2. General Assumptions

1. In each interval, up to one new request will be considered for service (one can easily relax this [apparently] restrictive assumption by aggregating thousands of requests to be a single "mega-request" and apply our formulation to this "mega-request").
2. Once a request arrives, a known bandwidth A_i ($i = 1, \ldots, m$) needs to be allocated.
3. The assignment of bandwidths occurs at the starting point of each time unit.
4. Instead of a best-effort allocation policy, an "all-or-nothing" policy is assumed that allocates to accepted requests the entire bandwidth A_i. R_i is the resulting revenue per request. To accommodate a best-effort default service, one can view R_i as the value differential between an assigned bandwidth and a best-effort class of service.
5. Unserved requests are lost without further impact on the system.

10.2.1.3. Request Durations

It is not necessary to model individual request durations. One can derive the probability (q_{it}) of a service request from class i leaving the system at t via the arrival and service time assumptions.

10.2.1.4. Optimality Equation

Consider the following action space $A = \{$accept, reject$\}$. When the system is at t with $\vec{N}$ requests in progress, a reward $R(\vec{N}, a)$ is given for action $a \in A$. The corresponding optimality equation is

$$V_t(\vec{N}) = \max_a \left\{ R(\vec{N}, a) + \sum_{\vec{L}} V_{t-1}(\vec{L}) P_{\vec{N}, \vec{L}}(a) \right\} \qquad (10.1)$$

subject to the *SLA* constraint and the boundary condition

$$V_0(0) = 0, \qquad V_0(\vec{N}) = -\infty \text{ when } \vec{N} \cdot \vec{A} > SLA \qquad (10.2)$$

where the summation in Equation 10.1 is over any $\vec{L} \leq \vec{N}$ or $\vec{L} \leq \vec{N} + 1$ depending on whether the action a is to accept or to reject. $P_{\vec{N}, \vec{L}}(a)$ denotes the transition probability from state $\vec{N}$ to state $\vec{L}$ under action a.

The above boundary conditions guarantee that SLAs are never violated. Note that the model also allows for violations of the SLAs via penalty functions $V_0(\vec{N})$.

More concretely, at each time period there are four possibilities: a request arrives and it is accepted, a request arrives and is rejected, no requests arrive, or no change (in arrival and departure) occurs. A more detailed description of the optimality conditions is as follows:

$$V_t(\vec{N}) = \sum_{i=1}^{m} \max \left\{ p_{it}(R_i + \sum_{\vec{L} \leq \vec{N} + e_i} V_{t-1}(\vec{L}) P_{\vec{N} + e_i, \vec{L}}), p_{it} \sum_{\vec{L} \leq \vec{N}} V_{t-1}(\vec{L}) P_{\vec{N}, \vec{L}} \right\}$$

$$+ \prod_{i=1}^{m} (1 - p_{it}) \sum_{0 < \vec{b} \leq \vec{N}} q_{\vec{b}t} V_{t-1}(\vec{N} - \vec{b}) + \prod_{i=1}^{m} (1 - p_{it}) q_{0t} V_t(\vec{N})$$

where q_{0t} means no departure.

It is not hard to see that the optimal policy is completely state dependent. Because of the curse of dimensionality, it could be quite hard to derive the optimal policy in an explicit analytical form. But this computation can be done off-line. Solving the dynamic program yields a lookup table which specifies for each period t and $\vec{N}$ whether bandwidth A_i should be allocated for the arriving request.

Additional assumptions may reduce the computational complexity. For instance, if we assume that one and only one of the following events occurs —

(1) an arrival of a request from class i, (2) some departures of class i from the system, or (3) no event — then the dynamic programming recursion can be written as:

$$V_t(\vec{N}) = \sum_{i=1}^{m} p_{it} \max\{R_i + V_{t-1}(\vec{N} + e_i), V_{t-1}(\vec{N})\}$$

$$+ \sum_{\vec{N} \geq \vec{b} > 0} q_{\vec{b}} V_{t-1}(\vec{N} - \vec{b}) + \left(1 - \sum_{i=1}^{m} p_{it} - \sum_{0 < \vec{b} \leq \vec{N}} q_{\vec{b}}\right) V_{t-1}(\vec{N})$$

(10.3)

This additional assumption is plausible and natural when one wants to approximate the corresponding continuous time problem with time discretization. For interested readers, Lippman and Stidham (1977) provide such applications for the airline seat control problem.

To further simplify the computations, one may wish to assume that:

- Interarrival time of customer requests is exponential with parameter λ_i for class i.
- Service time for class i is exponential with parameter μ_i.

Nevertheless, one needs to be careful in choosing an appropriate time unit to make all assumptions consistent.

10.2.1.5. Control Policy

The admission control policy is a simple threshold policy: Admit A_i at time t if the system has $\vec{N}$ requests in service when:

$$R_i + \sum_{\vec{L} \leq \vec{N} + e_i} V_{t-1}(\vec{L}) P_{\vec{N} + e_i, \vec{L}} \geq \sum_{\vec{L} \leq \vec{N}} V_{t-1}(\vec{L}) P_{\vec{N}, \vec{L}}$$

(10.4)

This development is similar to dynamic programming approaches to the reservation of airline seat allocation problem with cancellations studied by Subramaniam et al. (1999). The principal differences are that in our model we permit variable resource requests A_i and the exit probabilities q_{it} are class dependent. Moreover, their formulation relies heavily on a rather restrictive assumption that there is up to only one arrival or departure (not both) during one time period. It is worth pointing out that the approach in this section can be described in its most general form as an airline yield management problem with multiple fare classes, overbooking, and cancellations. (Interested readers are referred to McGill and van Ryzin [1999] for a survey of research in airline revenue management).

A similar problem was considered by Marbach et al. (2000). However, their formulation is an admission control for a discounted Markov decision problem with an infinite time horizon, whereas the problem considered in this section has a finite time horizon. The advantage of this approach is that the admission control policy can be adjusted to fit various traffic conditions by carefully choosing appropriate time windows. For example, lookup tables can be different for off-peak and peak hour traffic statistics. Also, Poisson arrival and service assumptions are crucial in the formulation of Marbach et al. (2000), while the formulation in this section can be applied to more general cases.

10.2.2. What If We Know Everything: Off-line Algorithms

In this subsection, we consider the off-line problem of bandwidth allocation strategies. This provides a benchmark against which to compare the dynamic programming allocation strategy. Each request specifies an arbitrary bandwidth and revenue. Assume that the requested bandwidth w_i, value v_i (revenue), start time t_i, and duration D_i of each request are known in advance. A subset of the requests is to be retained (called *intervals* in this subsection) that maximizes the sum of the retained values, subject to the constraint that at each time instant the sum of bandwidths of retained intervals that span that time instant is at most the total bandwidth capacity B.

This problem is NP-hard. There is a simple reduction from the knapsack problem (Garey and Johnson, 1979): for each item in the knapsack instance, construct a bandwidth request with value equal to that of the item with bandwidth equal to the item's weight.

Thus one turns to approximation algorithms. An algorithm has an *approximation ratio r* if the value of the solution returned is at least $1/r$ times the optimal value for maximization problems or at most r times the optimal value for minimization problems.

The allocation problem is isomorphic to the "general caching problem"; see Bar-Noy et al. (2000), for instance. However, in the general caching problem, the optimization criterion is complementary: the goal is to minimize the sum of the values of the discarded intervals (requests) rather than to maximize the value of those retained. Irani (1997) gives an algorithm for this problem with an approximation ratio logarithmic in the ratio of the cache size (which corresponds to total bandwidth) to the smallest page (smallest bandwidth of any request), for the special cases in which the values are the same for all intervals and in which they are proportional to the widths. Although this does not yield an approximation bound for the bandwidth allocation problem, the algorithm is appealing due to its simplicity, its natural adaptation to our problem, and its good performance in practice.

The algorithm classifies intervals by their widths, in geometrically increasing width classes. Class j comprises requests of widths between 2^j and 2^{j+1}. The algorithm makes a left-to-right (i.e., in order of increasing time) scan of the input set of intervals, maintaining a set of "live" intervals that are candidates for the solution. When the right endpoint of a live interval is passed, the candidate is added to the solution. When the left endpoint of an interval is passed, the interval is added to the live set, and then some number of intervals is discarded from the live set if necessary because the width bound B is exceeded. Once a class is chosen from which to discard an interval, the interval chosen within that class is the one whose right endpoint is furthest away (i.e., greatest). Irani uses the brute force approach of discarding from every class whenever B is exceeded, but this is not necessary and is only used to show that the algorithm has a worst-case approximation guarantee. We can instead discard only enough intervals to satisfy the size bound B again, but we need to decide which class or classes from which to discard.

Irani's algorithm can be adapted in a natural way to the bandwidth allocation problem. The idea is to balance the sums of the values of intervals discarded from each class. For each class, a counter is maintained; these counters are set to zero at the start of the algorithm. Each time an interval is discarded, the counter for the interval's class is incremented by the value of the interval. A victim class is chosen to minimize the maximum counter value, after incrementing the victim class's counter. As before, within a class, that interval whose right endpoint is greatest is chosen. This is repeated until the bound B is met again. Recently, Bar-Noy et al. (2000) gave a simple and elegant algorithm for the bandwidth allocation problem with a constant approximation ratio.

We implemented Irani's algorithm and a simple off-line algorithm that discards the request with the smallest ratio of revenue to remaining time until the end of the request. Results of these simulations are reported below as benchmarks against which to compare on-line policies.

10.2.3. Simulation and Comparison of Control Policies

In this subsection, two admission control policies — the dynamic programming (DP) policy and the greedy policy (which assigns resources based solely on availability) — are simulated by arrival rates and average service times derived from real HTTP log traces. The experiments show that the DP policy, depending on the revenue assumptions, beats the greedy policy by a wide margin in all occasions. In the rest of the subsection, the simulation setting and results are reported, followed by discussion and interpretation of the results.

10.2.3.1. Simulation Setting

The simulation environment tracks the admission control decisions made by two policies, DP and greedy. The arrival traffic processed by both policies is identical. However, due to different admission policies, the number of active requests is different and the number of completed tasks also differs. For easy comparison, only two classes of requests are assumed: gold and silver. This two-class assumption matches common distinctions of "browsing" and "shopping" customers in e-commerce. It is noted that multiclass arrivals can be easily handled by the DP formulation and solution developed in this section.

Arrival rates and average service time are derived from an actual one-day HTTP log trace from a major commercial Web site that recorded arrival times and requested file sizes. The time granulation of the log was on the order of several seconds. There were typically multiple arrivals in one second all sharing the same time stamp. The requested file sizes are generally different as the requests look for different files. Because of the insufficient temporal resolution and the single arrival per time slot assumption in the DP policy, the real traffic rates were estimated using an artificially generated arrival pattern.

The simulator estimates the arrival rates and service times in the following way:

■ The logged requests are divided randomly into gold group and silver group according to a given fixed probability ratio. The gold arrival rate is obtained by dividing the total number of gold requests by the time duration of the log trace (e.g., 24 hours). The silver arrival rate is the division of the number of silver requests and the time duration.

■ Average service times are computed from the requested file sizes. In the beginning of the simulation, the total available bandwidth (in SLA), the assigned bandwidth per gold request, and the assigned bandwidth per silver request are specified by user. Average service times are computed by dividing the average requested file size by the assigned class bandwidth.

■ The current simulation only applies the HTTP log traces to estimate rates. The interarrival times of every class are assumed to be i.i.d. Poisson and the service time of each class exponential.

The simulator also allows the assignment of revenues generated for each class. The revenue brought by each request is fixed regardless of how long the request stays in the system. This assumption reflects how most HTTP 1.0 requests are processed, which rarely involves long connections. In HTTP 1.1 and later, connections may be much longer since all elements (text and images) in a document are aggregated and sent through a single HTTP connection.

Nevertheless, the DP formulation can be easily modified to account for revenue rate if needed.

10.2.3.2. Greedy Policy

The greedy policy is used in conjunction with the DP policy as a reference benchmark. The greedy policy operates by the first-come/first-served rule and does not reject any request unless the SLA will be violated. It treats requests from different classes in the same way and ignores differential revenue brought by these requests. This simple policy reflects how most Web sites today handle HTTP requests.

10.2.3.3. Simulation Results

Example. Many rounds of simulations with different bandwidth and revenue assignments were conducted. Since their results do not differ qualitatively, a representative case is reported here. We assume that the ratio of service time between gold and silver is 2 and that:

- Estimated arrival rate of gold class (per time slot) is 4.5
- Estimated arrival rate of silver class is 8.6

10.2.3.4. Discussion

From the reported simulation results in Table 10.1, we observed:

1. The DP policy constantly beats the greedy policy.
2. The DP policy does not fully utilize bandwidth all the time.
3. The DP policy favors requests with higher revenue.

Separately, we noted that both greedy and DP policies deliver similar performance at the beginning of the simulation, when the system is largely empty and is nowhere near overloading.

Intuitively, a good admission control policy should accept any request when the system is empty and should be very selective about what is accepted when the system is near its capacity. This is exactly what the DP policy is performing. At the beginning, the DP policy is as aggressive as the greedy policy in accepting requests, regardless of how much revenue they bring. Therefore, both deliver similar performance. As time progresses, the system gradually approaches its capacity and the DP policy selectively reserves bandwidth for the more valuable gold requests and rejects most silver requests. Bandwidth reservation makes the

Table 10.1.   Comparison: DP Versus Greedy, On-line Versus Off-line

Total bandwidth (kbps)	1000	1000	1000	1000	1000
Gold bandwidth (kbps)	56	56	56	56	56
Silver bandwidth (kbps)	28	28	28	28	28
Gold revenue ($)	3	3	3	3	4
Silver revenue ($)	2	2	2	2	2
Gold arrival rate (/s)	10	15	10	10	10
Silver arrival rate (/s)	10	15	20	20	20
Average gold service time (s)	1.7	1.7	1.7	1.7	1.7
Average silver service time (s)	3.3	3.3	3.3	1.7	3.3
DP total revenue ($)	2597	2854	2590	3752	3388
Gold acceptance percent	72.94%	60.99%	74.67%	20.55%	82.34%
Silver acceptance percent	21.73%	4.14%	13.16%	77.72%	5.80%
Greedy total revenue ($)	2398	2436	2253	3605	2560
Gold acceptance percent	39.67%	23.99%	19.10%	38.76%	20.48%
Silver acceptance percent	59.84%	45.49%	42.27%	60.82%	43.64%
Ratio off-line total revenue ($)	3639	4746	4438	5234	5182
Counter off-line total revenue ($)	3613	4644	4221	5155	4954

overall utilization lower in order that it be available when high-revenue customers arrive. As the simulation shows, this aggressive-on-revenue approach enables the DP policy to generate more revenue than the aggressive-on-usage greedy policy.

It is well known that the DP approach can be very costly to implement, since the computational complexity grows exponentially with the increase of customer classes. It is worth pointing out that in some cases when greedy is near optimal to DP, we may choose to replace greedy algorithm for DP. As noted, when the system is lightly loaded, greedy policy is optimal. Also, it is not hard to see that when a fairly large amount of requests are being served in the system — so that in the next time unit the ratio between a possible new arrival and possible departures is low — the greedy policy can be as near optimal as DP. This was confirmed by our experimental results.

10.2.4. Implementation Issues

Most request dispatcher implementations emphasize low latency to prevent themselves from being the bottleneck. A request admission policy must also make decisions quickly. Fortunately, to implement the DP policy one only needs to keep the lookup table in memory. Admitting or dropping a request only involves table lookup and a comparison.

The only drawback of this approach is the potential large size of the lookup table. One option is to approximate the lookup table with some simple rules. For example, a rule may state that when the overall bandwidth usage is below

60%, all requests should be accepted. Another rule may state that when there are less than 20 gold-class customers and more than 80 silver-class customers, all new arrivals from silver-class customers should be rejected. These approximation rules are much less precise than the lookup table, but they are easy to implement and require much less memory to store. Another simplification is to develop rules that characterize states where greedy policy is optimal or near optimal.

10.2.5. Concluding Remarks

This section reports a successful implementation of revenue management control policies to the operational problem of service allocation to multiple user classes at a commercial Web hosting facility. Several conclusions and directions for further research are worth highlighting.

Revenue management appears to be an effective model for this purpose. Assigning revenue numbers to user requests does result in differentiated service. The service differentiation depends on the total free capacity available, so when there is capacity available, then all classes receive the highest grade of service. This strikes us as fair: since the marginal cost of service is nearly zero, why not give good service when there is room to do so? On the other hand, the method preserves capacity to allocate to future arrivals so the site will never be "jammed." A static allocation model (like the "Paris subway" [Odlyzko, 1997]) cannot do this.

The implementation includes several parameters that can be used for the tuning of differentiated services. These are revenue by class, bandwidth allocation (as a proxy for all other Web site resources) by class, and total capacity. Evidently, the setting of these parameters results in important service differentials. While one could outline an empirical procedure to assess the relative effects of tuning these parameters, one would like to have an analytical understanding of their impact on service level measurements. This is a topic for future research.

Solving the revenue management problem using dynamic programming techniques has obvious limitations. When the number of classes is more than two, there will be serious difficulties with the explosion of states. On the other hand, two classes may be enough for many applications. Certainly, the two-class problem is well within the capabilities of the dynamic program even for very busy Web sites. It may be possible to handle larger numbers of classes by clever approximation and/or learning techniques (Marbach et al., 2000). Refer also to Section 10.4.

Perhaps a more serious consideration arises when the stochastic assumptions on the arrival and service processes are not met. Service times may exhibit a subexponential or heavy-tailed distribution, and arrivals may exhibit a short-range or long-range dependence structure. Generalizing the assumption of exponential service time distribution will considerably complicate the calculation of the departure probabilities in the dynamic programming recursion. A possible way through this may be to analyze a broader class of on-line algorithms and rank them by their efficiency relative to the optimal off-line solution under the subexponential/heavy-tailed and short-range/long-range-dependent assumptions. Other approaches are considered in Sections 10.3 and 10.4.

To summarize, it appears that revenue management can be applied to the problem of resource allocation at Web sites and other IT service applications. A realistic implementation of such an idea appears in this section. Much interesting and important work remains to be done.

10.2.5.1. Appendix: Transition Probability for the DP Policy

We will compute the probability of the transition $\langle N \rangle \rightarrow \langle N' \rangle$ when the decision $1 \leq i \leq m$ (allocate bandwidth A_i to the arrived request) is taken.

If we are in state $\langle N \rangle = (n_1, \ldots, n_m)$ and the customer arrives, the available decisions (bandwidths) are subject to the capacity constraint. Suppose the decision A_1 is taken. At the next arrival, we can be at any state $\langle N' \rangle = (n_1', n_2', \ldots, n_m')$ with $n_1' \leq n_1 + 1, n_2 \leq n_2, \ldots, n_m' \leq n_m$.

For each individual bandwidth level i, the transition $n_i \rightarrow n_i$ means that n_i requests are not over by the next arrival and $n_i - n_i$ requests are over by the next arrival. For each individual request, the probability that it is over by the next arrival is $\mu_i/(\lambda_i + \mu_i)$, and correspondingly, the probability of not being over is $1 - \mu_i/(\lambda_i + \mu_i) = \lambda_i/(\lambda_i + \mu_i)$. This holds because the interarrival and service times are exponentially distributed with parameters λ_i and μ_i. Using a Bernoulli formula, the probability of transition $\langle N \rangle \rightarrow \langle N' \rangle$ under action A_1 can be derived.

10.3. DYNAMIC MULTIRESOURCE SCHEDULING

We formulate a revenue/penalty-based multiresource allocation problem for multiple QoS classes. In the present context, the control policies concern the load-dispatching router and the per-server resources, although our methods and results can be applied more generally. Most previous optimal resource allocation studies of this type have focused on QoS performance guarantees based on throughput or mean response time measures. However, a critical issue for Web hosting applications and services concerns the per-request efficiency with which the differentiated services are handled, since delays experienced by clients of each service provider customer can result in lost revenue and clients for the customer. Further, such QoS performance guarantees may not be fully captured by the more standard performance metrics. To address these issues, we consider a general class of SLA models that include the tail distributions of the per-class response times in addition to standard metrics. The decision variables of the corresponding optimization problem are concerned with allocating resources to maximize the profit of hosting the customer Web sites under these SLA constraints and a general cost model.

Our problem falls within the general class of optimal resource allocation problems, but based on the foregoing nonconventional performance metrics. Recently, Menascé et al. (2000) considered the related problem of resource scheduling in Web sites with the aim of maximizing revenue. A priority scheme is proposed for scheduling requests based on the states (navigation and purchase) of the client, who will lose patience if the response time is too long. Simulations were performed to evaluate the gains of such a policy in terms of revenue generated by the e-shopping carts. The study by Menascé et al. (2000) is the most closely related to our research in the literature, but it differs substantially from our study in several important respects (e.g., by considering a suboptimal allocation policy and by taking a simulation-based approach).

The general optimal resource allocation problem of interest involves decisions at different time scales. In this section, we present the general problem and consider the specific problem of optimal routing and scheduling of server resources at a relatively fine time scale, whereas Section 10.4 considers the related problem of optimal server assignments at a relatively coarse time scale. Specifically, we propose and investigate an analytic approach to obtain a provably optimal server capacity routing and scheduling policy with the use of methods from probability theory, queueing theory, and combinatorial optimization. The optimization of SLA profits is formulated as a network flow model with a separable set of concave objective functions at the servers that are based on queueing-theoretic formulas we derive to capture the system dynamics. Our solution is computed using the most efficient algorithms for this class of optimization problems, and we show this solution to be globally optimal within assumptions of our formulation. A large number of experiments are performed to evaluate the effectiveness of our approach for optimizing SLA profits, quantifying the significant benefits of the optimal solution over existing methods across a wide range of system loads.

The remainder of the section is organized as follows. Section 10.3.1 describes the set of mathematical models used in our study, and then in Section 10.3.2 we present our analysis of the resource allocation optimization problem. Our experimental results are provided in Section 10.3.3, and concluding remarks are presented in Section 10.3.4.

10.3.1. Formal Framework

We consider a Web hosting environment in which a common service provider hosts the Web sites for a set of N customers by providing Web applications and services to the clients of each customer. This includes the allocation of a set of M resources used to host the Web sites for these customers in order to satisfy the QoS performance requirements for every class of service. An SLA is created for every QoS class that a customer wants to provide to its clients, with an overall total of K SLA classes. The service provider gains revenue for all requests satisfying its per-class SLA and incurs a penalty otherwise. The only exceptions to this are best-effort requests, for which a flat-rate pricing policy can be defined. Our objective, then, is to find the optimal resource allocation control parameters that maximize the profit of hosting the customer Web sites. We assume that the revenues and penalties for the service provider are coupled with the corresponding revenues and penalties of each of the customers being hosted, and thus optimizing SLA profits benefits every customer as well as the service provider.

10.3.1.1. Web Hosting Environment

A Web server farm is a distributed computer system consisting of M heterogeneous servers that independently execute K SLA classes of request streams, where each request is destined for one of N different Web sites. To accommodate any and all restrictions that may exist in the possible assignments of class-site pairs to servers, we assume that these possible assignments are specified via a general mechanism. In particular, let $I(i, j, k)$ be the indicator function matrix for these assignments: $I(i, j, k)$ takes on the value 1 when class k requests destined for site j can be served by server i and 0 otherwise. This assignment function simply defines the set of class-site requests that can be served by a given server, with no implication that the requests will be served there. The problem of setting the values of the indicator matrix $I(i, j, k)$, which occurs at a coarser time scale due to the overheads involved in changing server assignments, is considered in Section 10.4.

We assume a system architecture in which there is a request dispatcher in front of the Web server farm that immediately routes all incoming class-site requests to one of the eligible servers. One of the optimization problems considered in this section is the control of the routing decisions between each pair of class-site requests and each server eligible to serve such requests. More precisely, we determine the optimal rate (or proportion) of traffic of different classes from different sites to be routed to each of the servers. Thus, our solution of the corresponding optimization problem will determine which requests are actually served by which servers.

10.3.1.2. Server Scheduling Policies

The primary policy for scheduling different classes of requests on each server is assumed to be preemptive priority scheduling (PPS), which is a natural candidate when the SLA classes have a strict ordering among the per-class performance guarantees, revenues, and penalties. It is quite reasonable to expect this to be the case for the class of Web hosting environments of interest, either in a strict sense or in a grouping sense (as discussed below). Moreover, class-based priority scheduling disciplines have been shown to be optimal for the scheduling of classes of differentiated service in single-server systems (e.g., refer to Smith, 1954; Klimov, 1974, 1978; and Avram et al., 1995). We shall therefore assume throughout this section a strict ordering among the SLA classes across all servers and all sites.

Of course, there will be instances of our general problem where such a strict ordering does not exist among all of the SLA classes. A common scenario for such cases consists of the hosting of multiple Web sites, each of which has levels of QoS performance guarantees that are very similar but not identical. Our proposed approach for this case consists of partitioning the individual SLA classes into groups, each containing those which have very similar yet not identical QoS performance guarantees, revenues, and penalties. The optimal solution among these equivalence groups of classes under the PPS discipline is obtained via the analysis of Section 10.2. The final step of our approach consists of taking this optimal resource assignment for each equivalence group and determining the optimal partition of this assignment among the SLA classes comprising the group under the generalized processor sharing (GPS) discipline. GPS is considered as a natural candidate for the deployment of QoS response time guarantees within each equivalence group because of its properties of isolation and proportional sharing among classes. In the interest of space, we do not consider here the details of our combined PPS-GPS approach, but instead refer the interested reader to Liu et al. (2001b).

Finally, we note that it is certainly possible to consider the resource allocation problem using GPS instead of PPS for scheduling different classes of requests on each server. This approach is considered by Liu et al. (2001a), and it yields a suboptimal solution to the resource allocation problem. Section 10.4 also considers a variant of the resource allocation problem of this section under the GPS server scheduling policy.

10.3.1.3. Queueing Network Model

The Web server farm is modeled by a queueing network composed of a set of M multiclass single-server queues and a set of $N \times K \times K$ single-class infinite-server queues. The former represents the collection of heterogeneous Web servers,

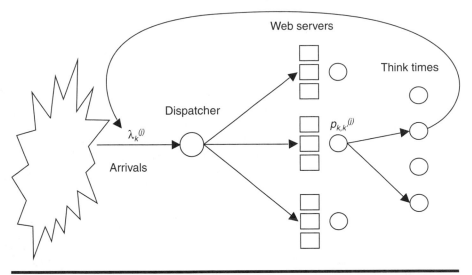

Figure 10.1. Queueing network model for Web server farm.

and the latter represents the client-based delays, or think times, between the service completion of one request and the arrival of the subsequent request within a client session. We shall henceforth index the Web servers by i, the delay servers by (j, k, k'), the Web sites by j, and the SLA classes by k, which are assumed to satisfy the natural conditions $i = 1, ..., M$, $j = 1, ..., N$, and $k = 1, ..., K$, unless noted otherwise. Figure 10.1 illustrates the queueing network model under consideration.

Without loss of generality, we assume that each of the M single-server multiclass queues representing the Web servers can accommodate all classes of requests subject to $I(i, j, k)$. PPS is used to control the allocation of resources among the different service classes on each server. Thus, class 1 has absolute priority over class 2, which in turn has absolute priority over class 3, and so on. We assume that the service times of class k requests on server i follow a general distribution with mean $b_{i,k} = C_i^{-1}\mu_{i,k}^{-1}$, where C_i is the capacity of server i. Requests within each class on every server are assumed to be executed in a first-come/first-served manner. This is a reasonable assumption within each class of a multiclass single-server queue under PPS, from both a practical and theoretical perspective. Furthermore, this use of first-come/first-served minimizes the waiting time variance within each class (Kingman, 1962).

Client sessions for site j that begin with a class k request arrive to the system from an exogenous source with rate $\lambda_k^{(j)}$. Upon completion of a class k request, the corresponding site j client session either returns as a class k' request with probability $p_{k,k'}^{(j)}$ following a delay at an infinite-server queue having mean

$(\delta_{k,k'}^{(j)})^{-1}$ or completes with probability $1 - \sum_{\ell=1}^{K} p_{k,\ell}^{(j)}$. Let $L_k^{(j)}$ denote the aggregate arrival rate of site j class k requests to the set of servers, which is determined by the exogenous arrival rates and the transition probabilities:

$$L_k^{(j)} = \sum_{k'=1}^{K} L_{k'}^{(j)} p_{k',k}^{(j)} + \lambda_k^{(j)} \qquad (10.5)$$

Define $p_k^{(j)} \equiv [p_{k,k'}^{(j)}]$ to be the corresponding request feedback matrix for site j, which is substochastic and has dimension $K \times K$. This matrix defines how each type of site j client session flows through the queueing network as a sequence of server requests and client think times, and thus it is used in our model to explicitly capture the correlations between the arrivals of class k and class k' requests of the same client session. The client think times can have arbitrary distributions, depending solely on the site j and the classes k and k'. It is important to mention that this model of client navigational behavior and its variants for capturing Web site traffic patterns are very general and are validated by various Web characterization studies (e.g., see Menascé et al. [1999] and Liu et al. [2001b] and the references cited therein).

There are two important aspects of our resource allocation problem in practice that have direct restrictions and implications on our formulation and solution approach. On the one hand, the navigational behavior of client sessions explicitly captured in our queueing network model creates per-class arrival processes that have strong dependence structures which in turn have a significant impact on the corresponding response time distributions. In particular, these types of complex arrival processes tend to result in response time distributions that have heavier, or longer, tails than the corresponding queue under simpler arrival processes (e.g., see Squillante et al., 1999). On the other hand, the speed at which the dispatcher operates prevents it from collecting detailed statistics about the per-class arrival processes, and typically the only available information is the corresponding mean arrival rates. Thus, the more detailed statistics required to properly characterize these arrival processes in order to obtain accurate tail distributions for the corresponding response times are simply not available to us. We therefore need an approach based solely on the mean arrival rate as the only characterization of the per-class arrival process that captures in a sufficient manner the tail of the corresponding response time distribution found in the Web hosting environments of interest.

Our approach is based on bounding from above the long-tail response time distributions of single-server queues under arrival processes with strong dependence structures by the response time tails of corresponding M/G/1 queues for relatively small response time values. More precisely, letting T_{LT} be the generic random variable for the response time process of a general single-server queue that has a long-tail response time distribution and letting $T_{M/G/1}$ be the generic random variable for the response time process of a corresponding M/G/1 queue with $E[T_{LT}]$ = $E[T_{M/G/1}]$, it then can be easily shown that $P[T_{LT} > x] \leq P[T_{M/G/1} > x]$ for sufficiently small values of x. While most recently published work on the tail of the response time distribution has focused on the asymptotic behavior of the tail distribution (i.e., characterizing $P[T > x]$ in the limit as $x \to \infty$), our interests here are quite different due to the very nature of the strict QoS performance guarantees motivating our study, which makes us more interested in characterizing (or bounding) the measure $P[T > x]$ for relatively small values of x. These and related arguments (Liu et al., 2001b) suggest that we can use the corresponding response-time tail distributions from a multiclass preemptive-priority M/G/1 queue as an upper bound on the per-class response-time tail distributions for each server under PPS. Our results in Section 10.3 clearly demonstrate the effectiveness of this approach, especially those results based on access logs from production commercial Web sites.

10.3.1.4. Cost Model

Our cost model is based on the notion that revenue is gained for each request satisfying its per-class SLA, and a penalty is paid otherwise. Let T_k be the generic random variable for the class k response time process, across all servers and all sites. Associated with each request of class k is an SLA constraint of the form

$$P[T_k > z_k] \leq \beta_k \qquad (10.6)$$

Our cost model is therefore based on receiving revenue $\mathbf{R}_k$ for each class k request having a response time of at most z_k and incurring a penalty $\mathbf{P}_k$ for each class k request which has a response time exceeding z_k. Our analysis can further handle multiple QoS performance guarantee intervals together with profit or loss parameters for each SLA class (Liu et al., 2001b).

As is common in practice, there is at least one additional request class that is assumed not to have an SLA contract and is instead served on a best-effort (BE) basis. Our cost model for each BE class k is based on the assumption that a fixed revenue $\mathbf{R}_k$ is gained for the entire class, independent of the number of class k requests executed, $k > K$. To help simplify the presentation, we will further assume that there is a single BE class $K + 1$, noting that it is straightforward to extend our analysis to handle multiple BE classes.

10.3.2. Optimization of SLA Profits Under PPS

We now consider the resource optimization problem of allocating server capacity among the set of class-site requests with the goal of maximizing profits under the above cost model. Let $\lambda_{i,k}^{(j)}$ denote the rate of class requests destined for site j that are assigned to server i. Our objective is to determine the optimal traffic assignments $\lambda_{i,k}^{(j)}$ that maximize SLA profits, given the matrix $I(i, j, k)$ and the exogenous arrival rates $\lambda_k^{(j)}$ which yield the aggregate arrival rates $L_k^{(j)}$ through the formula given in Equation 10.5.

Our analysis is based on the assumption that the routing decisions at the request dispatcher are probabilistic: A class k request for site j is routed to server i with probability $\lambda_{i,k}^{(j)} / \Sigma_{i'=1}^{M} \lambda_{i',k}^{(j)}$, independent of all else. When other routing mechanisms are used (e.g., weighted round robin), our optimal solutions in this probabilistic framework can be applied to set the parameters of these mechanisms (e.g., the per-class weights).

Our approach consists of first decomposing the queueing network into separate queueing systems and formulating each per-class optimization problem in terms of the profits of these queueing systems, and then solving the resulting optimization problems. In particular, we exploit the strict ordering of SLA classes and the properties of PPS to isolate the per-class queues at each server by decomposing the per-class performance characteristics of each server i in a hierarchical manner such that the analysis of the decomposed model for each class k in isolation is based on the solution for the decomposed models of classes $1, \ldots, k - 1$. To elucidate the exposition, we first provide the theoretical framework for our decomposition-based approach and the corresponding formulation of the optimization problem; then we present the algorithms used to efficiently compute our optimal solutions to these resource allocation problems.

10.3.2.1. Formulation of Optimization Problem

To simplify the analysis, suppose the optimal traffic assignments satisfy $\rho_{i,k} \equiv \lambda_{i,k}/(C_i \mu_{i,k}) < 1$. We then divide the optimization problem into separate formulations for the SLA classes and the BE class. Our formulation for the SLA classes is given by:

$$(\text{SLA}-\text{PPS}) \quad \max \sum_{i=1}^{M} \sum_{k=1}^{K} (\mathbf{R}_k \lambda_{i,k} - (\mathbf{R}_k + \mathbf{P}_k)\lambda_{i,k} P[T_{i,k} > z_k])$$

$$\text{s.t.} \quad P[T_{i,k} > z_k] \leq \beta_k \omega_k$$

$$\sum_{j=1}^{N} \lambda_{i,k}^{(j)} = \lambda_{i,k}$$

$$\sum_{i=1}^{M} \lambda_{i,k}^{(j)} = L_k^{(j)} \qquad (10.7)$$

$$\lambda_{i,k}^{(j)} = 0, \text{ if } I(i, j, k) = 0$$

$$\lambda_{i,k}^{(j)} \geq 0, \text{ if } I(i, j, k) = 1$$

where $1 \leq \omega_k \leq \beta_k^{-1}$. The $\lambda_{i,k}^{(j)}$ are the decision variables we seek to obtain, and $\mathbf{R}_k$, $\mathbf{P}_k$, C_i, $\lambda_k^{(j)}$, z_k, β_k, ω_k, $\mu_{i,k}$ are input parameters. Note that the first constraint represents the SLA relationship among the variables, which depends on $\lambda_{i,k}$. Note also that, by allowing $z_k = \infty$ for any k, or equivalently by setting $\mathbf{P}_k = -\mathbf{R}_k$, our cost model makes it possible to include the objective of optimizing the throughput for class k. Furthermore, we note that there exists an equivalent formulation involving only the per-class tail distributions in the objective function of (SLA-PPS); this differs from the original objective function value by a constant.

In our formulation of the optimal allocation problem for the BE class, we attempt to minimize the weighted sum of the mean response time for class $K + 1$ requests over all eligible servers subject to the decisions for the SLA classes, which yields the problem:

$$(\text{BE} - \text{PPS}) \qquad \min \sum_{i=1}^{M} \xi_{i,K+1} \left(\frac{\sum_{\ell=1}^{K+1} \lambda_{i,\ell} b_{i,\ell}^{(2)}}{2\sigma_{i,K}\sigma_{i,K+1}} + \frac{b_{i,K+1}}{\sigma_{i,K}} \right)$$

$$\text{s.t. } \lambda_{i,K+1} \leq \overline{C}_i \mu_{i,K+1}$$

$$\sum_{i=1}^{M} \lambda_{i,K+1}^{(j)} = L_{K+1}^{(j)} \qquad (10.8)$$

$$\lambda_{i,K+1}^{(j)} = 0, \text{ if } I(i, j, K + 1) = 0$$

$$\lambda_{i,K+1}^{(j)} \geq 0, \text{ if } I(i, j, K + 1) = 1$$

where $\sigma_{i,k} = 1 - \rho_{i,k}^{+}$, $\overline{C}_i = C_i\sigma_{i,K}$, $\xi_{i,K+1}$ is the relative importance factor for the mean response time of the BE class $K + 1$ on server i, $b_{i,\ell}$ and $b_{i,\ell}^{(2)}$ are the first two moments of the service times (recall that $b_{i,\ell} = C_i^{-1}\mu_{i,\ell}^{-1}$), and $\rho_{i,\ell}^+$ is the total load of classes $1, \ldots, \ell$: $\rho_{i,\ell}^+ = \sum_{\ell'=1}^{\ell}\rho_{i,\ell'} = \sum_{\ell'=1}^{\ell}\lambda_{i,\ell'}b_{i,\ell'}$. The $\lambda_{i,K+1}^{(j)}$ are the decision variables that we seek to obtain, and the remaining variables are input parameters. Note that the relative importance weights $\xi_{i,K+1}$ are included in our formulation as they may be of greater use when there are multiple BE classes.

The response time expression in the objective (Equation 10.8) is derived from known results for the multiclass preemptive-priority M/G/1 queue (e.g., see Takagi, 1991). Specifically, the set of SLA classes has absolute priority over the BE class of requests, and thus from the perspective of the BE class, the system behaves as a $K + 1$ class preemptive-priority queue where BE requests represent the lowest priority class. Moreover, following the bounding arguments made above and based on the approximations developed below, we use the Poisson arrival process for the higher priority (SLA) classes of requests.

In the above formulation of (SLA-PPS), we also introduced the scaling factors to generalize the optimization problem. Several practical considerations motivate the use of such scaling factors. Most importantly, the scaling factors $\omega_k > 1$ make it possible for the hosting company to violate the SLA to a controlled degree in an attempt to increase profits under Equation 10.7, whereas the hosting company will strictly follow the predefined SLA whenever $\omega_k = 1$. This can be particularly effective when the revenues and penalties for the hosting service provider are coupled with the corresponding revenues and penalties of each of the customer sites being hosted, as assumed in our study.

Another important aspect of the problem (SLA-PPS) concerns an explicit expression for the per-class response time tail distributions. Following the queueing-theoretic bounding arguments of Section 10.3, we consider this optimization problem within the context of a set of bounding multiclass preemptive-priority M/G/1 queues. Our approach within this framework depends upon the per-class service time distribution, where the exact response-time tail distribution for a single-class M/G/1 queue is used under exponential service times and a proposed approximation for the response-time tail distribution in a single-class M/G/1 queue is used under general service times. To elucidate the exposition of this approach, we shall consider here the specific case where class 1 service times are exponentially distributed and the other classes have general service time distributions. More generally, one would exploit the class 1 analysis below for each of the SLA classes with exponential service times and exploit the remaining analysis below (classes $2 \leq k \leq K$) for each of the SLA classes with a general service time distribution.

We first consider class 1 in isolation under the previously stated assumptions. Following the bounding arguments above, we suppose the arrival process to the class 1 queue at each server i to be a Poisson process. It then follows from standard results in the queueing theory (e.g., see Kleinrock, 1975) that the left-hand-side of the SLA constraint is given by $e^{-(C_i\mu_{i,1}-\lambda_{i,1})z_1}$. Hence, the SLA constraint (Equation 10.6) is satisfied when:

$$P[T_1 > z_1] = e^{-(C_i\mu_{i,1}-\lambda_{i,1})z_1} \le \beta_1 \tag{10.9}$$

As a result of Equation 10.9, and since the lower priority classes do not interfere with the execution of class requests under PPS, our formulation for the class optimal resource allocation problem (SLA(1)-PPS) is identical to (SLA-PPS) but with the objective function in Equation 10.7 replaced by:

$$(\text{SLA}(1)-\text{PPS}) \quad \max \sum_{i=1}^{M} \left(\mathbf{R}_1 \lambda_{i,1} - (\mathbf{R}_1 + \mathbf{P}_1)\lambda_{i,1}e^{-(C_i\mu_{i,1}-\lambda_{i,1})z_1} \right) \tag{10.10}$$

with the SLA constraint modified according to Equation 10.9 and with $k = 1$ in the remaining constraints. Note that the third constraint is the resource allocation constraint, which ensures all offered traffic will be allocated in an attempt to optimize SLA profits. However, if we instead change this constraint to be $\sum_{i=1}^{M}\lambda_{i,1}^{(j)} \le L_1^{(j)}$ and appropriately modify the objective function, then some fraction of the offered load might not be scheduled. In particular, whenever the optimal values of $\lambda_{i,1}^{(j)}$ sum to something less than the offered load, then admission control will be activated by denying service to the corresponding fraction of clients. Within the context of this formulation, all such clients can be assumed to be lowered to the BE class and assumed to not satisfy their SLA constraint with probability 1 (Liu et al., 2001b).

Upon solving (SLA(1)-PPS) to obtain the optimal decision variables $\lambda_{i,1}^{(j)*}$, we seek to approximate the tail distribution for the class queue within the same queueing-theoretic framework, which then will be used recursively to formulate and solve the optimization problem for the subsequent classes under the PPS ordering. Thus, for any class $k \ge 2$, we shall exploit results on preemptive priority M/G/1 queues to approximate the tail distributions of the response times at server i. More precisely, we assume that there exist constants $\gamma_{i,k}$ and $\theta_{i,k}$ such that:

$$P[T_{i,k} > z_k] \cong \gamma_{i,k}e^{-\theta_{i,k}z_k} \tag{10.11}$$

These types of approximations are justified by various known results in the queueing literature, including the exponential distribution of response times in an M/M/1 queue (e.g., refer to Equation 10.9 and Kleinrock, 1975), the heavy-traffic approximation of an exponential waiting time distribution in a GI/G/1 queue due to Kingman (e.g., see Kleinrock, 1976), the exponential upper and lower bounds on the response time in G/GI/1 queues (e.g., refer to Liu et al., 1997), the large-deviation upper and lower bounds on queues (e.g., see Chang, 2000 and Duffield and O'Connell, 1995), and the asymptotic results for single-server queues (e.g., refer to Abate et al., 1995).

Note that the exact tail distributions of the response times in preemptive-priority M/G/1 queues can be obtained by numerically inverting the corresponding Laplace transforms (e.g., refer to Takagi, 1991). However, such an approach will not be very useful for our optimal allocation problem. Indeed, for our solution approach, the cost functions should be concave in the rate variables $\lambda_{i,k}$, which does not hold true in general for the exact tail distributions.

Assuming that we have solved the optimization problem for the higher priority classes $1, \ldots, k-1$, then our formulation of the allocation problem for class k (SLA(k)-PPS) is identical to (SLA-PPS) but with the objective in Equation 10.7 replaced by:

$$\text{(SLA}(k)-\text{PPS)} \qquad \max \sum_{i=1}^{M} \left(\mathbf{R}_k \lambda_{i,k} - (\mathbf{R}_k + \mathbf{P}_k)\lambda_{i,k}\gamma_{i,k}e^{-\theta_{i,k}z_k} \right) \qquad (10.12)$$

In order to apply the efficient optimization algorithms of Section 10.2, we need to appropriately choose the parameters $\theta_{i,k}$ and $\gamma_{i,k}$. While different schemes can be envisioned, in this section we propose to fit the two parameters with the first two moments of the response time distribution. Since $E[X^m] = m\int_0^\infty x^{m-1}P[X > x]dx$ for any nonnegative random variable X, it then follows from Equation 10.11 that

$$E[T_{i,k}] = \gamma_{i,k}/\theta_{i,k} \quad \text{and} \quad E[T_{i,k}^2] = 2\gamma_{i,k}/\theta_{i,k}^2 \qquad (10.13)$$

and thus

$$\theta_{i,k} = \frac{2E[T_{i,k}]}{E[T_{i,k}^2]} \quad \text{and} \quad \gamma_{i,k} = \frac{2E[T_{i,k}]^2}{E[T_{i,k}^2]} \qquad (10.14)$$

Using the known formulas for $E[T_{i,k}]$ and $E[T_{i,k}^2]$, we have (Takagi, 1991)

$$E[T_{i,k}] = \frac{\sum_{k'=1}^{k} \lambda_{i,k'}b_{i,k'}^{(2)}}{2\sigma_{i,k-1}\sigma_{i,k}} + \frac{b_{i,k}}{\sigma_{i,k-1}} \qquad (10.15)$$

$$E[T_{i,k}^2] = \frac{\sum_{k'=1}^{k} \lambda_{i,k'} b_{i,k'}^{(3)}}{3\sigma_{i,k-1}^2 \sigma_{i,k}} + \frac{b_{i,k}^{(2)}}{\sigma_{i,k-1}^2}$$

$$+ \left(\frac{\sum_{k'=1}^{k} \lambda_{i,k'} b_{i,k'}^{(2)}}{\sigma_{i,k-1} \sigma_{i,k}} + \frac{\sum_{k'=1}^{k-1} \lambda_{i,k'} b_{i,k'}^{(2)}}{\sigma_{i,k-1}^2} \right) E[T_{i,k}]$$

(10.16)

where $b_{i,k}$, $b_{i,k}^{(2)}$, and $b_{i,k}^{(3)}$ are the first three moments of the class k service times on server i, and $\sigma_{i,k} = 1 - \rho_{i,k}^+$.

We now establish an important result based on this formulation that shows our solution to be globally optimal, within the assumptions of this section.

Theorem 1. Assume that the service time distributions of classes $1, ..., k$ at each server i belong to the family of mixtures of exponentials. Then, the objective functions in Equations 10.10 and 10.12 are concave in $\lambda_{i,k}$, for all i = $1, ..., M$.

Proof. The objective function in Equation 10.10 is obviously concave for each i as the first term is linear in $\lambda_{i,k}$ and the second term is negative and convex in $\lambda_{i,k}$. As for the objective function in Equation 10.12, it suffices to show that $\gamma_{i,k}$ is increasing and convex in $\lambda_{i,k}$ and that $\theta_{i,k}$ is decreasing and concave in $\lambda_{i,k}$. These properties are readily verified.

Indeed, we are confident that this result holds under more general assumptions. Furthermore, it follows from this theorem that we can recursively apply the network flow model algorithms of Section 10.2 to the K subproblems (SLA(k)-PPS) corresponding to classes $k = 1, 2, ..., K$.

10.3.2.2. Optimization Algorithms

We now present a brief description of the basic optimization algorithm employed in the solution for each class k. Additional details, generalizations, and references can be found in Liu et al. (2001b) and Ibaraki and Katoh (1988).

Consider a directed network with a single-source node and multiple sink nodes. There is a function associated with each sink node. This function is required to be increasing, differentiable, and concave in the net flow into that sink, and the overall objective function is the (separable) sum of these concave functions. We wish to optimize this objective function. There can be both upper (capacity) and lower bound constraints on the flows on each directed arc. We call this the network flow resource allocation problem

(NFRAP). To be precise, consider a directed network consisting of nodes **V** and directed arcs **A**. The arcs $a_{v_1v_2} \in$ **A** carry flow $f_{v_1v_2}$ from nodes $v_1 \in$ **A** to nodes $v_2 \in$ **V**. The flow is a real variable that is constrained to be bounded below by a constant $l_{v_1v_2}$ and above by a constant $u_{v_1v_2}$. That is, $l_{v_1v_2} \leq f_{v_1v_2} \leq u_{v_1v_2}$ for each arc $a_{v_1v_2}$. It is possible, of course, that $l_{v_1v_2} = 0$ or $u_{v_1v_2} = \infty$. There will be a single-source node $s \in$ **V** satisfying $\Sigma_{a_{sv_2}} f_{sv_2} = $ **R** > 0. This value **R**, the net outflow from the source, is a constant that represents the amount of resource available to be allocated. There are N sinks $v_2 \in$ **N** $\subseteq$ **A** which have the property that their net inflow $\Sigma_{a_{v_1v_2}} f_{v_1v_2} > 0$. All other nodes $v_2 \in$ **A** $- \{s\} -$ **N** are transshipment nodes that satisfy $\Sigma_{a_{v_1v_2}} f_{v_1v_2} - \Sigma_{a_{v_2v_3}} f_{v_2v_3} = 0$. There is a single increasing, concave, and differentiable function F_{v_2} of the net flow into each sink node j. Thus, the overall objective function is given by $\Sigma_{v_2 \in \text{N}} F_{v_2} (\Sigma_{a_{v_1v_2}} f_{v_1v_2})$, which we wish to optimize subject to the lower and upper bound constraints described above.

In addition to the source node s, there are N nodes corresponding to the sites, followed by a pair of M nodes corresponding to the servers, the latter set being the sinks. In the first group of arcs, the jth node has capacity equal to $L_k^{(j)}$. The second group of arcs corresponds to pairs (j, i) for which $I(i, j, k) = 1$, and these arcs have infinite capacity. The capacities of the third group of arcs on (i, k) correspond to the SLA constraints. All lower bounds are 0.

A special case of NFRAP is:

$$\max \sum_{v_2=1}^{N} (F_{v_2} (x_{v_2})) \qquad (10.17)$$

$$\text{s.t. } l_{v_2} \leq x_{v_2} \leq u_{v_2} \qquad (10.18)$$

$$\sum_{v_2=1}^{N} x_{v_2} = \text{R} \qquad (10.19)$$

where each $F_{v_2}(\cdot)$ is an increasing, concave, and differentiable function of the real decision variables x_{v_2}. The optimal solution for this so-called separable concave resource allocation problem (SCRAP) occurs at the place where the derivatives $F'_{v_2}(x_{v_2})$ are equal and the resource allocation constraint in Equation 10.19 holds, modulo the bound constraints in Equation 10.18. More precisely, the algorithm proceeds as follows. If $\Sigma_{v_2=1}^{N} l_{v_2} > $ **R** or $\Sigma_{v_2=1}^{N} u_{v_2} < $ **R**, there is no feasible solution and the algorithm terminates. Otherwise, the algorithm consists of an outer bisection loop that determines the value of the derivative D and a set of N inner bisection loops that find the value of $l_{v_2} \le x_{v_2} \le u_{v_2}$ satisfying $F'_{v_2}(x_{v_2}) = D$ if $F'_{v_2}(l_{v_2}) \le D$ and $F'_{v_2}(u_{v_2}) \ge D$. Otherwise, we set $x_{v_2} = l_{v_2}$ (in the first case) or $x_{v_2} = u_{v_2}$ (in the second). The initial values for the outer loop can be taken as the minimum of all values $F'_{v_2}(l_{v_2})$ and the maximum of all values $F'_{v_2}(u_{v_2})$. The initial values for the v_2-th inner loop can be taken to be l_{v_2} and u_{v_2}.

Now the general network flow problem is solved by recursive calls to a subroutine that solves the problem with a slightly revised network and with generalized bound constraints $l'_{v_1 v_2} \le f_{v_1 v_2} \le u'_{v_1 v_2}$ instead of those described above. As the algorithm proceeds, it makes calls to the SCRAP solver. More precisely, we start by solving the problem obtained by ignoring all but the source and sink nodes. Let x_{v_2} denote the solution to that optimization problem. In the next step, we add a supersink t to the original network, with directed arcs jt from each original sink, forming a revised network $(\mathbf{V}', \mathbf{A}')$. We set $l'_{jt} = 0$ and $u'_{jt} = x_{v_2}$ for all arcs connecting the original sinks to the supersink. For all other arcs, the lower and upper bounds remain the same. Thus $l'_{v_1 v_2} = l_{v_1 v_2}$ and $u'_{v_1 v_2} = u_{v_1 v_2}$ for all arcs $a_{v_1 v_2}$. We then solve a so-called maximum flow problem to find the largest possible flow $f_{v_1 v_2}$ through the network $(\mathbf{V}', \mathbf{A}')$ subject to the lower and upper bound constraints described above. A simple routine for the maximum flow problem is the so-called labeling algorithm combined with a path augmentation routine. Using the residual network, one can simultaneously obtain the so-called minimum cut partition. Those original sink nodes j which appear in the same partition as the supersink are now regarded as saturated. The flow $f_{v_2 t}$ becomes the lower and upper bounds on that arc. Thus we set $l'_{v_2 t} = u'_{v_2 t} = f_{v_2 t}$. For all remaining unsaturated arcs j, we set $l'_{v_2 t} = x_{v_2}$ and $u'_{v_2 t} = f_{v_2 t}$. Now we repeat the entire process, solving the SCRAP for the unsaturated nodes only, with suitably revised total resource, and then solving the revised network flow problem. This process continues until all nodes are saturated or we reach an infeasible solution.

10.3.3. Experimental Results

In this subsection, we discuss some experimental results to illustrate the effectiveness of our approach for optimizing SLA profits based on QoS performance guarantees. A large number of experiments have been conducted under a wide range of parameter settings. In each case, we numerically determine the optimal solution using the models and methods of Section 10.1 and Section 10.2, and then we investigate through numerical experiments and simulation the benefits of our approach. A representative set of these experiments are discussed here; additional results and details can be found in Liu et al. (2001b).

10.3.3.1. Configuration of Experiments

Throughout this subsection we shall focus on the following parameter settings: $M = 12$; $N = 3$; $K = 3$; $C_i = 1.0$ for $i = 1, \ldots, 6$; $C_i = 2.0$ for $i = 7, \ldots, 12$; and $\lambda_k^{(1)} = 0.08, 0.16, 1.2$; $\lambda_k^{(2)} = 0.06, 0.12, 0.08$; $\lambda_k^{(3)} = 0.04, 0.08, 0.4$; $\mu_{i,k}^{-1} = 0.15, 0.3, 0.6$; $\beta_k = 0.05, 0.1, 0.1$; $z_k = 0.6, 1.2, 1.8$; $\mathbf{R}_k = 0.3, 0.2, 0.1$; $\omega_k = 15, 8, 8$; for $k = 1, 2, 3$. There is a strict ordering of QoS performance guarantees, revenues, and penalties from class 1 to class 3. We shall consider the effect of the penalty-revenue ratio $r := \mathbf{P}_k/\mathbf{R}_k$ by using $\mathbf{P}_k = r \cdot \mathbf{R}_k$ in our experiments. (One would typically have $r \geq 1$, and usually $r \gg 1$.) We also have investigated the case where the SLA for class 3 is based solely on throughput by setting $\mathbf{P}_3 = -\mathbf{R}_3$, where the corresponding results are only slightly different from those provided below; refer to Liu et al. (2001b).

Although we are discussing experiments with a relatively modest number of servers, these results can be easily used to infer the results corresponding to Web server farms which are larger (in a uniform sense). For example, consider a system where each of the 12 servers actually represents 10 real servers that are identical in every way. In this case, the optimal solution for the 120-server farm can be easily inferred from the solution provided in our experiments.

A multiplicative load factor $\eta > 0$ is used to scale the base arrival rates $\lambda_k^{(j)}$ to consider different traffic intensities. Thus, the load factor η provides a relative scaling such that $\lambda_k^{(j)}\eta$ is used in the experiments for the site j class k arrival rate. Note that, at least for the experiments discussed below, the service requirements depend only on the classes k and not on the servers i.

We consider three configurations $I1$, $I2$, and $I3$ for the indicator matrix $I(i, j, k)$. Matrix $I1$ corresponds to the fully clustered server farm: any server can process requests for any class and any site. Matrix $I2$ corresponds to a partially clustered server farm: servers 1, 2, and 3 are dedicated to site 1 requests; servers 4 and 5 are dedicated to site 2 requests; and server 6 is dedicated to site 3 requests, whereas servers 7, 9, 10, and 12 are shared by site 1 and site 2 requests and servers 8 and 11 are shared by site 1 and site 3 requests. Matrix $I3$ corresponds to a fully partitioned server farm: servers 1, 2, 3, 7, 8, and 9 are dedicated to site 1 requests; servers 4, 5, 10, and 11 are dedicated to site 2 requests; and servers 6 and 12 are dedicated to site 3 requests.

For comparison with our optimal allocation algorithm, we consider the proportional assignment scheme that employs

$$\lambda_{i,k}^{(j)} = \frac{\lambda_k^{(j)} C_i \mu_{i,k} I(i, j, k)}{\sum_{\ell=1}^{M} C_\ell \mu_{\ell,k} I(\ell, j, k)} \tag{10.20}$$

$$\lambda_{i,k} = \sum_{j=1}^{N} \lambda_{i,k}^{(j)} \tag{10.21}$$

to allocate the per-class per-site traffic among the eligible servers. This is a natural way to assign the traffic and server capacity, and it is provably the best load-balancing scheme in terms of stability regions. Moreover, for a more competitive comparison with our optimal solution, we consider a PPS discipline at every server. If, on the other hand, existing Web server scheduling disciplines were used together with proportional allocation instead of PPS, then the results under our optimal solutions would provide significantly larger profits than those discussed in this subsection.

10.3.3.2. Comparison of Profits

We now quantitatively compare the profits obtained under our optimal resource allocation algorithm with those obtained under the proportional assignment scheme. For each of the experimental configurations considered, we only discuss profit results for the SLA classes, because the BE classes do not impact the profit value under our cost model. Various comparisons are discussed under different stochastic assumptions.

Poisson arrivals and exponential service times. Consider first the case where the arrivals form a Poisson process and the service times are exponentially distributed. We consider four values of r, starting with $r = 10$ and doubling up through $r = 80$. Since we are considering the profit per unit time, ideal performance under this metric corresponds to a linear function.

We observe that both algorithms yield a profit for small values of r, with considerably larger profits under the optimal assignment as well as strictly positive profits for somewhat higher values of r. For very large values of r, it is not possible to be profitable, with greater losses under proportional assignment than the optimal solution. At light to moderate loads, the profits under the optimal assignment essentially grow linearly, and the curves are nearly on top of each other. This is the ideal situation: penalties are rare. The profits do start to tail off at heavy loads. Naturally, the higher r values degrade more seriously, and the ordering of the curves is strictly determined by the value of r.

We also note that the optimal curves for $I2$ are, for all practical purposes, almost identical to those for the fully clustered matrix $I1$. Indeed, this is a further indication of the robustness of the overall optimal resource allocation algorithm. Even though the partially clustered and fully partitioned matrices correspond to distinctly different scenarios, there is enough flexibility to allow the optimizer to find solutions equivalent to the globally optimal solution given in the fully clustered case. Naive schemes such as proportional will not be as robust, which is further illustrated next.

Renewal arrival process and general service times. Now consider a more general case in terms of the distributional model assumptions. We focus on $I1$ with the penalty-to-profit ratio fixed at $r = 20$. The interarrival and service time sequences are each assumed to be independent and identically distributed, but otherwise arbitrary. We consider a comparison between the optimal solution and the proportional scheme under different coefficients of variation for these distributions, where coefficients of variation of 5 and 10 for the interarrival times and the service times are studied.

In comparison to the previous case where the coefficient of variation equals 1 for both interarrival and service times, the profits under both optimal and proportional solutions are decreased. These profits are decreasing in the coefficients of variation of both service times and interarrival times. This is not very surprising, as it is well known that the response times increase as the coefficients of variation increase. It is, however, important to note that the gaps in profits between the two solutions are increased with the increase of the coefficient of variation.

Access logs from a production commercial Web server. We next consider the case where the request arrival times and service times are taken from the access logs of a production commercial Web site, which exhibit long-range dependent arrival patterns with a Hurst parameter of around 0.78 and subexponential (Weibullian) service requirements. The corresponding results for I matrix configurations and various penalty-to-profit ratios r are studied.

It is interesting to observe from these results that the gap between the profits under both optimal and proportional solutions is even bigger than those discussed above for the stochastic interarrival and service processes. Moreover, we see that all of the trends observed under the above workloads are also discussed in the results based on a production commercial Web site.

10.3.4. Concluding Remarks

The growth in Web usage creates a vital need to provide QoS guarantees for each differentiated service class across a wide range of Web hosting environments. In this section, we explored the problem of optimizing profits under SLA contracts based on strict QoS performance guarantees and a general cost model. Our optimal resource allocation solution is obtained in a hierarchical manner using methods from probability theory, queueing theory, and combinatorial optimization.

Our results provide important insights into the fundamental problem of optimizing SLA profits in Web hosting environments. In particular, we observe that the optimal resource allocation algorithm provides significantly larger profits per unit time than those obtained under the natural scheme of proportional assignment combined with PPS. This also illustrates the validity of our overall approach, including the viability and profitability of the class of SLA contracts used in our study. The optimal allocation consistently provides large profits over a wide range of system loads, whereas the naive algorithm typically yields losses which can be quite considerable. While it is possible to increase the capacity of the system to make a profit under proportional allocation, much greater profits can be obtained under the optimal allocation algorithm with fewer system resources, thus making a profit in a more efficient manner. Our results further demonstrate the effective use of bounds and approximations on the per-class response time distribution when closed-form expressions are not known, at least within the context of our SLA contracts and related models. Finally, numerical experiments also demonstrate our methods to be extremely efficient in practice, making it possible to exploit them on-line in Web hosting environments.

10.4. DYNAMIC MULTIRESOURCE ASSIGNMENT

We continue our investigation of a general revenue/penalty-based multiresource allocation problem by building upon the optimal routing and scheduling of server resources at a relatively fine time scale of the previous section and by focusing on the related control problem of optimal server assignments at a relatively coarse time scale. In particular, one of the key tasks of the hosting service provider is to allocate servers to each of the Web sites to satisfy the agreed upon QoS performance guarantees for the different classes of incoming requests at each point in time, while maximizing its profits. Doing so requires consideration of what might happen over multiple periods of time. However, the number of scenarios to which the system can transition in just a short amount of time grows quickly with the system dimensions, making it computationally infeasible to find the optimal control policy for dynamically assigning servers, as well as adding new servers, within the context of the set of SLAs. We propose a solution to the Web server allocation problem based on approximate dynamic programming and compare our algorithm against a deterministic policy that optimizes the allocation based on the average Web site traffic.

The remainder of the section is organized as follows. Aspects of our formal framework for the resource allocation problem are presented in Section 10.4.1.

We then formulate the server allocation problem in the Markov decision process framework in Section 10.4.2 and discuss applications of approximate linear programming in Section 10.4.3. We demonstrate how problems stemming from state space and action space complexity can be addressed in Section 10.4.4 and Section 10.4.5. We present experimental results in Section 10.4.6 and offer closing remarks in Section 10.4.7.

10.4.1. Formal Framework

10.4.1.1. Solving the Scheduling and Routing Problems

We consider a variant of the formal Web hosting framework in Section 10.1 consisting of a collection of M Web servers that are shared by N customer Web sites. The scheduling policy at each Web server is GPS. We will solve the server capacity scheduling and routing problem over 2.5-minute intervals. The Web server assignments and arrival rates are assumed to remain fixed within each of these intervals. We use the symbol I to denote a particular encoding of the Web server assignment and let L denote a vector of aggregated endogenous/exogenous arrival rates L_k. The solution of the scheduling and routing problem is a function of the pair (I, L).

Using an approach based on stochastic bounds and approximations, our routing and scheduling decision variables reduce to $\lambda_{i,k}$, the arrival rate of class k requests routed to server i, and $\phi_{i,k}$, the fraction of server i capacity assigned to class k. The arrival rates across servers for any given class have to equal the total arrival rate for that class L_k. Furthermore, the total assigned capacity for any given server cannot exceed 1.

The SLA establishes that the response time T_k for each class k request must satisfy

$$P(T_k > z_k) \leq \beta_k$$

for given parameters z_k and β_k. As discussed by Liu et al. (2001a), we bound this constraint from above by

$$e^{(\lambda_{i,k} - \phi_{i,k}\mu_k)z_k} \leq \beta_k$$

via arguments based on stochastic bounds and approximations.

We also consider a simplified variant of the cost model in Section 10.3. In particular, a usage-based cost model is considered in which server usage is charged per time with rate $\mathbf{P}_k$ for class k. The expected time server i devotes to class k in each 2.5-minute interval is given by $\lambda_{i,k}/\mu_k$, provided that arrival rates and service times are expressed in the correct time scale, and therefore the expected profit generated by class k requests processed on server i is given by:

$$\mathbf{P}_k \frac{\lambda_{i,k}}{\mu_k}$$

We thus have the following optimization problem for determining server capacity scheduling and routing policies:

$$(\text{Usage} - \text{GPS}) \qquad \max \sum_{i=1}^{M} \sum_{k=1}^{K} \mathbf{P}_k \frac{\lambda_{i,k}}{\mu_k}$$

$$\text{s.t.} \quad \lambda_{i,k} \leq \frac{\ln(\beta_k)}{z_k} + \phi_{i,k}\mu_k, \text{ if } I(i,k) = 1, i = 1, \ldots, M, k = 1, \ldots, K$$

$$\sum_{i=1}^{M} \lambda_{i,k} \leq L_k, k = 1, \ldots, K$$

$$\lambda_{i,k} = 0, \text{ if } I(i,k) = 0, k = 1, \ldots, K, i = 1, \ldots, M \qquad (10.22)$$

$$\lambda_{i,k} \geq 0, \text{ if } I(i,k) = 1, k = 1, \ldots, K, i = 1, \ldots, M$$

$$\sum_{k=1}^{K} \phi_{i,k} \leq 1, i = 1, \ldots, M$$

$$\phi_{i,k} = 0, \text{ if } I(i,k) = 0, k = 1, \ldots, K, i = 1, \ldots, M$$

$$\phi_{i,k} \geq 0, \text{ if } I(i,k) = 1, k = 1, \ldots, K, i = 1, \ldots, M$$

The $\lambda_{i,k}$ and $\phi_{i,k}$ are the decision variables we seek to obtain. Here our use of $I(i, k)$ is a slight abuse of notation and it indicates whether server i is assigned to the Web site associated with class k.

The optimal value of problem (Usage-GPS) is denoted by $R(I, L)$, corresponding to the expected profit over a 2.5-minute interval when arrival rates are given by L and the Web server assignment is given by I.

The LP (Usage-GPS) can be solved analytically, which speeds up computation. Note that it decomposes into N smaller problems of scheduling and routing for each Web site. Moreover, we can show that the following greedy strategy is optimal:

1. Assign the minimum capacity $-\ln(\beta_k)/z_k\mu_k$ to each class k.
2. Assign the remaining capacity as needed to classes based on a priority scheme, serving classes according to profit $\mathbf{P}_k$.

Optimality of the procedure above is easily verified as follows. Suppose we have two classes k and k' with $\mathbf{P}_k < \mathbf{P}_{k'}$, with $\sum_i \lambda_{i,k'} < L_k$ and $\phi_{i,k} > 0$ for some i. Then we can reallocate server capacity according to $\overline{\phi}_{i,k} = \phi_{i,k} > 0 - \varepsilon$, $\overline{\phi}_{i,k'}$ $= \phi_{i,k'} + \varepsilon$, so that $\sum_i \lambda_{i,k'} + \varepsilon\mu_k \leq L_k$ and $\overline{\phi}_{i,k} \geq 0$, which is a new feasible solution to (Usage-GPS). This incurs a change in profit of

$$\frac{\mathbf{P}_{k'}}{\mu_{k'}} \varepsilon\mu_{k'} - \frac{\mathbf{P}_k}{\mu_k} \varepsilon\mu_k = \mathbf{P}_{k'} - \mathbf{P}_k > 0$$

We conclude that an optimal policy must serve all requests of the most expensive classes first; hence the greedy policy is optimal.

Note that the constraint

$$\lambda_{i,k} \leq \frac{\ln(\beta_k)}{z_k} + \phi_{i,k}\mu_k$$

corresponding to the SLA for class k, requires that a minimum server capacity be assigned to requests of class k even if that server is not processing any requests of that type. This is due to the fact that the SLA constraint is based on a stochastic bound, which is not tight for small (or zero) arrival rates $\lambda_{i,k}$. Ideally, problem (Usage-GPS) would be reformulated to correct for that, but this would lead to a nonconvex optimization problem. In a different relaxation of the original scheduling and routing problem, we may approximate the number of servers needed for serving all requests of class k by

$$\frac{L_k}{\mu_k + \dfrac{\ln(\beta_k)}{z_k}} \tag{10.23}$$

and assign the available servers to the classes associated with a Web site according to that number. In this situation, server capacity is not assigned to classes with no requests being processed in a given server. Expression 10.23 is motivated by the fact that if a server i is totally dedicated to class k requests ($\phi_{i,k} = 1$), it can process at most $\mu_k + [\ln(\beta_k)/z_k]$ requests of that type. With Expression 10.23 as an approximation for the number of servers needed for each class, we have a nearly optimal policy by assigning available servers greedily according to profit $\mathbf{P}_k/\mu_k$.

The Web server allocation problem will next be solved by dynamic programming. We will use the optimal value of problem (Usage-GPS) — $R(I, L)$ — as one-step rewards. Dynamic programming is called for due to the time-variant nature of arrival rates: changes in the incoming traffic will typically require adjustments in the number of servers allocated to each Web site. However, before tackling the Web server allocation problem, we will discuss the arrival rate process.

10.4.1.2. Arrival Rate Process

As explained in Section 10.3, there are two types of Web page requests in a Web server farm: exogenous, corresponding to users initiating a browsing session, and endogenous, corresponding to subsequent requests in an already initiated session. As mentioned before, we will consider the aggregated arrival rate, making no distinction between these two types of requests.

We consider the following model for the arrival rate process for requests of class k associated with Web site i:

$$L_k(t + 1) = \max(\overline{L}_k + a_k(L_k(t) - \overline{L}_k) + \sigma_k N_k(t) + M_k B_i(t), 0) \quad (10.24)$$

where $\{N_k(t), k = 1, ..., K, t = 0, 1, ...\}$ is a collection of independent standard normal random variables and $\{B_i(t), i = 1, ..., N, t = 0, 1, ...\}$ is a collection of independent Bernoulli random variables.

We interpret the arrival rate process in Equation 10.24 as follows. $\overline{L}_k$ represents a prediction for the average arrival rate associated with class k. We assume that arrival rates fluctuate around their average value $\overline{L}_k$, where a_k is a scalar between 0 and 1 representing how persistent deviations from the average arrival rate behave. The normal random variables $N_k(t)$ represent regular fluctuations around the average arrival rate, and the Bernoulli variables $B_i(t)$ capture arrival bursts. Note that the occurrence of a burst is associated with a Web site as a whole, not with any particular classes of users. We next turn to the Web server allocation problem, which is formulated in the dynamic programming framework.

10.4.2. Markov Decision Process Model for Web Server Assignment Problem

We model the Web server assignment problem in discrete time, with each time step corresponding to 2.5 minutes, which represents the time necessary to allocate or deallocate a server. The state of this model should contain all information that is important for the assignment decision. In the Web server assignment problem, with the simplified model in Equation 10.24 for arrival rates presented in Section 10.2, a natural choice for the state variable is the pair (I, L), where I indicates the servers assigned to each Web site and L is a K-dimensional vector of arrival rates.

Actions A take values on the same space as Web server configurations I and indicate new Web server configurations. Valid actions must satisfy the constraint that only currently deallocated servers can be assigned to a Web site. A state (I, L) under action A transitions to state $(A, \tilde{L})$ with probability $P(L, \tilde{L})$ determined by the arrival rate processes given by Lippman and Stidham (1977).

We have to specify rewards associated with each state-action pair. For simplicity, we will assume that the arrival rate L remains constant over each time step in the Web server assignment problem and consider the expected reward $R(I, L)$ for the static scheduling/routing decision given by the optimization problem (Usage-GPS).

We will seek to optimize the discounted infinite-horizon reward. We expect to use reasonably large discount factors (in the experiments, $\alpha = 0.99$) so that our criterion can be viewed as an approximation to average reward.

10.4.3. Approximate Linear Programming

In the previous subsection, we specified the parameters necessary to formulate the Web server assignment problem as a dynamic programming problem. Ideally, an optimal policy would be determined based on the *optimal value function* $J^*(I, L)$, which is the unique solution to Bellman's equation:

$$J^*(I, L) = \max_A \{R(I, Z(L, A)) + \alpha E[J^*(A, L(1)) \mid L_0 = L]\}$$

Function $Z(L, A)$ determines the servers available to each Web site when the configuration is changing from L to A (for instance, if a server is being added to a Web site, it will only be available in the next time step; however, if it is being removed from that Web site, it becomes unavailable right away).

An optimal policy A^* can be derived from J^* as follows:

$$A^*(I, L) = \arg \max_A \{R(I, Z(L, A)) + \alpha E[J^*(A, L(1)) \mid L_0 = L]\}$$

There are several algorithms for solving Bellman's equation. However, we observe that even with a reasonably simple model for the arrival rate processes such as that given by Lippman and Stidham (1977) — and certainly with more sophisticated models that one might eventually want to consider — our problem suffers from the *curse of dimensionality*. The number of state variables capturing arrival rate processes grows linearly in the number of Web sites being hosted, and the number of states for the mapping of servers to Web sites is on the order of $O(M^N)$. Clearly, for all but very small Web server farms, we will not be able to apply dynamic programming exactly, as it would require computing and storing the optimal value function over a huge state space. Alternatively, we use approximate linear programming (Schweitzer and Seidmann, 1985; de Farias and Roy, 2001a).

Approximate linear programming is based on the linear programming approach to dynamic programming (de Ghellinck, 1960; Denardo, 1970; D'Epenoux, 1963; Manne, 1960). It involves an approximation of the optimal value function by a linear combination of prespecified *basis functions* ϕ_i, $i = 1, ..., p$:

$$J^*(I, L) \approx \sum_{i=1}^{p} r_i \phi_i(I, L)$$

A reasonable set of weights r_i, $i = 1, ..., p$ to be assigned to each of the basis functions can be found by the solution of the following linear program:

$$\min_{r_i} \sum_i r_i \sum_{I,L} c(I, L) \phi_i(I, L)$$

$$\text{s.t. } R(I, Z(L, A)) + \sum_i r_i E[\phi_i(A, L(1)) \mid L_0 = L]$$

$$\leq \sum_i r_i \phi_i(A, L) \qquad \forall (I, L, A)$$

We refer to this problem as the *approximate LP*. The objective function coefficients $c(I, L)$ are *state-relevance weights,* and they determine how errors in the approximation of the optimal value function over different portions of the state space are weighted.

We face the following design decisions in the implementation of approximate linear programming:

- Choice of basis functions ϕ_i
- Choice of "state-relevance weights" c
- Development of a mechanism for dealing with the intractable number of constraints involved in the approximate LP

We address these design questions in the next subsection.

10.4.4. Dealing with State Space Complexity

A suitable choice of basis functions is dictated by conflicting objectives. On one hand, we would like to have basis functions that accurately reflect the advantages of being in each state. To satisfy this objective, we might want to have reasonably sophisticated basis functions; for instance, values of each state under a reasonably good heuristic could be a good choice. On the other hand, choices are limited by the fact that the implementation of the approximate LP in acceptable time involves the ability to compute a variety of expectations of the basis functions relatively fast. In particular, we need to compute or estimate the objective function coefficients $c^T\Phi$, which correspond to the vector of expected values of each of the basis functions conditioned on the states being distributed according to the state-relevance weights c. Expected values of the basis functions also appear in the approximate LP constraints; specifically, a constraint corresponding to state (I_k, L_k) and action A_k involves computing the expected value of the basis functions evaluated at (A_k, L_{k+1}), conditioned on the current arrival rates L_k. To keep the running time acceptable, we would like to have basis functions that are reasonably simple to compute and estimate. We would also like to keep the number of basis functions reasonably small.

Our approach was to extract a number of features from the state that we thought were relevant to the decision-making process. The focus was on having smooth features, so that one could expect to find a reasonable scoring function by using basis functions that are polynomial on the features. After some amount of trial and error, we have identified the following features that have led to promising results:

- Number of servers being used by each class, assuming that server capacity is split equally among all classes associated with each Web site. Denote by $I(i)$ the number of servers allocated to Web site i and by $N(i)$ the number of classes associated with that site. The number of servers U_k being used by each class k associated with Web site i is the minimum of $I(k)/N(k)$ and Expression 10.23 for the approximate number of servers needed by that class.
- Current arrival rates per class, given by L_k.
- Average server utilization for each Web site. This is computed as the ratio between the total number of servers being used by all classes associated with a given Web site, assuming that server capacity is split equally among all classes, and the total number of servers assigned to that Web site. More specifically, $\sum_k U_k / I(i)$.

We let server capacity be split equally among all classes associated with each Web site in the choice of features for the sake of speed, as that leads to simpler expressions for the features and allows for analytical computation of certain expected values of the features and functions thereof. We have a total of $N + 2K$ features, where N is the number of Web sites and K is the total number of classes. We consider basis functions that are linear in the features, for a total of $N + 2K +1$ basis functions.

We need to specify a distribution over pairs (I, L) to serve as state-relevance weights. Recall that states are given by pairs (I, L) corresponding to the current server assignment and arrival rates. Following the ideas presented by de Farias and Roy (2001b), we sample pairs (I, L) with a distribution that approximates the stationary distribution of the states under an optimal policy. Since the arrival rate processes are independent of policies, it is not difficult to estimate their stationary distribution. We use the following approximation to the stationary distribution of arrival rates:

$$ L_k(\infty) \approx \left(\overline{L}_k + \frac{\sigma_k}{\sqrt{1 - a_k^2}} N(0, 1) + J_i \sum_{t=0}^{\infty} a_k^t B_t, 0 \right)^+ $$

In choosing state-relevance weights, we have simplified the expression further and considered

$$ L_k(\infty) \approx \max\left(\overline{L}_k + \frac{\sigma_k}{\sqrt{1 - a_k^2}} N(0, 1) + \frac{J_i}{1 - a_k} B_0, 0 \right)^+ $$

We sample arrival rate vectors L according to the distribution above, and then select a server assignment I based on L. While the evolution of arrival rates is independent of decisions being made in the system in our model, the same is not true for server assignments. Hence, sampling Web server assignments I based on the arrival rates is a more involved task. Our approach is to choose a server configuration based on the approximate number of servers needed per class, according to Expression 10.23. Servers are greedily assigned to Web sites corresponding to classes with the highest profits P_k/μ_k. As discussed in Section 10.2.2 in the context of the scheduling and routing problems, such a procedure is nearly optimal for fixed arrival rates. Hence our underlying assumption is that an optimal dynamic server allocation policy should somewhat track the behavior of the short-run optimal allocation.

Naturally, we cannot expect that states visited in the course of running the system under an optimal policy would always correspond to pairs of arrival rates L and server assignments I that are optimal with respect to L. To account for that, we randomize the assignment being sampled for each vector of arrival rates by moving some servers between Web sites and between allocated and deallocated status with some probability, relative to the optimal fixed assignment. More specifically, the randomization is performed in two steps:

1. For each originally unallocated server, with probability p_a allocate it to a Web site chosen uniformly from all Web sites.
2. For each originally allocated server, with probability p_d deallocate it.

The choice of probabilities for the randomization step involved some trial and error. We found that relatively high values of p_a lead to the best performance overall, whereas p_d can be made reasonably small. Typical values in our experiments were $p_a = 0.9$ and $p_d = 0.1$.

The objective function coefficient $c^T \Phi$ is estimated by sampling according to the rules described above. Note that with our choice of basis functions, conditional expected values of $\phi_i(\cdot)$ involved in the constraints can be computed analytically.

To deal with the intractable number of constraints involved in the approximate LP, one approach is to sample state-action pairs according to the frequency with which they would be observed if the system were running under an optimal policy. It can then be shown that, for a sufficiently large and tractable number of samples, solving the approximate LP with only the sampled constraints yields a good approximation to the full problem; see de Farias and Roy (2001b). Determining the frequency of state-action pairs under an optimal policy is not feasible; alternatively, we choose a distribution that is only approximately representative of how often state-action pairs are visited.

In our constraint sampling scheme, we sample states according to the same procedure used for the state-relevance weights. Once a state (I, L) is sampled, we still need to sample an action corresponding to a new server assignment. We choose a feasible action as follows:

1. Compute the approximate expected arrival rates at the next time step as follows:

$$L_k(+) = \overline{L}_k + a_k(L_k - \overline{L}_k) + s_k + 20 * P[B_i = 1]M_k$$

2. Note that we overestimate the arrival rates; the true expected arrival rate at the next time step is actually given by $\overline{L}_k + a_k(L_k - \overline{L}_k) + P[B_i = 1]M_k$. However, experimental results suggested that overestimating future arrival rates led to improvements in the overall quality of the policy generated by approximate linear programming; it is helpful to plan for some slack in the capacity allocated to each Web site since true arrival rates are uncertain.
3. Compute the number of needed servers per class k for arrival rates $L_k(+)$, as given by Expression 10.23. For each class, with probability p_r ran-

domize the number of needed servers by multiplying it by a uniform random variable between 0 and 1.

4. Assign the unused servers according to need, with priority given to classes k with higher values of $\mathbf{P}_k/\mu_k$.

5. Determine the number of servers with usage less than a threshold value (in our experiments, 40%). With probability p_r, randomize the number of underused servers by multiplying it by a uniform random variable between 0 and 1.

6. Deallocate the underused servers.

In our experiments, p_r was set to 0.1. Note that the action sampling procedure corresponds to a randomized version of a greedy policy.

10.4.5. Dealing with Action Space Complexity

The Web server assignment problem suffers from complexity in the action space, in addition to having a high-dimensional state space. In particular, a naive definition of the problem leads to a large number of actions per state: there are two choices for each allocated server (to keep it allocated or to deallocate it) and $N + 1$ choices for each deallocated server (allocate it to each of the Web sites or keep it deallocated).

An approach to dealing with the large number of actions is to split them into sequences of actions, so that in each point in time it is necessary to choose from smaller sets of actions. A natural choice is to consider actions for each server in turn; we would have a sequence of M decisions, with each decision being a choice from at most $N + 1$ values. This approach does not fully solve the problem of having a large action space; instead, we transfer the complexity to the state space. As suggested in the discussion of the previous subsection, we choose an alternative approach: we "prune" the action space, using the structure present in the Web server allocation problem to discard actions that are most likely suboptimal in practice.

Our pruning of the action space is based on different rules for allocating and deallocating servers. In deciding how many servers to assign to each Web site, we first generate a rough estimate of how many extra servers each class will need, given by Expression 10.23, and we order the classes according to the associated profits $\mathbf{P}_k/\mu_k$. We then use the scoring function generated by approximate linear programming to decide on the *total number* of Web servers to be allocated, ranging from 0 to the total number of free servers. Servers are allocated based upon need, following the profit-based class ordering. In deciding how many servers to deallocate, we first estimate their usage over the current and next time steps and order servers based on usage. We then consider deallocating a number of servers ranging from 0 to the number of servers with usage under some threshold (in our experiments, 40%). We decide on the *total number* of servers to be deallocated based on the scoring function generated by approximate linear programming. Actual servers being deallocated are decided based on the usage ordering (least-used servers are deallocated first).

10.4.6. Experimental Results

To assess the quality of the policy being generated by approximate linear programming, we compared it to a fixed policy that is optimal for the average arrival rates $\bar{L}_k + M_k P[B_i = 1]/(1 - a_k)$. We considered problems with up to 65 Web servers and 10 Web sites, with 2 classes of requests per Web site ("browsers" and "buyers"), for a total of 20 classes.

The actual advantage of using approximate linear programming as opposed to a fixed allocation depends on the characteristics of the arrival rate processes. In particular, in our experiments the best gains were obtained when arrivals were bursty.

Tables 10.2 to 10.6 present data for a representative example with 65 servers and 10 Web sites. The two classes of requests per Web site — "browsers and buyers" — were assumed to have the same characteristics across Web sites. Service rates, price per unit of time, and SLA values for browsers and buyers are presented in Table 10.2. Characteristics of Web site traffic are presented in Tables 10.3 to 10.6. We let the probability $P[B_i = 1]$ of observing a burst of arrivals in any time step for each Web site i be the same and equal to 0.005.

Table 10.2. Characteristics of Browsers and Buyers

	Browsers	Buyers
Service rate (μ_k)	10	5
Profit (P_k)	1	3
Response time threshold (z_k)	1	2
Maximum fraction of requests with service time $\geq z_k$ (β_k)	0.1	0.2

Table 10.3. Average Arrival Rates $\bar{L}_k$

Class/Web site	1	2	3	4	5	6	7	8	9	10
Browsers	20	26	26	19	19	16	14	11	9.6	10
Buyers	5	3	4	4	2.5	2	4	4	2	5

Table 10.4. Persistence of Perturbations in Arrival Rates Over Time a_k

Class/Web site	1	2	3	4	5	6	7	8	9	10
Browsers	0.95	0.95	0.97	0.95	0.95	0.95	0.97	0.95	0.95	0.95
Buyers	0.95	0.95	0.97	0.95	0.95	0.95	0.97	0.95	0.95	0.95

Table 10.5. Arrival Rate Fluctuation Factors σ_k

Class/Web site	1	2	3	4	5	6	7	8	9	10
Browsers	1.92	1.28	2.56	0.64	1.60	1.28	1.60	0.96	0.64	0.64
Buyers	0.32	0.32	0.48	0.32	0.22	0.32	0.80	0.16	0.22	0.48

Table 10.6. Magnitude of Bursts in Arrival Rates M_k

Class/Web site	1	2	3	4	5	6	7	8	9	10
Browsers	60	100	170	80	100	58	130	53	50	70
Buyers	40	20	90	24	14	10	70	32	20	70

Simulation results comparing the policy generated by approximate linear programming with the fixed allocation policy optimizing for average arrival rates $\overline{L}_k + M_k/(1 - a_k)$ show that the policy generated by approximate linear programming led to average profits that are 15% higher than the profits obtained by the fixed policy, as well as to a dramatic increase in the QoS, with about half as many dropped requests. Furthermore, achieving approximately the same profit with a fixed allocation was empirically determined to require as many as 120 servers.

When the bursty component $M_k B_i(t)$ in the arrival rate processes is relatively small, the gains resulting from the use of approximate linear programming relative to that of the naive fixed allocation are smaller. Note that in this situation the fluctuations are driven by the term $\sigma_k N(t)$. We have two different possibilities in this case: σ_k is small, in which case there is little fluctuation and fixed policies should do well, and σ_k is large, in which case there is much fluctuation and one might think that dynamic allocations would do better. The problem with the latter is that there is a considerable amount of noise in the system, which makes it difficult for any dynamic policy to track the variations in arrival rates fast enough. In fact, in our experiments the policies generated by approximate linear programming in this case tended to perform few changes in the server allocation, settling on a fixed allocation that had average reward comparable to that of the fixed allocation that is optimized for average arrival rates.

The approximate linear programming algorithm was implemented in C++ and the approximate LP was solved by CPLEX 7.5 on a Sun Ultra Enterprise 6500 machine with Solaris 8 operating system and a 400-MHz processor. Reported results were based on policies obtained with approximate LPs involving 200,000 sampled constraints. The constraint sampling step took ~46 seconds on average and solution of the approximate LP took 17 minutes.

10.4.7. Closing Remarks

We proposed a model for the optimal resource allocation problem in Web hosting systems and developed a solution via approximate linear programming. The experimental results suggest that our approach can lead to major improvement in performance compared to the relatively naive approach of optimizing allocation for average traffic, in particular when Web site traffic is bursty.

Several extensions of the current model and solution may be considered in the future:

- More extensive comparison with other heuristics
- Refinement of the arrival rate processes, with the possibility of including forecasts and accounting for cyclical patterns often observed in Internet traffic
- Refinement of the choice of basis functions
- Further development of the action space pruning strategies
- Extending our model for the scheduling and routing problems to support priority scheduling at the servers, either instead of or in addition to the proportional scheduling policy considered herein
- Integration with the problems of scheduling and routing, by considering all of them within the dynamic programming framework, rather than solving the first two by stochastic bounds and approximations
- Consideration of capacity planning, where the number of servers does not remain fixed but may increase as new servers are acquired over time at some cost

ACKNOWLEDGMENTS

This chapter is a survey of a few years of work and discussions among our colleagues in IBM Research. Many of the sections are based on material that has been published in the academic literature. Section 10.2 is adapted from the IBM Research report by Yuan-Chi Chang, Xin Guo, Tracy Kimbrel, and Alan King (IBM Thomas J. Watson Research Center) that was never published (Chang et al., 2001); the authors acknowledge Dr. Shabbir Ahmed (Georgia Institute of Technology) and Dr. David Gamarnik (IBM Thomas J. Watson Research Center) for valuable comments and thank Menghui Cao (Columbia University) and Daniela de Farias (Stanford University) for their help in building the simulator and analyzing its runs during their summer internship at IBM. Section 10.3 is adapted from a paper by Zhen Liu, Mark Squillante, and Joel Wolf (IBM Thomas J. Watson Research Center) that appeared in the proceedings of the IEEE Conference on Decision and Control (Liu et al., 2002). Section 10.4 is adapted from a paper by Daniela de Farias (IBM Almaden Research Center), Alan King, Mark Squillante (IBM Thomas J. Watson Research Center), and Benjamin van Roy (Stanford University) that appeared in the proceedings of the INFORMS Revenue Management Conference (de Farias et al., 2002).

REFERENCES

Abate, J., Choudhury, G. L., Lucantoni, D. M., and Whitt, W. (1995). Asymptotic analysis of tail probabilities based on the computation of moments, *Annals of Applied Probability*, 5, 983–1007.

Avram, F., Bertsimas, D., and Ricard, M. (1995). Fluid models of sequencing problems in open queueing networks; an optimal control approach, in *Stochastic Networks*, Vol. IMA 71, Kelly, F. and Williams, R., Eds., pp. 199–234.

Bar-Noy, A., Bar-Yehuda, R., Freund, A., Naor, J. S., and Schieber, B. (2000). A unified approach to approximating resource allocation and scheduling, in *Proceedings of the Thirty-second Annual ACM Symposium on Theory of Computing*, ACM, May, pp. 735–744.

Bertsekas, D. (1995). *Dynamic Programming and Optimal Control*, Athena Scientific, Nashua, NH.

Bertsekas, D. and Tsitsiklis J. N. (1996). *Neuro-Dynamic Programming*, Athena Scientific, Nashua, NH.

Chang, C. S. (2000). *Performance Guarantees in Communication Networks*, Springer-Verlag, London.

Chang, Y.-C., Guo, X., Kimbrel, T., and King, A. (2001). Bandwidth Broker: Revenue Maximization Policies for Web Hosting, Technical Report, IBM Research Division.

de Farias, D. P. and Roy, B. V. (2001a). The linear programming approach to approximate dynamic programming, conditionally accepted to *Operations Research*.

de Farias, D. P. and Roy, B. V. (2001b). On constraint sampling in the linear programming approach to approximate dynamic programming, conditionally accepted to *Mathematics of Operations Research*.

de Farias, D. P., King, A., Squillante, M. S., and van Roy, B. (2002). Dynamic control of Web server farms, in *Proceedings of the INFORMS Revenue Management Section Conference*, June.

de Ghellinck, G. (1960). Les problèmes de décisions séquentielles, *Cahiers du Centre d'Etudes de Recherche Opérationnelle*, 2, 161–179.

Denardo, E. V. (1970). On linear programming in a Markov decision problem, *Management Science*, 16(5), 282–288.

D'Epenoux, F. (1963). A probabilistic production and inventory problem, *Management Science*, 10(1), 98–108.

Duffield, N. G. and O'Connell, N. (1995). Large deviations and overflow probabilities for the general single-server queue, with applications, *Mathematical Proceedings of the Cambridge Philosophical Society*, 118, 363–374.

Garey, M. and Johnson, D. (1979). *Computers and Intractability: A Guide to the Theory of NP-Completeness*, W.H. Freeman and Company, New York.

Gordon, G. (1999). Approximate Solutions to Markov Decision Processes, Ph.D. thesis, Carnegie Mellon University, Pittsburgh.

Ibaraki, T. and Katoh, N. (1988). *Resource Allocation Problems: Algorithmic Approaches*, The MIT Press, Cambridge, MA.

Irani, S. (1997). Page replacement with multi-size pages and applications to web caching, in *Proceedings of the Twenty-ninth Annual ACM Symposium on Theory of Computing*, El Paso, TX, May, pp. 701–710.

Kingman, J. F. C. (1962). The effect of queue discipline on waiting time variance, *Proceedings of the Cambridge Philosophical Society*, 58, 163–164.

Kleinrock, L. (1975). *Queueing Systems, Volume I: Theory*, John Wiley and Sons, Hoboken, NJ.

Kleinrock, L. (1976). *Queueing Systems, Volume II: Computer Applications*, John Wiley and Sons, Hoboken, NJ.

Klimov, G. P. (1974). Time sharing service systems I. *Theory of Probability and Its Applications*, 19(3), 532–551.

Klimov, G. P. (1978). Time sharing service systems II. *Theory of Probability and Its Applications*, 23(2), 314–321.

Lippman, S. A. and Stidham, Jr., S. (1977) Individual versus social optimization in exponential congestion systems, *Operations Research*, 25(2), March.

Liu, Z., Nain, P., and Towsley, D. (1997). Exponential bounds with an application to call admission, *Journal of the ACM*, 44, 366–394.

Liu, Z., Squillante, M. S., and Wolf, J. L. (2001a). On maximizing service-level-agreement profits, in *Proceedings of the ACM Conference on Electronic Commerce (EC'01)*, October.

Liu, Z., Squillante, M. S., and Wolf, J. L. (2001b). Optimal Control of Resource Allocation in E-Business Environments with Strict Quality-of-Service Performance Guarantees, Technical Report, IBM Research Division.

Liu, Z., Squillante, M. S., and Wolf, J. L. (2002). Optimal control of resource allocation in e-business environments with strict quality-of-service performance guarantees, in *Proceedings of the IEEE Conference on Decision and Control*, December.

Manne, A. S. (1960). Linear programming and sequential decisions, *Management Science*, 6(3), 259–267.

Marbach, P., Mihatsch, O., and Tsitsiklis, J. N. (2000). Call admission control and routing in integrated service networks using neuro-dynamic programming, *IEEE Journal on Selected Areas in Communications*, 18(2), 197–208, February.

McGill, J. and van Ryzin, G. J. (1999). Revenue management: Research overview and prospects, *Transportation Science*, 33(2), 233–256, May.

Menascé, D. A., Almeida, V. A. F., Fonseca, R., and Mendes, M. A. (1999). A methodology for workload characterization of e-commerce sites, in *Proceedings of the 1999 ACM Conference on Electronic Commerce*.

Menascé, D. A., Almeida, V. A. F., Fonseca, R., and Mendes, M. A. (2000). Business-oriented resource management policies for e-commerce servers, *Performance Evaluation*, 42, 223–239.

Odlyzko, A. (1997). A Modest Proposal for Preventing Internet Congestion, Technical Report, AT&T Labs–Research, September (http://www.research.att.com/~amo).

Paschalidis, I. C. and Tsitsiklis, J. N. (2000). Congestion-dependent pricing of network services, *IEEE/ACM Transactions on Networking*, 8(2), 171–184, February.

Schweitzer, P. and Seidmann, A. (1985). Generalized polynomial approximations in Markovian decision processes, *Journal of Mathematical Analysis and Applications*, 110, 568–582.

Smith, W. E. (1954). Various optimizers for single-stage production, *Naval Research and Logistics Quarterly*, 3, 59–66.

Squillante, M. S., Yao, D. D., and Zhang, L (1999). Web traffic modeling and web server performance analysis, in *Proceedings of the IEEE Conference on Decision and Control*, December.

Subramaniam, J., Stidham, Jr., S., and Lautenbacher, C. J. (1999). Airline yield management with overbooking, cancellations, and no-shows, *Transportation Science*, 33(2), 147–167, May.

Takagi, H. (1991). *Queueing Analysis: A Foundation of Performance Evaluation. Volume 1: Vacation and Priority Systems, Part 1*, North Holland, Amsterdam.

SEQUENTIAL RISK MANAGEMENT IN E-BUSINESS BY REINFORCEMENT LEARNING

Naoki Abe, Edwin Pednault, Bianca Zadrozny, Haixun Wang, Wei Fan, and Chid Apte

11.1. INTRODUCTION

Of the many types of information technology potentially useful for risk management in e-business, we are interested in decision support systems that help generate business rules that manage risks, while fulfilling other business objectives. This issue can be naturally thought of as the problem of deciding which actions to take in order to minimize the expected risk (or cost). Numerous off-the-shelf statistical and data-mining methods can be used to assess the risks associated with possible actions. Viewed this way, risk management becomes a traditional decision theoretic problem, and as such there is a large body of work in related fields such as decision theory, statistics, machine learning, and data mining that can provide a solid theoretical basis for it.

One aspect of the risk management problem that has not received proper attention is the intrinsically sequential nature of this problem. That is, it is hardly satisfactory to consider the risk of a single action in isolation, but rather it is necessary to consider the long-term risks of sequences of actions taken over time. For example, consider the problem of deciding to whom to make a certain campaign offer for the purpose of churn detention. In the isolated problem setting, one might conclude that the optimal decision is to make the offer just in case the expected profit resulting from that mailing exceeds the mailing cost. However, it may very well be the case that that customer is not easily convinced by a single offer, but that other related offers following this offer will eventually work and turn out to avoid the greater risk of churn and bring more profits in the long run. This will not be taken into account if the decision is based on the expected outcome of the single action in isolation.

Recently, there has been increasing interest within the machine learning and data-mining communities in what has become known as cost-sensitive learning, which addresses the issue of learning classification (decision) rules under non-uniform misclassification cost. There has been a significant amount of research on this subject from various perspectives (e.g., Domingos, 1999; Elkan, 2001; Fan et al., 1999; Margineantu and Dietterich, 2000; Turney, 2000; Zadrozny and Elkan, 2001). But, here again, the issue of sequential cost-sensitive learning and decision making had not been addressed until recently introduced in Pednault et al. (2002).

In this chapter, we propose to apply the framework of reinforcement learning to address the issues of sequential cost-sensitive learning and decision making, particularly for the purpose of e-business risk management. Reinforcement learning refers to a class of problems and associated techniques in which a learner learns how to make sequential decisions based on delayed reinforcement so as to maximize cumulative rewards.

In the past, reinforcement learning has been applied mostly in domains in which satisfactory modeling of the environment is possible, which can then be used by a learning algorithm to experiment with and learn from. This type of method, known as indirect or simulation-based learning methods, would be difficult to apply in the domain of business intelligence, since customer behavior is too complex to allow reliable modeling. For this reason, we propose to apply so-called direct reinforcement learning methods, that is, those that do not estimate an environment model used for experimentation, but directly estimate the values of actions from given data.

For a proof of concept, we test our approach on the well-known donation data set from the KDD Cup 1998 competition. This data set contains approximately two years of direct-mail promotional history in each donor's data record. We transformed this data set and applied a reinforcement learning approach to acquire sequential targeting rules. The results of our experiments show that, in terms of the cumulative profits obtained, our approach outperforms straightforward (repeated) applications of single-event targeting rules. We also compare and contrast the performance and behavior of two particular variants of the proposed approach and discuss their appropriateness in the context of e-business risk management.

The rest of this chapter is organized as follows. In Section 11.2, we describe our proposed approach including the reinforcement learning methods and the base learning algorithm we employ for function approximation. In Section 11.3, we explain our experimental setup, including the features employed and how the training data are generated from the original KDD Cup data set. We also describe the simulation model we use to evaluate the performance of our approach. In Section 11.4, we present experimental results. Section 11.5 concludes with a discussion of results and future research issues.

11.2. SEQUENTIAL DECISION MAKING

For illustrative purposes, we will use the domain of targeted marketing throughout this chapter. However, it should be noted that the approach set forth here is applicable to a wide variety of applications in e-business risk management. We will use the term *single-event targeted marketing approach* to mean one in which customers are selected for promotions based on maximizing the benefits obtained from each promotion when each is considered in isolation. A *sequential targeted marketing approach*, by contrast, is one in which a series of promotional actions are to be taken over time, and promotions are selected for each customer based on maximizing the cumulative benefits that can be derived from that customer. In an ideal sequential targeted marketing approach, each decision would be made with the goal of maximizing the net present value of all profits and losses expected now and in the future. The challenge in implementing a sequential targeted marketing approach lies in the fact that information about the future is available only in a delayed fashion. We appeal to the apparatus of reinforcement learning to resolve this difficulty.

11.2.1. Reinforcement Learning

As briefly explained in the introduction, we adopt the popular Markov decision process (MDP) model of reinforcement learning with function approximation. For an introduction to reinforcement learning, see, for example, Kaelbling et al. (1996) and Sutton and Barto (1998). The following is a brief description of an MDP.

At any point in time, the environment is assumed to be in one of a set of possible states. At each time clock (assumed to be discrete), the environment is in some state s, the learner takes one of several possible actions a, receives a finite reward (i.e., a profit or loss) r, and the environment makes a transition to another state s'. Here, the reward r and the transition state s' are both obtained with probability distributions that depend on the state s and action a.

The environment starts in some initial state s_0, and the learner repeatedly takes actions indefinitely. This process results in a sequence of actions $\{a_t\}_{t=1}^{t=\infty}$, rewards $\{r_t\}_{t=1}^{t=\infty}$, and transition states $\{s_t\}_{t=1}^{t=\infty}$. The goal of the learner is to maximize the total rewards accrued over time, usually with future rewards discounted. That is, the goal is to maximize the cumulative reward R,

$$R = \sum_{t=1}^{t=\infty} \gamma^{t-1} r_t \qquad (11.1)$$

where r_t is the reward obtained at the tth time step and γ is some positive constant less than 1. In financial terms, γ is a discount factor for calculating the net present value of future rewards based on a given interest rate.

Generally speaking, a learner follows a certain policy to make decisions about its actions. This policy can be represented as a function π that maps states to actions such that $\pi(s)$ is the action the learner would take in state s. An MDP theorem is that a unique optimum policy π^* exists that maximizes the cumulative reward given by Equation 11.1 for every initial state s_0.

In order to determine an optimum policy π^*, a useful quantity to define is what is known as the *value function* Q^π of a policy. A value function maps a state s and an action a to the expected value of the cumulative reward that would be obtained if the environment started in state s and the learner performed action a and then followed policy π forever after. It is thus defined as

$$Q^\pi(s, a) = E_\pi \left[\sum_{t=1}^{t=\infty} \gamma^{t-1} r_t \mid s_0 = s, a_0 = a \right] \qquad (11.2)$$

where E_π denotes the expectation with respect to the policy π that is used to define the actions taken in all states except the initial state s_0.

A remarkable property of MDPs is that the value function Q^* of an optimum policy π^* satisfies the following recurrence relation, known as the Bellman optimality equation:

$$Q^*(s, a) = E_r[r \mid s, a] + \gamma E_{s'}[\max_{a'} Q^*(s', a') \mid s, a] \qquad (11.3)$$

where $E_r[r \mid s, a]$ is the expected immediate reward obtained by performing action a in state s, and $E_{s'}[\max_{a'} Q^*(s', a') \mid s, a]$ is the expected cumulative reward of performing the optimum action in the state s' that results when action a is performed in state s.

The Bellman equation can be solved via fixed-point iteration using the following system of equations:

$$Q_0(s, a) = R(s, a)$$

$$Q_{k+1}(s, a) = R(s, a) + \Sigma_{s'} P(s' \mid s, a) \max_{a'} Q_k(s', a')$$

(11.4)

where $R(s, a)$ is the expected immediate reward $E_r[r \mid s, a]$ and $P(s' \mid s, a)$ is the probability of ending up in state s' when action a is performed in state s. This solution method is known as *value iteration*. In the limit, $Q_k(s, a)$ converges to $Q^*(s, a)$ as k tends to infinity. The optimum policy is then given by:

$$\pi^*(s) = \arg \max_a Q^*(s, a)$$

The use of Equation 11.4, however, requires knowledge of both the expected reward $R(s, a)$ for each state-action pair as well as the state transition *probabilities* $P(s' \mid s, a)$. In learning situations, however, these functions are unknown. The problem faced by a learner, therefore, is to infer a (near) optimum policy over time through observation and experimentation.

Several approaches are known in the literature. One popular reinforcement learning method known as *Q-learning*, due to Watkins (1989), is based on the Bellman equation (Equation 11.2) and value iteration (Equation 11.4). Q-learning estimates value functions in an on-line fashion when the sets of possible states and actions are both finite. The method starts with some initial estimates of the Q values for each state and then updates them at each time step according to the following equation:

$$Q(s_t, a_t) := Q(s_t, a_t) + \alpha(r_{t+1} + \gamma \max_{a'} Q(s_{t+1}, a') - Q(s_t, a_t)) \quad (11.5)$$

It is known that, with some technical conditions, the above procedure probabilistically converges to the optimal value function (Watkins and Dayan, 1992). The parameter α affects the rate of convergence of the update rule, as well as the asymptotic residual error in the estimate of the value function as the time step t tends to infinity. In order to obtain both a fast rate of convergence (which requires α to be large) and small asymptotic estimation error (which requires α to be small), the value of α is usually set up to be a decreasing function of time t. To ensure convergence, it is also necessary to repeatedly try every action in every reachable state in order to estimate the value function for every state-action pair

One drawback of Q-learning is that it has a tendency to aggressively pursue what appears to be the best possible policy based on current knowledge, even though parts of the state space have not yet been thoroughly explored. This property of Q-learning is especially alarming from the viewpoint of risk management, as we will elaborate further in the section on experimental results.

Another popular learning method, known as *sarsa* (Rummery and Niranjan, 1994), is less aggressive than Q-learning in the assumptions it makes about the current knowledge of the state space. Like Q-learning, sarsa learning starts with some initial estimates for the Q values that are then dynamically updated, but the update rule is somewhat different:

$$Q(s_t, a_t) := Q(s_t, a_t) + \alpha(r_{t+1} + \gamma Q(s_{t+1}, a_{t+1}) - Q(s_t, a_t)) \qquad (11.6)$$

In particular, there is no maximization over possible actions in the transition state s_{t+1}. Instead, the current policy π is used without updating to determine both a_t and a_{t+1}.

When the policy is not updated but is held fixed, it can be shown, with some technical conditions, that Equation 11.6 will probabilistically converge to the value function for the given policy. When the policy is updated in combination with what is known in the literature as an ε-*greedy search* (Sutton and Barto, 1998), improvements are made to the policy, but without the aggressive assumptions made by Q-learning.

11.2.2. Batch Reinforcement Learning with Function Approximation

In the foregoing description of reinforcement learning, two simplifying assumptions were made that are not satisfied in the current setting we are considering. The first assumption is that the problem space consists of a reasonably small number of atomic states and actions. Both the sarsa and Q-learning methods described above perform value updates for each state-action pair, which requires that the number of such pairs be finite. In many practical applications, including targeted marketing, it is natural to treat the state space as a feature space with a large number of both categorical and real-valued features. In such cases, the state space is prohibitively large to represent explicitly, which renders the above methods impractical.

The second assumption made is the availability of on-line interaction with the environment. In applications like targeted marketing, this situation is typically not the case. In fact, it is quite the opposite. In targeted marketing, one usually has access to a very large amount of data accumulated from past transaction history from which an effective targeting strategy is to be derived. Moreover, the targeting strategy (i.e., the policy) must make simultaneous decisions for an entire population of customers, not one customer at a time. On-line learning of policies, via reinforcement learning or otherwise, is not practical in these circumstances.

Bearing these factors in mind, we propose to use so-called batch reinforcement learning methods with function approximation. Batch reinforcement learning refers to a form of reinforcement learning in which the learning does not take place in an on-line fashion as the learner performs actions and the environment traverses states. Instead, batch learning makes use of a potentially large volume of static training data that represent prior experience. The training data consist of sequences of states, actions performed in those states, and the resulting rewards. Batch learning thus reflects the realities of such certain real-world applications as targeted marketing.

Function approximation amounts to representing the value function as some reasonable function of state features and actions (see, for example, Bertsekas and Tsitsiklis, 1996; Tsitsiklis and Roy, 1997; Wang and Dietterich, 1999). The usual on-line learning approach, by contrast, assigns explicit values to explicit state-action pairs. For targeted marketing purposes, the state features can include everything that is known about a customer, such as demographic information and past transaction history.

Given such training data, batch reinforcement learning with function approximation attempts to estimate the value function $Q(s, a)$ by reformulating value iteration (Equation 11.4) as a supervised learning problem. In particular, on the first iteration, an estimate of the expected immediate reward function $R(s, a)$ is obtained by using supervised learning methods to predict the value of $R(s, a)$ based on the features that characterize the input state s and the input action a. On the second and subsequent iterations, the same supervised learning methods are used again to obtain successively improved predictions of $Q(s, a)$ by using variants of sarsa (Equation 11.5) or Q-learning (Equation 11.6) to recalculate the target values that are to be predicted for each iteration.

Figures 11.1 and 11.2 present pseudo-code for two versions of batch reinforcement learning: one based on sarsa, the other based on Q-learning. In both cases, the input training data D are assumed to consist of, or contain enough information to recover, *episode* data. An episode is a sequence of *events*, where each event consists of a state, an action, and a reward. Episodes preserve the temporal order in which events were observed. States $s_{i,j}$ are feature vectors that contain numeric and/or categorical data fields. Actions $a_{i,j}$ are assumed to be members of some prespecified finite set. Rewards $r_{i,j}$ are real valued. The base learning module, Base, takes input a set of event data and outputs a regression model Q_k that maps state-action pairs (s, a), to their estimated Q values, $Q_k(s, a)$. In the two procedures shown here and in all variants considered in this chapter, we set α_k to be α/k for some positive constant $\alpha < 1$.

Premise:
A base learning module, Base, for regression is given.
Input data:
$D = \{e_i \mid i = 1, ..., N\}$ where $e_i = \{< s_{i,j}, a_{i,j}, r_{i,j} > \mid j = 1, ..., l_i\}$
(e_i is the i-th episode, and l_i is the length of e_i)

1. For all $e_i \in D$
   $D_{0,i} = \{< s_{i,j}, a_{i,j}, r_{i,j} > \mid j = 1, ..., l_i\}$
2. $D_0 = \cup_{i=1,...,N} D_{0,i}$
3. $Q_0 = \text{Base}(D_0)$
4. For $k = 1$ to final
   4.1 For all $e_i \in D$
       4.1.1 For $j = 1$ to $l_i - 1$
           4.1.1.1 $v_{i,j}^{(k)} = Q_{k-1}(s_{i,j}, a_{i,j}) + \alpha_k [r_{i,j} + \gamma Q_{k-1}(s_{i,j+1}, a_{i,j+1}) - Q_{k-1}(s_{i,j}, a_{i,j})]$
           4.1.1.2 $D_{k,i} = \{< s_{i,j}, a_{i,j}, v_{i,j}^{(k)} > \mid j = 1, ..., l_i\}$
   4.2 $D_k = \cup_{i=1,...,N} D_{k,i}$
   4.3 $Q_k = \text{Base}(D_k)$
5. Output the final model, Q_{final}

Figure 11.1. Batch reinforcement learning (sarsa learning).

Identical to Batch-RL (sarsa) except 4.1.1.1 is replaced by:
           4.1.1.1 $v_{i,j}^{(k)} = Q_{k-1}(s_{i,j}, a_{i,j}) + \alpha_k [r_{i,j} + \gamma \max_a Q_{k-1}(s_{i,j+1}, a) - Q_{k-1}(s_{i,j}, a_{i,j})]$
           4.1.1.2 $D_{k,i} = \{< s_{i,j}, a_{i,j}, v_{i,j}^{(k)} > \mid j = 1, ..., l_i\}$
   4.2 $D_k = \cup_{i=1,...,N} D_{k,i}$
   4.3 $Q_k = \text{Base}(D_k)$
5. Output the final model, Q_{final}

Figure 11.2. Batch reinforcement learning (Q-learning).

Note that the only difference between the two methods is the equation used to recalculate target Q values at each iteration. In the case of Figure 11.2, Equation 11.6 is used at line 4.1.1.1; in the case of Figure 11.1, Equation 11.5 is used.

11.2.3. Base Regression Method: ProbE

As the base learning method, we employ the multivariate linear regression tree method implemented in the IBM ProbE™ data-mining engine (Apte et al., 2001; Natarajan and Pednault, 2002). This learning method produces decision trees with multivariate linear regression models at the leaves. Regression models are constructed as trees are built, and splits are selected to maximize the predictive accuracies of the regression models in the resulting child nodes. Feature selection is performed as part of both the tree-building process (i.e., split selection) and the regression-modeling process (i.e., variable selection). Likewise, pruning is performed both on the trees and on the regression models at the nodes.

In our experiments, we compared the conventional single-event targeting strategy of selecting customers for each marketing campaign so as to maximize the profit of each campaign when viewed in isolation, versus the proposed sequential targeting strategy of selecting campaigns for each customer so as to maximize the cumulative profits generated by each customer. To ensure a fair comparison, ProbE's multivariate linear regression tree method was used to construct models for both targeting strategies. A single-event targeting strategy was constructed by applying the procedure shown in Figure 11.2 with *final* set to a value of zero. Doing so causes the reinforcement learning loop at line 4 of Figure 11.1 to be omitted, thereby producing a policy that maximizes immediate reward. Because the same base learning algorithm is used for constructing both single-event and sequential marketing strategies, any differences in performance observed should reflect inherent differences in the strategies.

11.3. EXPERIMENTAL SETUP

As mentioned in the introduction, we performed preliminary evaluation experiments using an existing benchmark data set in the general domain of targeted marketing, in addition to simulations. We use the well-known donation data set from KDD Cup 1998, which contains demographic as well as the promotion history data as our *episode* data. The episode data are used in two ways:

1. A series of event data is generated from the episode data and is used for reinforcement learning to obtain a targeting policy.
2. Models of response probability and donation amount are estimated using similar event data generated from the episode data, which are used to obtain a model of MDP.

We then use this MDP to run simulation experiments for evaluating the acquired targeting policy.

11.3.1. Data Set

The data set we use, the donation data set from KDD Cup 1998, is available from the UCI KDD repository (Bay, 2000) along with associated documentation. This data set contains information concerning direct mail promotions for soliciting donations and contains demographic data as well as the promotion

Table 11.1. Features Used in Our Experiments

Feature	Description
age	Individual's age
income	Income bracket
ngiftall	Number of gifts to date
numprom	Number of promotions to date
frequency	Number of gifts to date/number of promotions to date
recency	Number of months since latest gift
lastgift	Amount in dollars of latest gift
ramntall	Total amount of gifts to date
nrecproms	Number of recent promotions (past six months)
nrecgifts	Number of recent gifts (past six months)
totrecamt	Total amount of recent gifts (six months)
recamtpergift	Recent gift amount per gift (six months)
recamtpergift	Recent gift amount per promotion (six months)
promrecency	Number of months since latest promotion
timelag	Number of months between first promotion and gift
recencyratio	Number of months since latest gift/number of months between first promotion and gift
promrecratio	Number of months since latest promotion/number of months between first promotion and gift
action	Whether mailed in current promotion (0,1)

history of 22 campaigns conducted monthly over an approximately two-year period. The campaign information contained includes whether an individual was mailed, whether he or she responded, and how much was donated. In additional, if the individual was mailed, the date of the mailing is available (month and year), and if the individual responded, the date of the response is available. We used the training data portion of the original data set, which contains data for approximately 100,000 selected individuals.* Out of the large number of demographic features contained in the data set, we selected only the age and income bracket. Based on the campaign information in the data, we generated a number of temporal features that are designed to capture the *state* of that individual at the time of each campaign. These include the frequency of gifts, recency of gift and promotion, number of recent promotions in the past six months, etc. and are summarized in Table 11.1.

It should be noted that many of these features are not explicitly present in the original data set, but are computed from the data by traversing through the campaign history data. In the terminology of general batch reinforcement learning introduced in Section 11.2, the demographic and campaign history data for each individual constitute an episode, from which the sequence of events —

---

* This is contained in cup98lrn.zip at http://kdd.ics.uci.edu/databases/kddcup98/kddcup98.html.

state, action, and reward triples — may be recovered. For example, the feature called numprom in the original KDD Cup data takes on a single value for each individual and equals the total number of promotions mailed to that individual prior to the latest campaign. In our case, numprom is computed for *each campaign* by traversing the campaign history data backwards from the latest campaign, subtracting one every time a promotion was mailed in a campaign. Similarly, ngiftall in the original data set is merely the total number of gifts to date as of the latest campaign, but here this is computed for each campaign by starting at the latest campaign and subtracting one each time a gift was made.

We note that we did not make use of the RFA codes included in the original data, which contain the so-called recency/frequency/amount information for the individuals, since they did not contain enough information to recover their values for each campaign.

11.3.2. Evaluation by Simulation

We evaluated our approach via simulation using an estimated MDP for the donation data set. The MDP we constructed consists mainly of two estimation models: one model $P(s, a)$ for the probability of response as a function of the state features and the action taken, and the other $A(s, a)$ for the amount of donation *given* that there is a response, as a function of the state features and the action. The $P(s, a)$ model was constructed using ProbE's naive-Bayes tree modeling capability, whereas $A(s, a)$ was constructed using linear-regressions tree modeling. Given these two models, it is possible to construct an MDP in the following way. First, the immediate reward $r(s, a)$ for a given state-action pair can be specified using the two models as follows: Flip a coin with bias $P(s, a)$ to determine whether there is a response. If there is no response, then the amount of donation is zero. If there is a response, then determine the amount of donation as $A(s, a)$. The reward obtained is the amount of donation minus mailing costs, if any. Next, the state transition function can be obtained by calculating the transition of each feature using the two models. For example, ngiftall (number of gifts to date) is incremented by 1 if the above coin with bias $P(s, a)$ came up heads and remains unchanged otherwise. Similarly, numprom (number of promotions to date) is incremented if the action taken was 1 and remains constant otherwise. Using the above two features, frequency (ngiftall/numprom) can be computed. Updates for other features are computed similarly.

Given the above functional definition of an MDP, we conducted our evaluation experiment as follows. Initially, we selected a large enough subset (5000) of individuals, and set their initial states to be the states corresponding to their states prior to a fixed campaign number (in experiments reported here, campaign number 1 was used). We then *throw* all these individuals to the MDP and use the value function output by our batch reinforcement learning procedure to make decisions about what actions to take for each of them. Utilizing the response probability model and the expected amount model, we compute the rewards and next states for all of them. We record the rewards thus obtained, and then go on to the next campaign. We repeat this procedure 20 times, simulating a sequence of 20 virtual campaigns.

The use of a simulation model for evaluation raises a question concerning our premise that on-line interaction with an MDP is infeasible. A natural inclination may be to use the above MDP as a model of the environment and to use an on-line learning method (such as on-line versions of sarsa and Q-learning) to estimate the value function from interactions with it. Our view is that the human behavior in application domains such as targeted marketing is too complicated to be well captured by such a simplified model of MDP. We use the simulation model to evaluate the policy obtained by our method only as a preliminary experiment prior to a real-world evaluation experiment.

11.4. EXPERIMENTAL RESULTS

We report on the results of our preliminary experiments using a simulation model. We evaluate our proposed approach with respect to a number of performance measures, including total lifetime profits obtained and the qualitative behaviors of the acquired targeting rules.

11.4.1. Lifetime Profits

We first consider the most obvious, and arguably most important, measure of total cumulative benefits — lifetime profits — obtained by the competing methods. In particular, we compare the lifetime profits obtained by two variants of reinforcement learning with those obtained with the single-event targeting method. Here, the single-event method is obtained by using the base regression module to learn a model of the expected immediate rewards (profits) as a function of state features and the action, and then mailing to an individual just in case the expected immediate reward for mailing exceeds that for not mailing, at each campaign. Note that since the state features contain temporal information such as recency, frequency, and the number of recent promotions, the targeting decisions obtained this way are sensitive to the campaign number and the past history.

Figure 11.3 shows the total lifetime profits obtained by the sarsa learning version of batch reinforcement learning, plotted as a function of the number of value iterations performed. The plots were obtained by averaging over five runs,

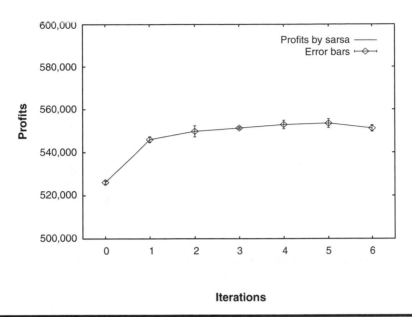

Figure 11.3. Total lifetime profits obtained by batch reinforcement learning (sarsa).

each run with episode data size 10,000, which translates to a training data size of 160,000 for reinforcement learning.

The total profits are obtained using the simulation model as described in the previous section and totaled over 20 campaigns. The error bars shown in the graph are the *standard errors* calculated from the total profits obtained in the five independent runs, namely

$$\sigma = \sqrt{\left(\sum_{i=1}^{i=n} (P_i - \tilde{P})^2 / (n-1) \right) / n}$$

where P_i is the total profit obtained in the ith run, $\tilde{P}$ is the average total profit, and n is the number of runs (five in this case). Note that the iteration number 0 corresponds to the single-event targeting method. Thus, the total lifetime profits obtained by models (policies) obtained in the later iterations represents a statistically significant improvement over the single-event approach.

11.4.2. Rule Behavior: Number of Mailings

In addition to the profits attained by the produced policies, we also examined how the behavior of the obtained models differs. Figure 11.4 shows the number

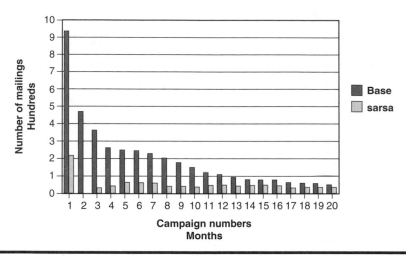

Figure 11.4. Number of mailings by a policy obtained by batch reinforcement learning (sarsa).

of mailings done in each of the 20 campaigns. The number of individuals considered in each campaign was 10,000 for this experimentation. Clearly, the policy obtained by sarsa learning is significantly more cost-containment oriented than the policy produced by the single-event strategy. It is also interesting to note that the model produced by reinforcement learning seems to exhibit rather sophisticated temporal characteristics. That is, it initially mails to a large number of individuals, waits to observe the responses, and then starts sending again to very selected segments. This type of sequential targeting strategy seems to make sense intuitively, but it also appears highly unlikely that a real-world retailer would actually do something like this. It appears to be a rather surprising and nontrivial discovery made by our reinforcement learning approach to sequential targeted marketing.

11.4.3. Rule Behavior: Profits per Campaigns

How can a cost-containment-oriented policy generated by our reinforcement learning approach achieve higher profits? To probe into this question further, we examined how the amount of profits obtained changes over time as the campaigns proceed. Figure 11.5 shows the profits obtained by each policy per campaign for the 20 campaigns run in the simulation. The graph clearly shows that the policy produced by the reinforcement learning approach settles for lower profits in the beginning for the sake of higher profits in later campaigns.

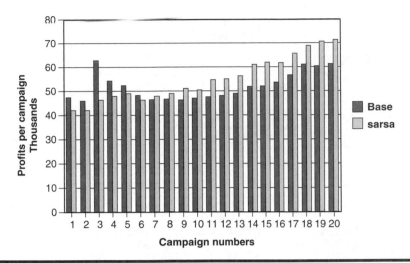

Figure 11.5.   Profits per campaign obtained by batch reinforcement learning (sarsa) and single-event method.

This is an indication that the reinforcement learning approach, which takes into account the long-term effects, is indeed successful at finding targeting rules that maximize lifetime profits rather than immediate profits.

11.4.4. Q-learning, Sarsa Learning, and Risk Management

Next, we compare and contrast the performance and behavior of targeting rules obtained by different versions of batch reinforcement learning methods, sarsa and Q-learning. We begin by comparing the total profits obtained by the two methods. Figure 11.6 shows the total profits obtained by these two versions, again using 10,000 episode data and averaged over five runs. These results show that, in this particular case, Q-learning resulted in a more profitable policy than sarsa learning, although the statistical significance of the difference was unconvincing with our limited experimentation. This is indeed not surprising considering that Q-learning attempts to obtain the optimal policy, whereas sarsa learning tries to perform a local improvement based on the current policy. In the context of batch reinforcement learning, this current policy is in fact the policy that was used in practice when the data were obtained.

When we examine the *qualitative behavior* of the policies obtained by the two methods, the situation becomes less clear. It was found that in many cases the policies obtained by the Q-learning version were policies that mail to almost all individuals. It was indeed the case that the simulation model we used cred-

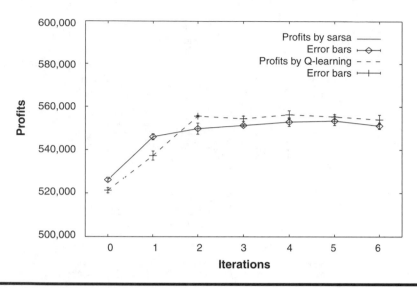

Figure 11.6. Total profits obtained by batch reinforcement learning (sarsa) and batch reinforcement learning (Q).

ited even higher profits to this strategy.* Since Q-learning deviates more from the current policy and searches for a global optimum, it appears to have found a policy that was significantly different in nature from the current policy but was more profitable. Sarsa learning, on the other hand, works more closely with the current policy and tries to improve it, and as a result appears to obtain a similar policy to the current one, but is more cost-containment oriented and more practical. This kind of distinction in the properties of the two methods was noted by Sutton and Barto (1998), where an illustrative example is provided wherein a simulated robot using Q-learning repeatedly runs itself off a cliff in order to better estimate the exact shape of the cliff edge in an attempt to find the best possible path to a goal state.

This is particularly interesting when one considers the issue of *risk management* in e-business. The profitability of a policy is obviously an important criterion in the choice of e-business marketing strategies. When one views this

---

* We note that this is not as unlikely as it may seem. The KDD Cup 98 data set contains data about individuals who used to actively contribute and then stopped being active. The test data used for the cup competition were the data for the last campaign. Hence the models tried to find a strategy that somehow determines who among these defectors is likely to be won back. This is not the case in our simulation. We took a certain campaign number in the first half of the two years, when most individuals were still active, and then started simulating from there.

problem as an instance of a more general problem of risk management, in which the aim is to maximize profit *subject to* fulfillment of various other business imperatives, there are clearly additional considerations that impact decision making. Observations such as the above may prove, for example, that the relatively conservative sarsa learning is more acceptable than the relatively aggressive Q-learning method from this broader perspective.

11.5. CONCLUSIONS

We presented a novel approach to sequential e-business risk management based on the framework of reinforcement learning and reported on the results of preliminary experiments performed using a simulation model. In the future, we plan to conduct large-scale, real-world experiments to further demonstrate the effectiveness of the proposed approach, as well as to assess its practicality in specific application problems.

ACKNOWLEDGMENTS

We thank Fateh Tipu for his generous help in setting up the environment for our experiments.

REFERENCES

Apte, C., Bibelnieks, E., Natarajan, R., Pednault, E., Tipu, F., Campbell, D., and Nelson, B. (2001). Segmentation-based modeling for advanced targeted marketing, in *Proceedings of the Seventh ACM SIGKDD International Conference on Knowledge Discovery and Data Mining (SIGKDD)*, ACM Press, New York, pp. 408–413.

Bay, S. D. (2000). UCI KDD Archive, Department of Information and Computer Sciences, University of California, Irvine (http://kdd.ics.uci.edu/).

Bertsekas, D. P. and Tsitsiklis, J. N. (1996). *Neuro-Dynamic Programming*, Athena Scientific, Belmont, MA.

Domingos, P. (1999). MetaCost: A general method for making classifiers cost sensitive, in *Proceedings of the Fifth International Conference on Knowledge Discovery and Data Mining*, ACM Press, New York, pp. 155–164.

Elkan, C. (2001). The foundations of cost-sensitive learning, in *Proceedings of the Seventeenth International Joint Conference on Artificial Intelligence*, Morgan Kaufmann, San Francisco, pp. 973–978.

Fan, W., Stolfo, S. J., Zhang, J., and Chan, P. K. (1999). AdaCost: Misclassification cost-sensitive boosting, in *Proceedings 16th International Conference on Machine Learning*, Morgan Kaufmann, San Francisco, pp. 97–105.

Kaelbling, L. P., Littman, M. L., and Moore, A. W. (1996). Reinforcement learning: A survey, *Journal of Artificial Intelligence Research*, 4, 237–285.

Margineantu, D. D. and Dietterich, T. G. (2000). Bootstrap methods for the cost-sensitive evaluation of classifiers, in *Proceedings 17th International Conference on Machine Learning*, Morgan Kaufmann, San Francisco, pp. 583–590.

Natarajan, R. and Pednault, E. (2002). Segmented regression estimators for massive data sets, in *Second SIAM International Conference on Data Mining*, Arlington, VA (available at http://www.siam.org/meetings/sdm02/proceedings/sdm02-33.pdf).

Pednault, E., Abe, N., Zadrozny, B., Wang, H., Fan, W., and Apte, C. (2002). Sequential cost-sensitive decision making with reinforcement learning, in *Proceedings of the Eighth ACM SIGKDD International Conference on Knowledge Discovery and Data Mining*, ACM Press, New York, pp. 259–268.

Rummery, G. A. and Niranjan, M. (1994). On-line q-learning Using Connectionist Systems, Technical Report CUED/F-INFENG/TR 166, Engineering Department, Cambridge University, Cambridge.

Sutton, R. S. and Barto, A. G. (1998). *Reinforcement Learning: An Introduction*, MIT Press, Cambridge, MA.

Tsitsiklis, J. N. and Roy, B. V. (1997). An analysis of temporal difference learning with function approximation, *IEEE Trans. Automatic Control*, 42(5), 674–690.

Turney, P. (2000). *Cost-Sensitive Learning Bibliography*, Institute for Information Technology, National Research Council, Ottawa, Canada (http://extractor.iit.nrc.ca/\\bibliographies/cost-sensitive.html).

Wang, X. and Dietterich, T. (1999). Efficient value function approximation using regression trees, in Proceedings of the IJCAI Workshop on Statistical Machine Learning for Large-Scale Optimization, Stockholm.

Watkins, C. J. C. H. (1989). Learning from Delayed Rewards, Ph.D. thesis, Cambridge University, Cambridge.

Watkins, C. J. C. H. and Dayan, P. (1992). Q-learning, *Machine Learning*, 8, 279–292.

Zadrozny, B. and Elkan, C. (2001). Learning and making decisions when costs and probabilities are both unknown, in *Proceedings of the Seventh International Conference on Knowledge Discovery and Data Mining*, KDD'01, pp. 204–213.

PREDICTING
AND OPTIMIZING
CUSTOMER BEHAVIORS

Louis Anthony Cox, Jr.

12.1. INTRODUCTION

Capital and expense budgeting, capacity forecasting and planning, and marketing campaign designs by telecommunications companies all typically require useful sales forecasts for at least the next 12 to 24 months. Even experienced carriers are frequently surprised by actual demand growth over this horizon. Enthusiastic customer responses to a new marketing initiative (e.g., introduction of the Digital One Rate price plan by AT&T Wireless Services in 1998) can easily exceed anticipated growth and swamp existing and planned capacity. Conversely, demand forecasts that overestimate actual demand can lead to excess and possibly to stranded capacity and can create a financial strain on the company that invested in it. The Iridium satellite network is a recent example. Marketing pressures to forecast what individual customers are likely to do and to identify which customers are most (and least) likely to respond to specific product offers also drive a need for improved prediction methods (Schober, 1999; Strouse, 1999). Increasingly, predictions of likely customer behaviors must be based on only a small amount of historical data, both because new products do not have long histories and because data warehouse administrators retain only a limited number of months worth of data. Forecasting probable future product-purchasing behaviors down to the level of individual households or accounts, based largely or entirely on short-term data, with enough accuracy to be useful in target marketing requires a fundamentally different approach to predictive modeling. The aggregate time series trending and allocation models long used by telecommunications companies for both high-level financial planning and more detailed budgeting are often no longer useful.

This chapter introduces a new approach to modeling individual purchasing behaviors. It addresses the need to forecast from relatively short histories by quantifying instantaneous transition rates of individuals among product ownership *states* (Aoki, 1996) rather than trying to forecast aggregate product sales levels from their own past values and from values of other macrolevel variables. Predictive models and algorithms are based on estimating state-dependent transition rates from short-term data. Predictively useful information is partitioned into a *macrostate* that summarizes each customer's current product profile and a *microstate* that summarizes aspects of history (i.e., information about past states and times spent in them) and any other covariates that are found to significantly affect transition rates among macrostates.

Individual customers or accounts are treated as the units of analysis. Their transition rates among product ownership states are dependent variables. The independent variables and covariates that affect individual transition rates are incorporated into state definitions. The methodology is illustrated and tested by application to telecommunications customer data provided by the US WEST Communications Marketing Intelligence and Decision Support (MIDS) group.

12.2. DATA AND BASIC METHODS OF ANALYSIS

12.2.1. From Raw Data to State Transition Models

Table 12.1 shows example data for three customers and a selection of telecommunications products over a 13-month observation period. It records the products owned by each customer at the end of each month; 1 means that the product was owned by the customer in column 1 at the end of the month in column 2, whereas 0 means that it was not. Thus, for example, customer 1 adds call waiting (CW) in month 8 and drops voice messaging (VM) in month 10. Customer 2 adds custom ring (CR) in month 12 and call waiting ID (CWID) and caller ID (CID) in month 13. Customer 3 had no product transitions over the period of observation. From such data, we wish to predict the change in total demand for each product (i.e., the aggregate of product adds and drops from approximately 11 million customers, by month) for each product over the 24 months following the end of the observation period.

To this end, we adopt the general framework of *state transition modeling* (Lancaster, 1990). Initially, and somewhat naively, the entire product profile

Table 12.1. Raw Data from Which to Predict Customer Demands

Cust ID	Month	CW	ADD	CF	TWY	VM	TP	CR	CWID	CID	CC	PCS
1	1	0	1	0	0	1	0	0	0	1	0	0
1	2	0	1	0	0	1	0	0	0	1	0	0
1	3	0	1	0	0	1	0	0	0	1	0	0
1	4	0	1	0	0	1	0	0	0	1	0	0
1	5	0	1	0	0	1	0	0	0	1	0	0
1	6	0	1	0	0	1	0	0	0	1	0	0
1	7	0	1	0	0	1	0	0	0	1	0	0
1	8	1	1	0	0	1	0	0	0	1	0	0
1	9	1	1	0	0	1	0	0	0	1	0	0
1	10	1	1	0	0	0	0	0	0	1	0	0
1	11	1	1	0	0	0	0	0	0	1	0	0
1	12	1	1	0	0	0	0	0	0	1	0	0
1	13	1	1	0	0	0	0	0	0	1	0	0
2	1	1	1	0	1	1	0	0	0	0	0	0
2	2	1	1	0	1	1	0	0	0	0	0	0
...												
2	12	1	1	0	1	1	0	1	0	0	0	0
2	13	1	1	0	1	1	0	1	1	1	0	0
3	1	0	0	0	0	1	0	0	0	1	0	0
3	2	0	0	0	0	1	0	0	0	1	0	0
...												
3	12	0	0	0	0	1	0	0	0	1	0	0
3	13	0	0	0	0	1	0	0	0	1	0	0

Key: CW = call waiting, ADD = additional line, CF = call forwarding, TWY = three-way calling, VM = voice messaging, TP = toll plan, CR = custom ring, CWID = call waiting ID, CID = caller ID, CC = custom choice, PCS = wireless.

that a customer has at the end of a month (a row in Table 12.1) might tentatively be viewed as a single state. Adds and drops of products are then represented by transitions of customers among states. Quantifying the rates at which these transitions take place would provide a Markov model for predicting the frequency distribution of customers among states over time, starting from any initial frequency distribution, via the recursion

$$E[X(t + 1) \mid X(t)] = AX(t)$$

where

- $X(t)$ = frequency distribution of customers among states at time t, represented as a column N-vector with one component for each of the N possible states. $X_i(t)$ is the number of customers in state i at time t and $E[X_i(t)]$ is its expected value. Equivalently, after dividing by the population size (ignoring customer arrivals and departures for the moment), $X_i(t)$ may be interpreted as the probability that a randomly selected customer at time t will be in state i.

- $A = N \times N$ matrix of one-step transition rates (i.e., probability per month of making a transition from each possible state to each possible next state).

Attractive though this Markov modeling approach may be in principle, there are at least two things wrong with it in practice. The first is that there are too many possible states: 2^n for n products. For the 11 products shown in Table 12.1, this means 2048 states, yielding A, a matrix of $2048 \times 2048 = 4,194,304$ elements, which is far too large to estimate comfortably from available data. The other problem is that product combinations may not contain all the relevant information needed to be a state in Markov modeling theory.

The defining requirement for a state variable is that the probability density of the next state (and hence all future states) be *conditionally independent* of the past history of states (i.e., the initial state and the subsequent state trajectory leading from it to the present state), given the current state. Intuitively, the future is conditionally independent of the past, given the current state. It is not especially plausible that the current set of products satisfies this requirement. For example, if a customer has already tried a particular product and dropped it, then he or she may be less likely to add it again. Therefore, a customer's current set of products may have to be augmented with some additional historical information to create a set of information that truly functions as a state variable for modeling purposes. This increases the combinatorial profusion of potential states even further.

Classification tree analysis (Biggs et al., 1991; Breiman et al., 1984) provides algorithms that can address both problems. As explained below, the potential combinatorial explosion of states is restrained by searching for relatively small combinations of variable values that have high predictive power, while the conditional independence property is arrived at by incrementally refining initial state definitions until it is satisfied. Figure 12.1 helps illustrate the main ideas. It shows a classification tree for a specific transition, namely adding CW. The first split shows that, among customers without CW, those with CID ($= 1$) are almost twice as likely as those without CID ($= 0$) to add CW (denoted by CWA $= 1$). Those with CID but no additional line (CID $= 1$, ADD $= 0$) add CW at an average rate of 1.4% per month, compared to only 0.5% per month among customers with ADD $= 1$ and CID $= 0$. The other nodes in the tree are interpreted similarly. In general, classification tree algorithms recursively partition populations of customers into finer and finer subsets by "splitting" successively

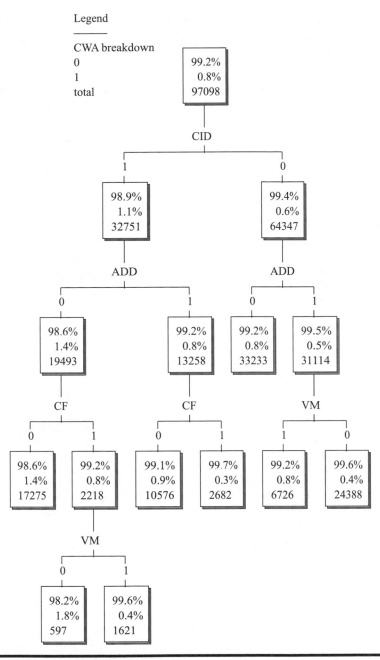

Figure 12.1. Classification tree for adding call waiting (CWA). CID = caller ID, ADD = additional line, CF = call forwarding, VM = voice messaging.

the variables that best separate (using entropy, F-tests, or other statistical criteria) the conditional distributions of the dependent variables obtained by conditioning on the splits.

Although classification trees can undoubtedly be useful in identifying the subsets of customers who are most (or least) likely to buy specific products next, they share with regression and neural net methods the limitation of considering only one dependent variable at a time. This limitation is overcome in state transition models that predict probabilistic transitions among states with multiple products as components. Before considering how to construct such a model from data, it is worth previewing what one looks like and how it is used.

Tables 12.2 to 12.4 show a set of 32 product ownership states and various lookup tables for making predictions based on them. Figure 12.2 shows the state transition diagram relating them. Section 12.3 explains how these states and the structure of the state transition model as well as quantitative values for transition rates (see Table 12.3) are derived from the data in Table 12.1. The derivation applies an iterative state construction algorithm that repeatedly invokes classification tree analysis as a subroutine.

These states exploit the fact that the full set of product-add behaviors of interest can be predicted relatively well from knowledge of which *core products* a customer currently owns. Core products are defined as those that (1) allow probable addition rates for themselves and all other (noncore) products to be predicted as well as if the full product set were used to make the prediction and (2) contain no proper subset with this property. The example in Tables 12.2 to 12.4 and Figure 12.2 has five core products, namely, ADD, CW, call forwarding (CF), VM, and CID. (Section 12.3 discusses algorithms for determining core product sets — or, more generally, core macrostates — from data.) A complete (macro-) state is merely a subset of the core products. These states may be used to predict all product addition probabilities (or, more generally, all transition rates) of interest. If the transition intensities change slowly, the core products and corresponding macrostates may also be used to make probabilistic predictions of both individual and population purchase patterns over time. We review these uses next and then explain the derivation of the state transition model.

Figure 12.2 shows the structure of the state transition model. The numbers represent common product combinations (i.e., macrostates) among which transitions take place. (States that occur infrequently, as indicated by the empirical frequencies in Table 12.2, column 2, are not shown.) Arrows indicate product adds. A customer who adds a core product makes a transition from one state to another. The product added is indicated in the leftmost column of Table 12.2 (for vertical arrows) or in the topmost row (for horizontal transitions) except for the 9 → 13 and 25 → 29 transitions, where the product added is CF. Bold

Table 12.2. Initial States, Frequencies, and Lookup Table for Selected Product Penetrations

State	%	ADD	CW	CF	VM	CID	TWY	TP	CR	CWID	CC
0	31.4	0.0	0.0	0.0	0.0	0.0	0.0	0.05	0.01	0.0	0.0
1	9.7	0.0	0.0	0.0	0.0	1.0	0.0	0.06	0.01	0.00	0.01
2	3.9	0.0	0.0	0.0	1.0	0.0	0.0	0.05	0.02	0.00	0.0
3	2.05	0.0	0.0	0.0	1.0	1.0	0.1	0.04	0.01	0.00	0.05
4	0.11	0.0	0.0	1.0	0.0	0.0	0.2	0.11	0.22	0.00	0.22
5	0.38	0.0	0.0	1.0	0.0	1.0	0.8	0.07	0.18	0.04	0.64
6	0.04	0.0	0.0	1.0	1.0	0.0	0.5	0.0	0.0	0.00	0.50
7	1.1	0.0	0.0	1.0	1.0	1.0	1	0.03	0.09	0.00	0.74
8	11.3	0.0	1.0	0.0	0.0	0.0	0.1	0.05	0.01	0.03	0.01
9	8.8	0.0	1.0	0.0	0.0	1.0	0.2	0.03	0.01	0.59	0.08
10	3.1	0.0	1.0	0.0	1.0	0.0	0.1	0.05	0.02	0.06	0.01
11	2.45	0.0	1.0	0.0	1.1	1.0	0.3	0.06	0.03	0.80	0.19
12	0.75	0.0	1.0	1.0	0.0	0.0	0.7	0.08	0.05	0.38	0.52
13	6.3	0.0	1.0	1.0	0.0	1.0	1.0	0.03	0.08	0.68	0.83
14	0.24	0.0	1.0	1.0	1.0	0.0	0.9	0.09	0.16	0.64	0.79
15	3.4	0.0	1.0	1.0	1.0	1.0	1.0	0.05	0.10	0.73	0.89
16	4.5	1.0	0.0	0.0	0.0	0.0	0.0	0.06	0.02	0.00	0.0
17	0.88	1.0	0.0	0.0	0.0	1.0	0.0	0.04	0.02	0.00	0.0
18	0.77	1.1	0.0	0.0	1.0	0.0	0.0	0.04	0.06	0.00	0.0
19	0.56	1.1	0.0	0.0	1.1	1.0	0.1	0.03	0.09	0.00	0.0
20	0.17	1.0	0.0	1.0	0.0	0.0	0.0	0.0	0.0	0.00	0.0
21	0.13	1.3	0.0	1.5	0.0	1.0	0.3	0.0	0.25	0.00	0.0
22	0.14	1.3	0.0	1.0	1.0	0.0	0.7	0.0	0.67	0.00	0.33
23	0.47	1.1	0.0	1.1	1.0	1.0	0.8	0.08	0.32	0.00	0.64
24	1.8	1.0	1.1	0.0	0.0	0.0	0.1	0.03	0.01	0.02	0.01
25	1.4	1.1	1.1	0.0	0.0	1.0	0.2	0.06	0.04	0.60	0.10
26	0.79	1.1	1.1	0.0	1.1	0.0	0.2	0.06	0.09	0.12	0.03
27	0.80	1.0	1.1	0.0	1.2	1.0	0.3	0.04	0.10	0.85	0.15
28	0.30	1.1	1.0	1.0	0.0	0.0	0.5	0.05	0.15	0.20	0.25
29	1.1	1.1	1.1	1.1	0.0	1.0	1.0	0.05	0.06	0.71	0.72
30	0.15	1.2	1.0	1.1	1.0	0.0	0.7	0.0	0.27	0.53	0.40
31	0.96	1.1	1.1	1.1	1.1	1.0	1.0	0.04	0.13	0.75	0.63
All		0.2	0.6	0.3	0.3	0.6	0.3	0.05	0.04	0.32	0.24

Key: ADD = additional line, CW = call waiting, CF = call forwarding, VM = voice messaging, CID = caller ID, TWY = three-way calling, TP = toll plan, CR = custom ring, CWID = call waiting ID, CC = custom choice.

arrows indicate the most common transitions. Product drops could be represented by other arrows, and account drops could be indicated by transitions to a special state (labeled Drop Acct. in Table 12.4 and DISC in Table 12.3). For simplicity, Figure 12.2 only shows the arrows representing product adds.

Table 12.3. State Lookup Table for Predicting Selected Product Add and Account Disconnect Rates (= L)

State	ADDADD	ADDCW	ADDCF	ADDVM	ADDCID	DISC
0	0.0018	0.0062	0.0018	0.0019	0.008	0.018
1	0.0011	0.01245	0.0029	0.0022		0.019
2	0.0009	0.0136	0.0018		0.011	0.025
8	0.0041		0.00815	0.0048	0.028	0.022
9	0.0032		0.012	0.0049		0.024
13	0.0028			0.0148		0.025
15	0.0053					0.036
16		0.0072	0.0024	0.0080	0.0087	0.023
All	0.0024	0.0081	0.0043	0.0043	0.013	0.021

Key: ADD = additional line, CW = call waiting, CF = call forwarding, VM = voice messaging, CID = caller ID, DISC = rate of account disconnects.

Table 12.4. Part of a State Transition Intensity Matrix (= A)

From State	Drop Acct.	0	1	2	8	9	13	15	16
0	1.8%	96.98%	**0.34%**	0.13%	0.10%	0.32%	0.13%	0.01%	0.17%
1	1.9%	0.43%	96.4%	0.00%	0.00%	**0.97%**	0.22%	0.04%	0.00%
2	2.5%	**0.98%**	0.09%	96.1%	0.18%	0.09%	0.00%	0.09%	0.00%
8	2.2%	0.46%	0.03%	0.03%	94.53	**2.04%**	0.53%	0.12%	0.00%
9	2.4%	0.24%	0.71%	0.00%	0.40%	95.08%	**1.07%**	0.04%	0.00%
13	2.5%	0.28%	0.22%	0.00%	0.39%	0.11%	95.09%	**1.38%**	0.00%
15	3.6%	0.00%	0.10%	0.00%	0.00%	0.00%	**0.31%**	95.99%	0.00%
16	2.3%	**0.08%**	0.00%	0.08%	0.00%	0.00%	0.00%	0.00%	97.55%

		CF		CID		VM		CID		VM		VM	
			19	←	18	←	16	→	17	→	*19*		
ADD			↑		↑		↑		↑		↑		
			3	←	2	←	*0*	→	1	→	3		
CW							↓		↓				
	15	←	11*	←	10	←	8	→	9*	→	13	→	15
ADD	↓		↓		↓		↓		↓	CF	↓		↓
	31	←	27*	←	26	←	24	→	25*	→	29	→	*31*

*Transitions also occur from 9 to 11 and from 25 to 27 (by adding VM).

Figure 12.2. A simple state transition diagram. CF = call forwarding, CID = caller ID, VM = voice messaging, ADD = additional line, CW = call waiting.

The product combination represented by each state is determined by the sequence of arrows leading from the origin (state 0) up to it. For example, state 13 = {CW, CID, CF}. This information can also be read from Table 12.2, in which the initial columns ADD to CID list the state definitions. Absence of an arrow (e.g., from state 3 to state 13) indicates a transition that seldom or never takes place. Table 12.4 lists observed transition rates between states in units of expected transitions per customer per month.

Table 12.2 enumerates the complete set of 32 product states for the five core products ADD, CW, CF, VM, and CID. Column 1 lists state numbers, from 0 = no core products to 31 = all core products. Column 2 lists the frequency distribution of the states in the complete data set (of which Table 12.1 is a small extract). From this frequency distribution, it is apparent that states 4 to 6, 20 to 23, 28, and 30 can be eliminated (i.e., replaced with a single *other* state) with little loss of model accuracy, as these states are seldom used. They do not appear in Figure 12.2. Thus, once n core products have been used to generate 2^n logically possible states, some may be pruned because they occur too seldom to make a significant contribution to predictions.

Columns ADD to CID in Table 12.2 define the states. The entries in these columns indicate the average number of each product (measured in universal service order codes [USOCs]) for customers in each state. Rounding to 0 and 1 values gives the logical definition of each state, where we simplify by only considering whether each customer has each product and not how many USOCs of it he or she has. For example, a customer in state 19 has ADD, VM, and CID, but not CW or CF.

The remaining columns of Table 12.2 list the average number of USOCs for each of several noncore products (three-way calling, toll plan, custom ring, etc.) for each state. These illustrate how states may be used to make predictions. For example, Table 12.2 predicts that a randomly sampled customer in state 9 is almost 20 times more likely to have CWID than a randomly sampled customer in state 8 (0.59% versus 0.03%).

12.2.2. Predicting Customer Behaviors: State Lookup Tables

Table 12.3 provides a lookup table to predict future behaviors — specifically, the rates at which individual core products are expected to be added in each of the eight most frequent states. (Blanks indicate products that are already owned in the corresponding states and that therefore cannot be added again.) In this table, DISC is the rate of account disconnects. It is included to illustrate how a state lookup table can be used to predict account attrition or churn. Table 12.4 shows the average transition rates (per customer per month) among the eight most frequent states. For example, starting from state 0, the most common transition is to Drop Acct. (i.e., account disconnect). The next two most frequent transitions are to state 1 (adding CID) and to state 9 (adding both CID and CW). Such information can help marketers design *bundles* of products to offer or promote together.

To predict product and account adds and drops in a *population* of customers, one first predicts transitions of customers among the core states over time. For any cohort of customers, this is done via the equation

$$E(X_{t+1} \mid X_t) = AX_t \qquad (12.1)$$

where

- X = 32-component column vector of probabilities that a randomly selected individual is in each state (or, equivalently, the population frequency distribution of states).
- A = 32 × 32 state transition matrix (a 32 × 32 extension of Table 12.4 with account drop rates in column 1 deleted and the array transposed).

The variance-covariance matrix for X_{t+k} given X_t can be calculated equally easily from A using standard Markov chain theory (Elliott et al., 1995).

The extension to multiple-birth cohorts, with new customers entering each month, is straightforward. It is based on the linear difference equation

$$E(N_{t+1} \mid N_t) = AN_t + a(t) - d(t) \qquad (12.2)$$

in which

- N_t = vector giving the number of people in each state at the start of period t.
- A = the state transition matrix (the transpose of the full array of which Table 12.4 is an extract).
- $a(t)$ = recruitment vector describing how many new customers are "born" into each state in each period (e.g., from people moving into the region or from young people aging and acquiring their own new accounts).
- $d(t)$ = account drop vector, obtained by multiplying the components of $N(y)$ by the state-specific drop rates (e.g., those in the first column in Table 12.4).

Joint confidence regions for the components of N_{t+k} given N_t and the error characteristics of predicted values for $a(t)$ are easily derived. Predictions from such simple models, with projected values of $a(t)$ purchased from data vendors, have proved quite accurate over a forecast horizon of several years (Cox, 2001).

Add and drop rates for noncore products and account disconnect rates within each period are predicted directly from the state vector via the equation

$$E[R(t) \mid X_t] = L^T X_t \qquad (12.3)$$

where

- $R(t)$ = transition indicator vector with $R_i(t) = 1$ for an individual if transition i occurs in the next month and $R_i(t) = 0$ otherwise.
- $L_{ij} = \Pr(R_j = 1 \mid X_i = 1)$.

Table 12.3 gives a portion of L, the lookup matrix mapping states to noncore transition probabilities. Blanks in this table correspond to structural zeros (i.e., to transition rates for transitions that have already happened). They should be filled with zeros when Equation 12.2 is used for numerical calculations. Table 12.3 lists only a few selected product add rates and the account disconnect rate, DISC (= Drop Acct. in Table 12.4), but a full version would include add rates and drop rates for each product from each state.

Thus, *once states have been defined,* the mechanics of prediction are both conceptually and computationally simple. The evolution of the core state vector over time is determined by Equation 12.1 for a cohort and by Equation 12.2 more generally. Equation 12.3 predicts account drops and noncore product adds and drops. Moreover, the key data arrays needed to make these predictions, namely, A, L, and X_t, can all be estimated directly from count data such as those in Table 12.1. While sophisticated algorithms are available for optimally estimating these quantities from incompletely observed data (Elliott et al., 1995), the count data in Table 12.1, which are typical of corporate data warehouse data, yield sample values of X. These allow naïve point estimates of A to be formed from any two consecutive values of X, say X_t and X_{t+1}. Namely, A_{ij} is estimated as the fraction of customers in state j at the start of month t who are in state i at the start of period $t + 1$. In our experience with real consumer data, the values of A obtained from two different pairs of consecutive values of X taken about eight months apart (based on several disjoint samples of between 10,000 and 100,000 customer-months of observation) agree in almost all elements to two significant digits. (For small sample sizes, the naïve estimates of elements of A may break down because the ratios become ratios of small integer counts, which may be far from the expected value of the ratio. With a database of several million customers, however, large enough samples can be taken to avoid this problem and to make the naïve estimates reliable.) Similarly, point estimates of L, formed by taking the ratios of observed noncore transition counts in any period to the sizes of the components of N in that period, also tend to be stable (or perhaps slowly changing) and accurate enough so that more so-phisticated estimation algorithms are unnecessary.

12.2.3. Optimizing Customer Behaviors

Pure predictions of customer demands for products can be very useful for capacity planning. For example, knowing (a) the number of people in each macrostate expected within a geographic area (from Equation 12.3), perhaps augmented with confidence bands) and (b) the rates at which people in each macrostate add lines (from the first column of Table 12.3, extended to all states) allows one to estimate the (approximately Poisson-distributed) number of ad-ditional lines that will be demanded in that area. However, marketers typically want not merely to predict future demands, but to help shape them. They can use state lookup tables such as Table 12.3 to actively manage demand by guiding target marketing efforts to increase the likelihood of offering customers the products (or product bundles, price plans, or other offers) that they are most likely to purchase.

To illustrate, consider the following typical marketing decisions:

1. Which product(s) to offer to a customer who has either called in (i.e., contacted a sales rep) or logged in to the company's e-business site.
2. Which customers to target for a product-specific direct mail campaign.
3. Which geographic areas or markets to introduce which new product(s) (e.g., a net-based service or a DSL high-speed residential data service) into next in order to maximize near-term sales and revenue yield.

Table 12.3 can be used as follows to help optimize these decisions:

1. Given the customer's current state (one of the rows of Table 12.3), offer the product with the highest add probability. For example, a customer now in state 0 should be offered CID. A customer in state 1 should be offered CW. If more than one product can be offered, then use Table 12.4 to identify the most likely product combination(s) to add next (i.e., the most likely transitions from the current state) and offer those product combinations.
2. For a specific product (i.e., column in Table 12.3), target those customers with the highest add probabilities. For example, a CID product manager should target customers in state 8 first and then, budget permitting, customers in state 2. More generally, the product manager can calculate how great the purchase probability must be to make it worthwhile to send

direct mail to a customer and then target all and only those customers in states for which the estimated purchase probability is sufficiently great.

3. For each geographic area being considered, calculate the population state vector N from customer product records (typically stored in the billing database). Calculate $L^T N$ for each area, where L is the matrix of product add rates for each state. In each area, offer the product(s) corresponding to the greatest component(s) of $L^T N$ (i.e., the products that will generate the greatest number of expected sales [= adds] per unit time). (Note that L must be estimated from data for areas where the new products have already been introduced, so that this method only helps plan a geographic rollout of products after some initial customer response data are available.)

The recommendations in these examples are based only on the information in Table 12.3, for purposes of illustration. The planner's goal in each case is assumed to be to maximize short-term sales by offering customers the products that they are most likely to want to buy next. These may be called the *next logical products* (NLPs) for the customers. The causal assumption motivating NLP calculations is that offering customers the product(s) that they are most likely to want to purchase next will tend to make them buy sooner, thus advancing the revenue streams generated by successfully matching products to customers. Since purchases are rare events and populations are large, the number of purchases per unit time will be approximately Poisson distributed. This provides decision-analytic justification for the use of expected values to set priorities: ordering Poisson-distributed random variables by their means also orders them by first-order stochastic dominance and hence by expected utility for any utility function that increases with number of sales (Shaked and Shanthikumar, 1994).

The simple prescriptive framework of Tables 12.3 and 12.4 can be extended in several useful directions. Important extensions include the following:

- **On-line dynamic decision support**: State lookup tables can be used to help optimize real-time adaptive sales decision making by including information about customer responses to offers made so far in the state definitions. For example, suppose that a caller or Web site visitor in macrostate 0 in Table 12.3 is offered CID but refuses it. Based on this information, the customer may be modeled as making a transition to a new microstate, where microstates augment product ownership information with response-to-offer information. The next product to offer will be determined by the microstate, which may change several times during a session.

- **Causal modeling of marketing effects**: Rather than simply assuming that customers tend to make purchases sooner if they receive appropriate direct mail or other marketing initiatives, the causal impact of initiatives can be estimated from preliminary data collected in trials. (Surrogate data from surveys, probabilistic choice models, or focus groups may also be used for this purpose, although usually with less confidence.) Whether a customer receives a particular offer or stimulus is represented as a controllable component of his or her state vector, and differences in state-dependent purchase rates are used to decide which customers should receive which stimuli to maximize sales probabilities or expected incremental revenues.

- **Optimal resource allocation**: Instead of matching product offers to customers to maximize sales (the NLP approach), one may seek to maximize expected incremental *revenues*. This may be called the next optimal product approach. Suppose that there is an entire set of alternative marketing initiatives (e.g., alternative advertising and promotion campaigns or different rules for matching product offers to customers) to choose among for a specific market area. Indexing the decision alternatives by α, one seeks the alternative that maximizes $rL^T(\alpha)N$, where $L(\alpha)$ is the product-add rate matrix (with a column for each state and a row for each product, including core products) associated with choice α. N is the column vector of state counts for the market area, and r is a compatible row vector giving the average revenue per customer in each state. In this formulation, choosing a particular alternative α affects the state-dependent purchase rates of different products and hence the expected incremental revenue. Given the costs of each α and a budget constraint (or multiple constraints, if implementing α requires multiple resources), the budget-constrained resource allocation problem may be formulated as being to choose the α that maximizes $rL^T(\alpha)N$ while meeting all constraints. An unconstrained formulation chooses α to maximize $rL^T(\alpha)N - c(\alpha)$, where $c(\alpha)$ is the cost of implementing α.

- **Long-term value (LTV) optimization**: Maximizing short-term sales or revenue increase may be less important than maximizing the expected net present value of the future revenue stream generated by each customer. A formula for LTV of customers may be developed as follows. Let v be the *state value vector* giving the expected discounted value of future revenues for a customer starting in each state. Then v must satisfy the recursion

$$v = r + \rho A v$$

where r is the vector of state-specific per-period revenues, ρ is the one-period discount factor, and A is the one-step transition probability matrix. In other words, the expected revenue value of a customer starting from the present state is the sum of the revenue generated this period (given by the appropriate component of r) and the value of the revenue stream starting from the state that the customer will be in one period from now, weighted by the corresponding state probabilities and discounted by one period ($\rho A v$). Hence,

$$v = (I - \rho A)^{-1} r \qquad (12.4)$$

This formula can also be obtained as the expected net present value, that is,

$$v = r + \rho A r + \rho^2 A^2 r + \dots$$

and then summing this vector geometric series. If A depends on the decision variable a, then so does v, and the LTV optimization problem is to choose α to solve the program:

$$\max_{\alpha} v^T(\alpha)N = N^T v(\alpha) = N^T [I - \rho A(\alpha)]^{-1} r = \text{LTV}$$

Note that in this formulation, A includes product drops as well as product adds (i.e., it is the full state transition matrix). Account attrition is represented by a transition to an absorbing, zero revenue state. Thus, maximizing the LTV of a population of customers described by N requires considering not only how likely they are to buy different products, but also how long they are likely to keep them and any effects that offers may have on customer retention.

   Although we will not pursue these extensions in greater detail here, it should be clear from these examples that *once states are defined,* the state-transition modeling framework can provide a rich source of guidance for predicting and optimizing customer purchase behaviors. However, its predictions and prescriptions are only justified if the underlying state transition model (Equations 12.1 to 12.3) accurately describes behaviors. This provides a powerful motivation for seeking state definitions that will make Equations 12.1 to 12.3 hold. The following section introduces algorithms for identifying such states from data, including the time series count data illustrated in Table 12.1.

12.3. DEFINING STATES FROM DATA

A state transition model may be built from data using a two-phase process consisting of an iterative state refinement inner loop within a core state selection and optimization outer loop.

12.3.1. Iterative State Refinement Loop: Building Microstates

Suppose that an initial candidate set of states has already been generated, perhaps as the power set of a small set of core products, as in Table 12.2. To be completely satisfactory, the states should make next-state transition probabilities or rates conditionally independent (CI) of all other variables. This is a statistically testable property. Testing it using classification trees reveals where, if anywhere, the CI property breaks down and indicates how to amend the state definitions to repair CI violations.

As soon as a set of states is proposed, its adequacy with respect to CI can be diagnosed by creating a new variable representing the next state and growing a tree for it. If the CI property for state transitions holds, then only the current state should appear in the tree for next state (i.e., the tree should have only one split). If this ideal is not achieved, then the additional information that helps to determine the probable next state from the current one can be incorporated into a refined set of state definitions. Thus, splitting the next-state variable (which we will call the *to* state) first on the current state (which we will call the *from* state) and then allowing splits on other variables helps both to assess the adequacy of current-state definitions and, where needed, to improve them. This process is iterated, generating increasingly fine state descriptions, until no further predictively useful refinements can be discovered. (One state description is said to be "finer than" another if it discriminates between individuals not distinguished by the coarser description. In effect, refining a tree by splitting its leaves into subtrees creates a finer probability measure, and hence a better informed one, for predicting the dependent variables. Laffont [1990, Chapter 4] discusses and compares information values of probability measures partially ordered by refinement).

Figure 12.3 shows the initial results of this state refinement step for states 0 and 1 in Table 12.2. *To* is the next-state variable. The code -1 (the top entry in each box) represents an account disconnect. *From* is the current-state variable. For brevity, only the initial refinements of two of states 0 and 1 are shown. The full refinement tree, of which Figure 12.3 shows the start, confirms that none of the products excluded from the core appears to offer useful information for predicting the probable next state. (The test data set used in Figure 12.2 is disjoint from the training data set used to identify core products

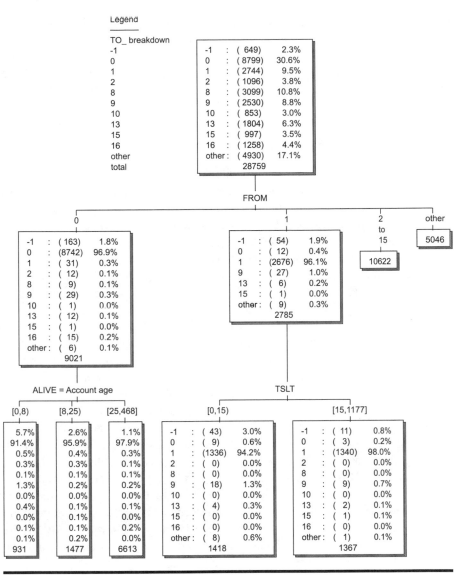

Figure 12.3. Refining macrostates to obtain microstates.

and states in Table 12.2.) Thus, the set of core products in Table 12.2 passes this diagnostic test. However, Figure 12.3 also reveals that some additional information *does* help to predict *to*, given the initial (32-macrostate) definition of *from*, and should therefore be incorporated into the state definitions. Specifically, *time since last transition* (TSLT) is a useful predictor of the probable next state, even after conditioning on *from*. *Account age* (*alive*) is also relevant for some states. Therefore, the 32 macrostates in *from* must be augmented with TSLT and account age information to make the next state CI of all other information in the data set. Further iterations of this state refinement procedure show that the products acquired when a new account is started may also help to predict later transitions. All these variables are derived from the raw data fields in Table 12.1, but classification tree analysis does not automatically create such derived variables: they must be created manually or by another program.

Refining the macrostate definitions with these new items of information is easy. Each leaf in the state refinement tree represents one of the new states. In other words, each leaf represents a combination of (1) one of the original macrostates and (2) the additional information required to refine it so that the CI criterion will be satisfied. The states defined by these leaves will be called *microstates*. Thus, the state refinement tree-growing step provides a technique for refining the initial set of states until no further improvement can be discovered.

States are used not only to predict state transition probabilities, but also to predict adds and drops of noncore products. Therefore, when a set of states has been constructed that satisfies the CI property for state transitions, it must be checked to make sure that it also contains all predictively useful information for these other variables. Again, classification trees provide a constructive procedure: Split each variable to be predicted on the final *from* variable (i.e., on the current state, using the final-state definitions) first. Then, confirm that no other variables enter the tree after conditioning on the *from* state. If another variable does enter, then refine the state definition accordingly. (Variables to be predicted are obtained from count data such as those in Table 12.1 by recoding them to create *transition rate indicator variables*, discussed below.)

For computational and conceptual purposes, it is often useful to treat states as two-level hierarchical entities rather than as unstructured vectors of variables. Specifically, product combinations (for core products) define macrostates, and all other predictively useful information defines microstates within the macrostates. This two-level hierarchy avoids the need to consider the full Cartesian product of all variables used to make predictions.

In an application to a database of over 10 million residential telephone customers, state refinement produced 81 microstates, starting with the 32 macrostates identified in Table 12.2 and augmenting the fields in Table 12.1 with over 100 other demographic and account history variables. The entire state transition and state lookup table modeling framework of Equations 12.1 to 12.3 applies to the refined set of states, but with 81 microstates instead of 32 macrostates. Several of the microstates include discretized ranges of TSLT and *alive* values, generated by the state refinement trees, as in Figure 12.3, among their components. The refined set of states improves predictive accuracy, both because the model Equations 12.1 to 12.3 describe customer behaviors better and because the refined states yield conditional transition rates that differ more widely (and hence that are more useful for decision making) than those in Tables 12.3 and 12.4. Section 12.4 discusses state-transition model validation and performance results in more detail.

12.3.2. Initializing the State Refinement Loop by Identifying Initial States

The state refinement procedure must be initialized with a starting set of states. Several different algorithms with varying computational requirements have proved useful for this purpose. The following approach is simple to implement and creates classification trees as intermediate outputs that may be useful for gaining insight into the drivers of specific transitions of interest. A more mechanical and more CPU-intensive approach, discussed below, also produces good starting states, as evaluated by the methods in Section 12.4.

1. **Create transition rate indicators**: For each transition of interest (i.e., for each product and account add and drop), create a *transition rate indicator variable* indicating the rate (per customer per unit time) at which the specified transition took place over the period of observation. This variable is defined as 1 for a customer who was eligible to make the specified transition in a time period and did so, 0 for a customer who was eligible to make the transition but did not do so, and missing if the customer was not eligible to make the transition then (e.g., because he or she has already made it or was not a customer then). (This definition allows for interval-censored data.) As an example, the transition indicator variable for adding call waiting, denoted by CWA, has a value of 1 for month 8 and for customer 1 in Table 12.1. It has a value of 0 for all other months for all three of the customers in Table 12.1.

2. **Identify potential state variables via classification tree analysis of transition indicator variables**: As discussed above, a classification tree ideally makes its dependent variable (at the top, i.e., root of the tree) CI of all variables not in the tree, given the values of the variables that are in it. (Otherwise, the tree would continue to grow.) This is precisely the property needed to search for potential state variables. In practice, limitations on sample sizes and classification tree algorithms make real trees approximations to this ideal — but often very useful approximations.

To initialize the process, each transition rate indicator in turn is treated as a dependent variable, and a tree for it is grown using all of the product indicator variables in Table 12.1 as candidate independent variables. Thus, Table 12.1 is augmented with a column of 0–1 missing values for the transition rate indicator variable. This column (i.e., variable) is then treated as a dependent variable and split on the other product indicator variables in Table 12.1. Only variables that appear in one or more trees need be considered further.

Figure 12.1 shows a classification tree for the CWA transition rate indicator variable, as an example. Of the 11 products in Table 12.1, only 4 are retained in the tree. Already, several fragments of potential macrostates can be discerned, as follows:

Partial State	Frequency (in 97,098)	VM	CF	ADD	CID	CWA
0	33,233	—	—	0	0	0.008
1	17,275	—	0	0	1	0.014
2	24,388	0	—	1	0	0.004
3	10,576	—	0	1	1	0.009
4	2,218	—	1	0	1	0.008
5	6,726	1	—	1	0	0.008
6	2,682	—	1	1	1	0.003

Each row in this table represents a *partial state* (i.e., a set of values for some of the independent variables), together with *don't care* conditions (indicated by dashes) for the rest. These partial states suffice to make the CWA variable CI of the values of the *don't care* variables and of the variables (e.g., three-way calling, toll plan, wireless, etc.) not shown in Figure 12.1.

The tree in Figure 12.1 predicts CWA from the current product configuration. As discussed above, such trees may later be refined by considering additional candidate-independent variables constructed from those in Table 12.1, such as account age, products subscribed to when an account is opened, products ever owned, products ever dropped, products prior to the most recent transition, and time since last transition. To respect causality, only values known prior to a transition may be used in growing a tree for it, so when columns representing historical variables are added to Table 12.1, each row only contains values derived from data in previous months. Thus, time until the next transition, for example, may not be used, even though it can be calculated from the data in Table 12.1.

When all of the derived variables just mentioned are included in a tree analysis, only account age, time since last transition, and selected current products turn out to be useful for predicting product add and drop rates. Thus, a time-varying (nonhomogeneous) semi-Markov process well describes the transitions of individuals among product profiles over time. Had other information been available and turned out to be relevant, such as variables describing customer demographics and customer service events history, it could be included using the state refinement process.

Once a tree has been grown for each transition of interest, the set of all candidate state variables can be restricted to those that appear in at least one tree. Splits on products are given priority, in keeping with the principle of nesting microstates within product combination macrostates. The trees automatically discretize any continuous or ordered categorical-independent variables, such as account age, by partitioning them into consecutive intervals. The final set of information used to construct potential states is the set of variables identified by the transition rate trees. For continuous and ordered categorical variables, possible values are discretized into a finite number of consecutive intervals, namely, the join of the intervals for those variables in individual transition trees. If the number of combinations of values for the predictor variables is sufficiently small (e.g., a few hundred), then no further processing is needed. Otherwise, the information in the trees may be further reduced to a smaller core set of facts that suffice to make future transitions approximately CI of information not in the core.

In principle, a complete state consists of a combination of values for all of the state variables (i.e., *don't care* conditions are removed by filling in all logically possible combinations for their values) that make all possible transitions starting from it CI of information not in the state definition. Moreover, the final set of states should be closed under state transitions (i.e., each account or product add or drop that takes place in one state results in another state). A computationally practicable approximation to this ideal partitions the full set of products into core products and peripheral (i.e., noncore) products. Only core products are used in the state definitions, and the set of states is closed only under additions and deletions of core products. However, the current state can be used to predict the rates at which peripheral products are likely to be added or dropped, as in Tables 12.3 and 12.4.

Several different heuristics are approximately equally effective for selecting core products, when effectiveness is assessed by ability to predict the next transition of a randomly selected customer (via lift curves, discussed in Section 12.4). The simplest is to select the products that appear in the greatest number of transition rate trees. In effect, each transition rate tree, such as Figure 12.1, casts one vote for each product that appears in it. Core products are those with the most votes; other products are pruned. The number of products included in the core is determined by adding products until including further products makes no significant improvement in lift. Then, products are dropped (i.e., pruned) from the core if doing so creates no significant deterioration in lift. Finally, pairwise swaps of products in the core with products outside it are tried to see whether a further improvement in lift can be obtained. This greedy approach requires very little computational effort.

A more CPU-intensive search procedure that yields similar results in the problems we have worked on is to evaluate each of the product subsets of size k, for $k = 1, 2, \ldots$, up to some small number (e.g., $k = 7$) for which it is practical to enumerate possibilities. Each is evaluated by first generating all of its subsets as macrostates (as in Table 12.2), pruning those that are seldom or never used, and refining the remaining ones via the state refinement iteration. The predictive value of the resulting model, given by Equations 12.1 to 12.3 with these state definitions, is then assessed by the evaluation methods in Section 12.4. The *smallest* subset with predictive power is not significantly different from that of the *best* subset found.

Interestingly, traditional factor analysis (with Varimax or Quartimax rotation, for example) and scree plots often identify factors whose dominant components are the core products identified by other methods, even though the usual assumptions for factor analysis (multivariate linearity and normality) may not hold.

Another approach to generating core products that is less computationally demanding than the systematic enumeration and evaluation of subsets just described is as follows. Begin with an empty list of product combinations. (If the data set is very large, a simple random sample of its records first may be extracted, ordered randomly, and then the following procedure used.)

Core Product Selection Procedure

1. **Enumerative clustering**: Beginning with the first record in the sample, do the following. If the next record encountered does not match any of the combinations formed so far, then add it to the combination list and set its frequency count equal to 1. Otherwise, find the product combination that it matches and augment the frequency count for this combination by 1.
2. **Prune small clusters**: Number the product combinations in order of decreasing frequency. Keep the k most frequent ones and discard the rest.
3. **Extract core products**: Grow a classification tree with the combination number as its dependent variable, using all products that appear in any pattern as its candidate independent variables. Products that appear in the resulting combination identification tree are the core products.

Extensive literature on clustering, vector quantization, and the mathematics of rough sets (e.g., http://www.cs.uregina.ca/~roughset/) suggests that there may be many other good algorithms for generating core products and macrostates. The set of core products is often not unique. Other core extraction heuristics, perhaps based on random generation followed by adaptive modification of candidate product sets, might also help to identify one or more core product sets, which could then be compared for predictive value using the methods in Section 12.4. However, the approaches outlined above have been useful for many applications when it was necessary to identify a starting set of core products and resulting macrostates to initialize state refinement.

12.4. RESULTS

The main idea of the predictive model in Equation 12.1 is to use rates of change and initial conditions to predict changes in product demand over time. Rates of change are expressed in A and can be estimated from short-term data. Initial conditions, X_0, are obtained directly from data such as those in Table 12.1. If the model in Equation 12.1 accurately describes the evolution of product adds and drops over time, then the frequency distribution of product states for any cohort of customers can be predicted from the solution to Equation 12.1. For example, the frequency distribution of customers among microstates predicted for the end of a planning horizon of h months, given the current frequency distribution $X(t)$, would be:

$$E[X(t + h) \mid X(t)] = A^h X(t) \qquad (12.5)$$

The predicted add and drop rates for noncore products are given by Equation 12.3 with a suitably defined L matrix for the conditional (state-dependent) transition rates of interest.

12.4.1. Lift Charts for Comparing and Evaluating Models

The above predictive modeling framework can be applied equally easily whether the states have been chosen well or badly. However, the quality of the predictions will vary depending on how well the defined states suffice to predict the future via Equation 12.1. If the states used do not satisfy conditional independence, then the accuracy of forecasts based on Equation 12.4 may deteriorate rapidly as the forecast horizon, h, increases. If the states are insufficiently refined, such that there is little separation between the values of state-conditioned rates for the transitions of interest, the information value of the model will suffer and its prescriptions for action will be less valuable (Laffont, 1990). Thus, it is important to evaluate the quality of the predictions from the model after its parameters have been estimated.

Predictive validity can be assessed using *model cross-validation* (Hjorth and Urban, 1994). First, multiple randomly selected disjoint subsets of customer data are used to fit the model, thereby creating multiple model replicates. The replicates are created using data available up to some time period, *t*. Each replicate is then used to predict the next-state transitions and future states of several thousand randomly selected customers, none of whom was used in fitting the model replicates. The predictions are made over periods $t + 1$, $t + 2$, ..., $t + h$, where *h* is the forecast horizon (e.g., 12 months). Finally, predicted behaviors (i.e., product add and drop probabilities and account drop probabilities) are compared to actual behaviors to assess the predictive utility of the model.

Predictions from Tables 12.3 and 12.4 were tested via model cross-validation in samples of customers not included in the data used to construct the model. The criterion for predictive usefulness was the *lift* provided by the model in predicting which customers are most likely to undergo attrition, buy specific products next, etc.

Lift is a marketer's term. Suppose that we wish to predict the 1% of customers who are most likely to buy an additional line (ADD) next month, based on the data in Table 12.1. Table 12.3 indicates that state 15 contains these customers and that, although randomly selecting 1% of the customers would yield an average of only 0.0024 additional line purchasers per sampled customer, selecting the customers from among those in state 15 more than doubles the expected yield, from 0.0024 to 0.0053. The ratio of 0.0053/0.0024 = 2.2 is called the *lift ratio,* achieved by using Table 12.3 compared to random selection of customers. (Actually, of course, it is only an *estimate* of the lift ratio. Repeating this calculation for many random samples of customers gives a frequency distribution of estimates for the lift ratio [i.e., the cross-validation estimate]. In 100 cross-validation replicates, the mean lift ratio was also slightly greater than 2.)

As long as the fraction of the population is less than about 3.6%, customers can be selected from state 15. Once all customers in state 15 (i.e., about 3.6% of them, according to Table 12.4) have been selected, however, the next highest yield state in Table 12.3 becomes state 8, with a lift ratio of only 0.0041/0.0024. Continuing in this way creates an entire *lift chart* or lift curve, showing the lift obtained (compared to randomly selecting customers) by using states to predict the *x*% of the population that is most likely to add a line in the next month, for all $0 \le x \le 100\%$. The lift curve consists of consecutive piecewise linear segments. Each segment corresponds to a specific state, and the slopes of the

Table 12.5. Average Lifts for Several Products (Nonpremiers)

		ADD	CC	CF	CID	CR	CW	CWID
10%	Model based	73.90	580.80	253.24	478.13	58.33	227.02	348.06
	Random	29.28	123.19	67.69	213.28	11.14	92.12	100.61
	10% lift	2.52	4.71	3.74	2.24	5.23	2.46	3.46
50%	Model based	202.95	1168.07	589.47	1283.46	100.39	571.77	872.98
	Random	146.43	615.98	338.44	1066.44	55.72	460.63	503.07
	50% lift	1.39	1.90	1.74	1.20	1.80	1.24	1.74

Key: ADD = additional line, CC = custom choice, CF = call forwarding, CID = caller ID, CR = custom ring, CW = call waiting, CWID = call waiting ID.

segments indicate the yield rate of the corresponding state for the transition being analyzed.

Table 12.5 shows the mean lift ratios at $x = 10\%$ and $x = 50\%$, estimated by averaging over 100 cross-validation replicates, achieved by state-based predictions for several products and for a subset of customers (the nonpremier customers, representing the majority of telephone account holders). These ratios are based on the average number of customers making each product purchase transition in a randomly selected $x\%$ of the population, for $x = 10\%$ and $x = 50\%$, compared to the average number making the same transition among the $x\%$ of the population identified by the model as being most likely to make it. This testing was carried out in a different set of customers from those used to define states and estimate transition rates.

The lifts in Table 12.5 were calculated for a three-month forecast horizon ($h = 3$); with longer horizons of up to a year, lifts gradually decline. However, extrapolating from short-term estimates of transition rates and initial conditions provides useful forecasts out to a year, the longest horizon tested. For example, the 10-month forecast for attrition in a particular hotly contested market area, based on attrition rates estimated from 3 months worth of data, was 0.23, compared to an observed rate of 0.19.

Lift charts can be used to compare predictive models. In general, one model is more useful than another for predicting a specific transition if it yields a higher lift curve for that transition. In the framework of Section 12.3, a choice of core products determines a model. The core states imply a set of macrostates (e.g., Table 12.2). These, with a database, generate a set of microstates via the state refinement procedure. The microstates yield predictions via Equations 12.1 to 12.3, and the predictions can be compared to actual transitions to create lift charts. Thus, finally, comparing lift charts allows evaluation of the initial choice of core products based on the lifts that they generate.

Since the same set of states can be used to predict multiple transitions, choosing a "best" set of states may require reducing multiple criteria to one. We have used each of the following as an evaluation criterion:

1. **Average lift**, evaluated at $x = 5\%$ (the size of population that might be addressed by targeted promotions or mail campaigns). This is the lift from use of state-based predictions, averaged over all transitions of interest (i.e., product and account adds and drops) weighted by their relative frequencies.
2. **Maximin lift**, which prescribes choosing state definitions to maximize the smallest lift obtained for any of the transitions of interest.

For both criteria, the five core products in Table 12.2 yield higher lifts than other choices for the core products.

12.4.2. Estimating the Prescriptive Value of a Model

Lift charts help to quantify the predictive value of a model for marketers, but they do not quantify the success of decisions based on the model. Table 12.6 shows examples of prescriptions from a state transition model. (The states shown are the most frequent of 81 microstates obtained from the macrostates in Table 12.2 via state refinement. The frequency counts shown are for a large sample of customers disjoint from the data sets used in earlier examples.) NLP1 to NLP3 are, respectively, the most likely, next most likely, and third most likely products to be purchased from each state.

To assess the economic value of such a table, it must be turned into recommended actions. The revenue consequences of the actions must be estimated and compared to those from the actions that would otherwise have been taken. This agenda is being pursued at US WEST as part of an ongoing project. The project is creating a real-time advisory system to advise sales agents about what products individual customers are most likely to want, given all available data about them (and subject to customer privacy and information protection and usage constraints). Until the results of that effort become available, the value of prescriptions based on state transition models can be estimated as follows:

1. Assume that a sales agent with access to Table 12.6 will offer each of the top three recommended products to a customer (i.e., NLP1 to NLP3) based on the customer's current microstate. (This does not consider dynamic revision of microstates as offers are made and accepted or rejected. Such adaptation may be implemented later.)

Table 12.6. Next Logical Product Prescriptive Lookup Table

State	Frequency	NLP1	NLP2	NLP3
1	15,635	CID	TP	CW
2	39,729	CID	TP	Toll
3	16,192	Toll	TP	CID
4	5,318	Toll	TP	CID
6	5,696	CW	VM	CC
7	5,046	Toll	CW	TP
8	9,600	Toll	CW	CC
15	3,131	CID	TP	CW
32	3,005	CID	CWID	TP
34	13,510	CID	Toll	TP
36	3,668	Toll	CID	TP
40	12,116	CC	CF	TWY
42	3,483	CID	CWID	TP

Key: CC = custom choice, CF = call forwarding, CID = caller ID, CW = call waiting, CWID = call waiting ID, TP = toll plan, TWY = three-way calling, VM = voice messaging.

2. Assume that the customer accepts an offered product at the time it is offered if it is one that he or she would otherwise have bought within the next six months. (Actual customer choices are known from count data over time, as in Table 12.1. If the sales agent successfully offers the next product that a customer will buy, then we assume that the purchase date and resulting revenue stream occur now instead of later.)

3. Assume that a sales agent without access to Table 12.6 always offers the three most popular products that the customer does not yet have. Again, offers are assumed to be accepted if they correspond to what the customer would have bought anyway within the next six months.

This simple model of sales agent offers and customer purchase behaviors allows one to simulate resulting sales and revenues with and without the prescriptions implied by Table 12.6. The result is that the average net present value per customer can be increased by over 10% for customers in many microstates by following the prescriptions in Table 12.6.

More realistic modeling of customer behaviors and of the economic value of state transition models for optimizing offers will be undertaken as data are collected on offers and responses for individual customers. However, it appears that product history data (Table 12.1) and prescriptions based on them (Table 12.6) already suffice to target products to customers in a way that can significantly increase the average economic values of many customers.

12.5. SUMMARY AND CONCLUSIONS

Our procedure for defining the states of a state-transition predictive model from historical data such as those in Table 12.1 can be summarized as follows:

1. **Identify core products** using any of the heuristics described in Section 3. This step eliminates from the core any products that can be well predicted from the products in the core.
2. **Create initial macrostates**. Generate all logically possible combinations of the core products. Find the frequencies of these combinations and prune (or combine into an *other* category) any combinations that occur too infrequently to significantly affect state-based predictions of transition rates. The surviving combinations are the initial macrostates.
3. **Refine the initial macrostates** by augmenting them (via a state refinement tree-growing step that iteratively splits the next-state frequency distributions on other variables) with the information needed to make transition rates among them CI of the data, given the augmented state definitions. These new states are called (core) microstates.
4. **Make predictions**. The refined set of states can be used to create *state lookup prediction tables* (Tables 12.3 and 12.4) for predicting probable next core states and for predicting probable product and account adds and drops from each core microstate.
5. **Evaluate predictions with lift charts**. The average or maximin lift (or other criteria, depending on the decisions to be supported) from the state lookup prediction tables measures the utility of the defined states in predicting customer behaviors. If desired, this evaluation can be fed back to step 1 to guide the search for the most useful set of core products to be used in defining states. This iterative loop is relatively CPU-intensive compared to using classification tree voting or other noniterative heuristics to identify core products.

In applications to US WEST Communications data, this procedure has yielded lift ratios (evaluated at $x = 10\%$ of the population) of between 2 and 6 for most product adds (see Table 12.5). Most of these lift ratios are more than twice as great as the ones obtained from previous predictive models that used logistic regression, rather than a state transition framework, to predict probabilities of customer behaviors. Thus, the approach appears promising as a guide for predicting customer purchasing behaviors and optimizing product offers, as well as for predicting account attrition rates, forecasting product demands, and planning marketing campaigns (Section 12.3). That it can be implemented using only a few months worth of data (to estimate A and X_0) may be a decisive advantage in settings where more extensive historical data are not available.

Finally, from a methodological perspective, the approach of this chapter complements a rich literature on estimation, filtering, and prediction techniques (Elliott et al., 1995) by focusing on how data can be used to best *define the states* of a state-space (Markov) prediction model. This complements methods that focus on optimal estimation of states and of transition rate parameters from data, taking the definitions of the states as given.

REFERENCES

Aoki, M. (1996). *New Approaches to Macroeconomic Modeling,* Cambridge University Press, Cambridge, U.K.

Biggs, D., de Ville, B., and Suen, E. (1991). A method of choosing multiway partitions for classification and decision trees, *Journal of Applied Statistics,* 18(1), 49–62.

Breiman, L., Friedman, J., Olshen, R., and Stone, C. (1984). *Classification and Regression Trees,* Wadsworth Publishing, Belmont, CA.

Cox, L. A., Jr. (2001). Forecasting demand for telecommunications products from cross-sectional data, *Telecommunications Systems,* 16(3), 439–456.

Elliott, R. J., Aggoun, L., and Moore, J. B. (1995). *Hidden Markov Models: Estimation and Control,* Springer-Verlag, New York.

Hjorth, J. and Urban, S. (1994). *Computer Intensive Statistical Methods: Validation, Model Selection, and Bootstrap,* Chapman & Hall/CRC, Boca Raton/London.

Laffont, J. J. (1990). *The Economics of Uncertainty and Information,* MIT Press, Cambridge, MA.

Lancaster, T. (1990). *The Econometric Analysis of Transition Data,* Cambridge University Press, New York.

Schober, D. (1999). Data detectives: What makes customers tick? *Telephony,* 237(9), 21–24.

Shaked M. and Shanthikumar, J. G. (1994). *Stochastic Orders and Their Applications,* Academic Press, New York.

Strouse, K. A. (1999). Weapons of mass marketing, *Telephony,* 237(9), 26–28.

INDEX